McDonnell Douglas DC-10 and KC-10

Wide-Body Workhorses

Arthur A C Steffen

McDonnell Douglas DC-10 and KC-10 Extender
© 1998 Arthur A C Steffen

ISBN 1 85780 051 6

Published by Midland Publishing Limited
24 The Hollow, Earl Shilton
Leicester, LE9 7NA, England
Tel: 01455 847 815 Fax: 01455 841 805
E-mail: midlandbooks@compuserve.com

Worldwide distribution (except North America):
Midland Counties Publications (Aerophile) Limited
Unit 3, Maizefield, Hinckley Fields
Hinckley, Leics., LE10 1YF, England
Tel: 01455 233 747 Fax: 01455 233 737
E-mail: midlandbooks@compuserve.com

North American trade distribution:
Specialty Press Publishers & Wholesalers Inc.
11481 Kost Dam Road, North Branch, MN 55056
Tel: 612 583 3239 Fax: 612 583 2023
Toll free telephone: 800 895 4585

Design concept and layout
© 1998 Midland Publishing Limited
and Stephen Thompson Associates

Edited by Ken Ellis

Printed in Hong Kong
via World Print

Aerofax is an imprint of
Midland Publishing Limited

Contents

Photograph on the previous page:
Former Lufthansa Fleet Captain Hans-Jürgen Leweck and crew demonstrating the impressive view from the DC-10's superbly aerodynamic cockpit. The DC-10 nose profile, incidentally, lives on in the C-17 Globemaster III military airlifter. Lufthansa

Photograph on this page, below:
Late night departure from Frankfurt/Main Airport to the Far East by Lufthansa DC-10-30 D-ADCO *Frankfurt*, August 1977. 'Charlie Oscar' was one of eleven Series 30s operated by the German flag carrier that had a registration / call-sign ending in 'Oscar'. Lufthansa

Photograph on the opposite page:
Another aspect of the DC-10 cockpit, this time on an American Airlines example. American Airlines

Introduction

During a news conference at the Waldorf Astoria Hotel in New York on 25th April 1968, McDonnell Douglas (MDC) announced the birth of a new wide-body tri-jet airliner, the DC-10. History was to show that this would be the last in the famous and successful series of 'DC' or 'Douglas Commercial' airliners.

When the first two DC-10s were delivered to American Airlines and United Airlines on 29th July 1971, Donald W Douglas declared the type the 'best DC yet'. James S McDonnell, then chairman and chief executive officer of the McDonnell Douglas Corporation, expressed feelings upon the delivery of the first DC-10s:

'The DC-10 represents the dedicated efforts of many organisations and thousands of individuals. This teamwork is the finest manifestation of the creative free enterprise system that has made the United States a great nation and brought it world leadership in aerospace'.

The years have proved him right. DC-10s have established an enviable reputation for reli-ability and profitability. They have shown them-selves to be both enduring and adaptable.

The European presentation of the DC-10 to aviation officials took place at the 29th Interna-tional Air Show in Paris in 1971. The aircraft, christened *The Spirit of St Louis - 1971*, was piloted by D L 'Don' Mullin, Douglas' Chief Pilot for Commercial Programs, and performed the non-stop 4,518 mile (7,270km) flight from St Louis, Missouri, to Le Bourget Airport, Paris, in a record time of 7 hours, 45 minutes.

Once in service, the DC-10 proved to be the workhorse it was designed to be. When the last aircraft, a Series 30, was delivered to Nigeria Airways on 25th July, 1989, a total of 446 had been built of which 60 were KC-10A Extender tanker/cargo versions for the US Air Force.

As of 31st December 1997, 413 of the total of 446 were still in service with 58 operators around the world. Since their introduction in 1971, airline DC-10s have carried 1,111,729,484 passengers, flown 11,491,941,710 statute miles and undertaken a total of 24,146,150 revenue hours. Such impressive figures are achieved by reliable aircraft and their operators.

Once German flag-carrier Lufthansa started phasing out their DC-10 Series 30 fleet, I was given the opportunity to accompany one of the aircraft to its temporary resting place. Under the command of Fleet Captain Hans-Jürgen Leweck and Check Captain Hans-Georg Geest and Flight Engineer Gerd Haack, D-ADCO was ferried to Evergreen's well-known Pinal Air Park at Marana, Arizona on 24th January 1994. At that time *Charlie Oscar* was the highest hour DC-10 in the world, with 87,749 hours and 18,861 cycles. Unlike many other aircraft stored at the Evergreen premises, the rugged workhorse would not stay for long. After con-version to a freighter, the aircraft entered ser-vice with Gemini Air Cargo and after nearly 20 years in worldwide service with Lufthansa, the grand old lady will continue to serve her new owner well for many years to come.

During 1997 another milestone was clocked up by DC-10 operators. Two Series 30s, Northwest N220NW (fuselage number 114 formerly Swissair HB-IHC) and DAS Air Cargo 5X-JOE (f/n 115, formerly Sabena OO-SLA) were the first of their type to exceed 100,000 flight hours.

Like other Douglas products, it is clear that the type will have a long service life. DC-10s were initially ordered by the world's flag carriers and the loyalty they established has passed the baton on to its replacement, the MD-11 – which remains in production. As well as the already mentioned military Extender, as major airlines have selected more modern equipment, the DC-10 has found a niche with charter operators and an increasing following in the pure freight world. The freighter DC-10 will evolve further during 1998 with the appearance of the first 'second generation' MD-10s with 'glass cockpits' and other refinements.

Two major accidents overshadowed the success of the airliner in its early years. After the THY disaster near Ermenonville, France on 3rd March 1974, the DC-10 became the centre of major controversy because of a faulty door locking mechanism and the improper operation of the door system by the ground staff. The vulnerability of a wide-body aircraft after a sudden depressurisation in the cargo hold however, was recognised.

The Federal Aviation Administration (FAA) required the reinforcement of cabin floors and an improved floor venting system not only on the DC-10, but also on all Boeing 747s, Lockheed L-1011 TriStars and Airbus A300s.

The American Airlines crash at Chicago O'Hare International Airport on 25th May 1979 was the worst domestic airliner accident in the USA. Although design flaws were criticised, the accident was attributed to improper maintenance procedures applied by the airline. The removal and the installation of the engine and pylon in one piece, a practice used by American Airlines as well as Continental Airlines at that time, was more than questionable.

On 6th June 1979 the FAA suspended the type certificate of the DC-10, which would last 38 days. It was a major blow to the DC-10 programme. Carriers outside the USA – especially in Europe – opposed the grounding.

Thorough inspections showed no defects at all on any of the DC-10s operated in Europe. The decision by the FAA was even considered an over reaction. During a conference in Zurich, Switzerland on 19th June, which was attended by representatives from the European DC-10 operators, the aviation authorities and the manufacturer, it was decided to lift the ban.

Within two weeks after the grounding in Europe, the DC-10 fleet of the KSSU group (KLM, SAS, Swissair and UTA) and the ATLAS group (Alitalia, Lufthansa and Sabena) were back in operation, showing the complete confidence in the safety of the aircraft. Their DC-10s were dispatched on all routes except the USA until the US civil aviation authorities reissued the airworthiness and operating certificate on 13th July.

It must also be said that, after these two crashes, no matter how small the event, the DC-10 always was an important target for the US and international media. This is a great pity, because its performance day-on-day has proved what a hard-working and reliable airliner and airlifter it is.

On 1st August 1997 it was announced that Boeing had acquired McDonnell Douglas. For all of the production history of the DC-10 and KC-10 these aircraft have been McDonnell Douglas products and they are termed as such throughout this book. See Chapter Eight for more details of the merger.

As the last of the 'DC' line, the mighty DC-10 is a living tribute to a pioneering aircraft manufacturer.

Arthur A C Steffen
Dreieich
Germany   January 1998

Bibliography

Aviation-Letter
Lundkvist Aviation Research, Pahoa, Hawaii, USA.

British Aviation Review
British Aviation Research Group, Surrey, UK.

DC-10 Jetliner
Aero Publishers Inc, Fallbrook, California, USA.

The Evolution of the DC-10 Wide-Body Tri-jet and its Impact on Air Transportation
Robert E Hage, Vice-President, Engineering, Douglas Aircraft Company, McDonnell Douglas Corporation. Presentation to the 13th annual Israel Conference on Aviation and Astronautics, 3rd March 1971 in Tel Aviv.

Jet Airliner Production List
J R Roach & A B Eastwood,
The Aviation Hobby Shop, West Drayton, Middlesex, England.

JP Airline Fleets International
Ulrich Klee, Bucher & Co. Publikationen, Zurich Airport, Switzerland.

Luftfahrt Journal
Hamburg, Germany.

Pedigree of Champions – Boeing since 1916
Boeing, Seattle, Washington, USA.

Acknowledgements

After 25 years of service as a flight attendant and purser with Air Canada and Lufthansa, I look back on 20 years of safe DC-10 flying. My enthusiasm for this aircraft led to the idea of a book on this wide-body workhorse. First of all, my thanks to the people at Midland Publishing for their support of the project.

I would like to record my appreciation to the following persons particularly: Don Hanson, Douglas Aircraft Company Media Relations; Harry Gann, retired Douglas Aircraft Company Historian; James W Ramsey, Media Relations Manager C-17 Program; Gerd Rebenich, Lufthansa Photo Archives; Ingrid Friedl, Lufthansa Internal Media; Marlyse Bartis, Swissair Photo Archives; Major Joseph E Davis, United States Air Force – Headquarters Air Mobility Command, Scott AFB; Bob Smith – Aviation Slides and Prints; Frank E Bucher – Bucher & Co; Mark Busseniers – Exavia; Eddy Gual – Aviation Photography of Miami; Reiner Geerdts – Luftfahrt Journal; Michael Hald, Theo Handstede, Derek Hellman, Manfred Kaspczak, Andreas Lang, Fred Lerch, Jean M Magendie, Nick Mills, Vickey Mills, Malcolm Nason, Neville Parnell, Nicky Scherrer – VIP Photoservice, G Schütz, Bob Shane, John Stephenson, Michel St Felix – Avimage, Rolf Wallner, Bernd Weber, Christofer Witt, Kai Ziehl and Andries Zwikker.

I would also like to express my thanks to the following companies, institutions and organisations for supplying documentation and photographic material: Adrian Meredith Photography, AeroLyon, African Safari Airways, Air Canada, Air France, Alitalia, American Airlines, Biman Bangladesh Airlines, the Boeing Company – Historical Archives, British Airways, Buena Vista International Belgium, Canadian Airlines International, Condor, Continental Airlines, Federal Express, Finnair, Flite-Line-Photos, Garuda, General Electric Aircraft Engines, Iberia, Icelandair, LOT Polish Airlines, Martinair, Military Aircraft Photographs, Newell and Sorell, Northwest Airlines, Orbis, Philippine Airlines, Premiair, Royal Netherlands Air Force – Eindhoven AFB Public Affairs, Sabena, SAS, Singapore Airlines, Thai Airways International, Turkish Airlines, United States Air Force – March AFB Public Affairs, McGuire AFB Public Affairs, Seymour Johnson AFB Public Affairs, and Travis AFB Public Affairs, United Technologies – Pratt & Whitney and World Airways.

Opposite:
The flight line at Long Beach in November 1972. Several aircraft of the different series are being readied for delivery. The second aircraft from the bottom is the first DC-10 built, N10DC, stripped of the McDonnell Douglas house colours, soon to receive the American Airlines livery. It was delivered to that carrier on 8th December 1972 as N101AA. McDonnell Douglas

Chapter One

Birth of a Wide-Body

In 1964, Boeing, Douglas and Lockheed received contracts from the US Air Force to design and develop a large cargo transport. The Cargo Experimental – Heavy Logistics System (CX-HLS) Transporter project would later be given the designation C-5. In the end, Lockheed was awarded the contract to build the massive aircraft, to be known as the Galaxy.

At Douglas, studies based on this proposal, were under way to build a transport capable of carrying up to 100 tons of cargo or 550 passengers. This huge four-engined aircraft would feature a two-aisle cabin layout with seven-abreast seating on the upper deck and eight-abreast seating on the lower deck, with a maximum of three seats between aisles. If the response of airlines were to prove positive, Douglas would proceed with the development of this aircraft,

named the DC-10. The outcome though would be completely different.

The evolution of the DC-10 can be considered as commencing in March 1966, when American Airlines released its requirements for a wide-body twin-engined aircraft to several manufacturers. The aircraft would be powered by two advanced technology high-bypass-ratio turbofans and carry 250 passengers over ranges up to 1,850 nautical miles (3,428km). A further and challenging requirement was the capability to operate with 250 passengers and 5,000lb (2,268kg) of cargo from New York's La Guardia Airport to Chicago. Weight restrictions were imposed by the limited strength of the runways at La Guardia – partially built on piers. Due to the short field lengths, low approach speeds became a requirement.

Quoting Robert E Hage, then Vice President, Engineering, Douglas Aircraft Company, from his presentation at the Israel Conference on Aviation and Astronautics in Tel Aviv on 3rd March 1971:

'The evolution of the DC-10 has occurred in an environment of increasingly severe social and economic pressures. This has necessitated the careful balancing of the gains resulting from advanced technology against the social and economic pressures. The social considerations include demands for improved services, increased safety, the elimination of smoke and the reduction of noise. The economic pressures include improved utilisation of limited resources such as ground and airspace, increasing costs, disappointing load factors and decreasing fares. These conflicting social and economic pressures on the air transportation system result in two types of aircraft design requirements, those that relate directly to the aircraft and those that ensure the compatibility of an efficient air transportation system with its environment. The most efficient airplane, if not compatible with its environment, cannot be successful. This has established new and challenging design requirements for the DC-10'.

The required characteristics for the aircraft included: wide-body dual aisle comfort, speed, safety, all weather capability, low direct operating costs and growth potential. The environmental characteristics required an optimised use of crowded ground and airspace, operation from small congested airports, compatibility with runway strength and existing terminal facilities, no smoke and low noise.

A 1967 International Civil Aviation Organisation (ICAO) forecast of free world operators formed the basis of determining the size of the DC-10. This was the result of carefully balancing the requirements: minimum physical size for heavily congested airports versus maximum size for low direct operating costs and the correct size for the market. Airline traffic requirements led to the selection of a 'new dimension' 270-passenger aircraft, filling the gap between the 210-passenger Douglas DC-8 Series 61/63 and the 380-passenger Boeing 747 four-jets.

Another important decision to be taken in the evolution process was the engine-configuration. Although a four-engine version was considered, it was rejected for two reasons. Firstly, the unavailability of a suitable size advanced technology engine and secondly, the lack of interest on the part of the airlines.

The decision between the two- and three-engine configuration was made in favour of the latter. In case of an engine failure during take-off, a three-engine aircraft would still have 67% of its thrust available, while the remaining thrust for a two-engine version would be 50%. Furthermore, a three-engine aircraft would require less runway length.

The significant increase in range compensated for the slightly higher take-off weight resulting from a third engine installation. The range flexibility also was an important factor in the development and growth of the DC-10 family.

Already during the configuration development space had been provided in the fuselage

centre bay for an additional landing gear required by a heavier long range aircraft. This proved to be a key factor in the success of the DC-10 in comparison to the Lockheed L-1011 TriStar which simply did not have the necessary endurance for a true long range aircraft.

The tri-jet design portfolio proposed by Douglas was accepted by American Airlines and following the order of United Airlines the go-ahead for the DC-10 Series 10 (or DC-10-10) was given. The aircraft was the result of refined design techniques evolved from long Douglas experience. Flight test programmes on three versions of the DC-8 and five versions of the DC-9 twin-jet provided a wealth of data that afforded a sound basis for the design of this new family of subsonic transports. An extensive development programme provided wind tunnel data on aspects that represented advances over DC-8 and DC-9 flight experience.

Over 14,000 wind tunnel test hours were completed to establish and refine the configurations for the domestic and intercontinental versions of the DC-10. From the smoothly contoured nose section and V-shaped windshield to the minimum upsweep rear fuselage section, results of the aerodynamic design tests were applied whenever beneficial.

More than 3,000 hours of high and low speed wind tunnel testing were devoted to the development of the wing and high-lift system design. The DC-10 wing combines advanced airfoil designs and 35° of sweep to provide a maximum operating efficiency for long range operations at a Mac 0.82 cruise and a high speed cruise of Mach 0.85. The Series 10 and 15 have a wingspan of 155ft 4in (47.35m) and a wing area of 3,550ft² (329.79m²). The long range Series 30 and 40 figures are 165ft 4in (50.39m) and 3,647ft² (338.80m²) respectively.

Wings on all series feature full-span leading edge slats, developed from those successfully used on the DC-9-30. Coupled with the powerful large-chord double-slotted trailing edge flaps, an extremely effective high-lift system is formed. For lateral control, all-speed inboard ailerons and spoilers, in conjunction with low speed outboard ailerons, are installed.

The tail section features a two-segment rudder for directional control. Longitudinal control is provided by the large elevators and horizontal stabiliser trim. The span of the horizontal stabiliser, at 71ft 2in. (21.69m), is greater than the length of the venerable Douglas DC-3, which measures 64ft 6½in. (19.67m).

There is a remarkable difference between the DC-10 and the L-1011 tail engine installation. While Lockheed adapted an S-type bend of inlet, Douglas selected a straight inlet duct for the DC-10. This aerodynamic design feature assures an optimal performance and freedom from inlet distortion and the associated operational losses. Further advantages of this configuration were the ease of assembly and the optimum utilisation of the rear fuselage. Staying with the DC-3 comparison, with a diameter of 95in (2.41m), the fuselage of a 'Dakota' would easily fit into the duct of the DC-10 aft engine installation, which is 108in (2.74m) in diameter.

In the initial design, the result of over 2,000 fatigue development tests conducted on the DC-8 and DC-9 were used in conjunction with an additional 1,700 DC-10 fatigue development tests to verify that the structure had a crack-free long life. The DC-10 structure was designed and tested for a life of 120,000 hours and 84,000 flights. This assures a high probability of crack-free service life for 20 years or 60,000 flight hours and 42,000 landings.

Prior to the production start, a development fixture was built to the exact dimensions of the aircraft. With parts coming from a worldwide network of subcontractors and suppliers, the fixture permitted the early trial and development of wiring, cockpit, cabin and avionics installations, amongst others.

There are 210,000 parts in a DC-10, exclusive of engine components. The airframe contains 1,750,000 fasteners, including 1,250,000 solid aluminium alloy rivets, 400,000 locking bolts and 100,000 screws and shear bolts. Laid end to end, the electrical wiring in a typical DC-10 would stretch between 40 and 50 miles (64 and 80km). The wire consists of 30,000 strands attached to 60,000 electrical terminators.

Opposite: **A family of fine and reliable transports. Clockwise from bottom left the following aircraft are depicted: Stewart Air Service C-47A-65-DL ('DC-3') N67578, Pacific Southwest Airways C-54A/R5D-1 ('DC-4') N93267, US Air Force C-118A Liftmaster (military DC-6), United Air Lines DC-7 N6353C and the first Douglas DC-8 – N8008D, first flown on 30th May 1958.**
Douglas Aircraft Company

Right: **Cutaway model representing a mid-1960s Douglas proposal for a double-deck high-capacity commercial jet transport, named DC-10.**
Douglas Aircraft Company

Because of their sheer size of deployment, two sequences of the operations were eye-catching. The wings of the DC-10 were manufactured by McDonnell Douglas-Canada at its Malton, Ontario plant, adjacent to Toronto's L B Pearson International Airport. Upon completion, they were shipped by boxcars to the plant in Long Beach, California.

General Dynamics' Convair Division in San Diego was the subcontractor for the manufacture of the main fuselage sections. In the beginning the sections were flown to the Long Beach facilities in an Aerospacelines Super Guppy (a radically converted Boeing 377/C-97 for the transportation of outsize cargo), but were later transported by barges to Long Beach Harbor. In order to avoid a disruption in the DC-9 and still ongoing DC-8 production, a new separate final assembly plant was built for the DC-10.

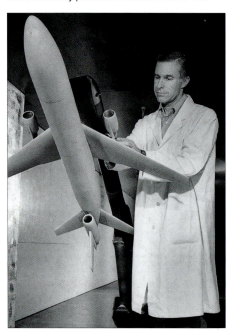

It is of interest that there actually never was a prototype. The complete test and certification programme was carried out by five DC-10s which were ultimately delivered to customer airlines. Once the first DC-10s were built, a comprehensive test programme to verify structural integrity and reliability was started. This programme included: proof-testing of a production airframe prior to first flight, instrumental structural demonstration flights, fatigue and fail-safe tests on full-scale airframe sections and ultimate strength tests on components.

The control system was proof-tested and the system operation was demonstrated on the first production aircraft before it made its maiden flight from Long Beach on 29th August 1970. Piloted by Project Pilot Clifford L Stout and crew members Harris C van Valkenburg, J D Chamberlain and Shojun Yukawa, DC-10-10 N10DC flew for 3 hours, 26 minutes on its first test flight from its home base to the USAF flight test centre at Edwards Air Force Base, California.

The second production aircraft was used for the actual proof-test during which distributed tail loads, dynamic response due to gust, landing, and taxi loads were determined during flight and ground tests. Instrumentation was calibrated to the proof-loads for the subsequent flight structural demonstration programme. This included all the critical design manoeuvre conditions and selected landing conditions and also included operations in

A flight test crew and a DC-10-10 test aircraft are well illustrated in this contemporary publicity artwork. McDonnell Douglas

Large scale models were used in extensive wind tunnel tests to determine the shape of the wing roots, engine pods and other components. McDonnell Douglas

smooth and turbulent weather. The aircraft was fully instrumented and calibrated by a matrix computer programme which provided data that verified the external loads and stress levels used in the analysis.

Aircraft No.3 conducted evaluation tests on engine installation and performance, engine compartment cooling on ground, as well as during take-off and climb. Further tests included the evaluation of airstarts at various speeds and altitudes, engine fire detector system and climb performance. Also part of this aircraft's programme were rejected take-off stopping distance, two-engine take-off performance and minimum control flight speed tests.

Although many representative structural component tests were conducted during the development programme, the fourth production aircraft was fatigue tested to a flight-by-flight repeated-load spectrum of 120,000 hours and 84,000 landings. Any design changes necessary to improve fatigue-sensitive areas as revealed by the fatigue test programme were included in early production parts.

After the final structural assembly of the fatigue test aircraft was completed, it was transferred to the test laboratory and divided into three major sections: forward fuselage, wing and centre fuselage and aft fuselage and empennage. Fatigue tests were then carried out simultaneously on all three sections to rapidly isolate possible fatigue-sensitive areas and implement remedial action.

Finally, the fifth aircraft conducted 150 hours of functional and reliability tests as required by the Federal Aviation Administration (FAA).

A 'first' for the aviation industry was the introduction of a long range data link system by Douglas. This advanced system permitted the collection and evaluation of flight test information on the DC-10 while the aircraft was in the air. The data from the on-board instrumentation was processed by airborne computers for telemetry transmission to a remote tracking station atop an 8,400ft (2,560m) mountain near Wrightwood, California. A microwave link then relayed the signals to the new flight test control centre at the plant in Long Beach.

The Xerox Data Systems Sigma 7 computer and cathode ray tube screens enabled flight test engineers at the centre to perform immediate data analysis. The system was also used for post-flight analysis of the data collected on airborne tape recorders. The flight test control centre was at all times in contact with the flight crew and test engineers on board during testing. In case a certain test was not satisfactory, it could be repeated immediately without the aircraft having to land first and analysing the airborne tape recorders thereafter.

To obtain the FAA type certificate, the five aircraft conducted the rigorous flight test and development programme over eleven months. Flight tests were conducted from Long Beach, the Douglas flight test facility at Yuma, Arizona and Edwards Air Force Base, California.

Noise certification tests were carried out at

the FAA's acoustical test range at Atlantic City, New Jersey. With the new FAR (Federal Aviation Regulation) Part 36 noise levels coming into effect, the DC-10 was the first aircraft to be certified under those stringent regulations.

The DC-10 came out with flying colours with take-off, landing and sideline noise measurements well below FAA requirements. Besides the certification flights at Atlantic City, flights were conducted at several US airports to demonstrate the aircraft's low noise and smoke levels to airport officials.

On 18th July 1971 the flight test programme was completed, nearly three months ahead of schedule. Together the test aircraft had logged more than 1,500 hours prior to FAA certification for airline service on 29th July 1971. That same day, deliveries of the first aircraft were jointly made to American Airlines and United Airlines.

Ten years later, on 1st February 1981, Donald Wills Douglas passed away at the age of 88. Nearly 350 DC-10s were already in service worldwide, proudly carrying the name of the founder of the Douglas Aircraft Company.

The development fixture, built to the exact dimensions of the aircraft, permitted early development of wiring, cockpit, avionics and other installations before the start of production. McDonnell Douglas

In the beginning, the three main fuselage sections, manufactured by subcontractor Convair, were flown from San Diego to Long Beach in an Aerospacelines Super Guppy. Later they were transported by barges to Long Beach Harbor and trucked to the plant. McDonnell Douglas

A tail-mounted engine support structure is moved on a rollered cradle to mate with the rear fuselage section. Note the substantial engine support beam. McDonnell Douglas

An airframe in an advanced stage of assembly, with the undercarriage installed.

A completed American Airlines DC-10 is towed across Lakewood Boulevard to receive its engines and tail fin.

With all three engines installed, British Caledonian Series 30 G-BEBM has its tail fin attached. All McDonnell Douglas

Photographs on the opposite page:

The final assembly line with three Series 10s. Before it was delivered to United Air Lines, the aircraft in the foreground, N1803U, served as the functional and reliability test aircraft. The American Airlines example shows the preliminary 'Astroliner' title, which was replaced by the name 'Luxury Liner'.

A DC-10 parked on the compass rose at the Long Beach plant to check the aircraft's magnetic navigation instruments.
Both McDonnell Douglas

Chapter Two

A Renowned Family

As explained in Chapter One, the DC-10 has adaptability designed into it. This allowed for growth in terms of combinations of gross weight, range and passenger capacity. Not only this, the airframe has proven to be a superb freighter and its capacity for military (see Chapter Five) and other special uses (Chapter Three and Chapter Four) well established. From the original design has come a family that is still expanding.

Pioneering Series 10

The first member of the DC-10 family was the Series 10 (DC-10-10). This medium range transport is powered by General Electric CF6-6Ds. It was designed for service on routes of 300 to 3,800 statute miles (480 to 6,114km) carrying 250 passengers in a mixed class or 380 passengers in an all-economy configuration. When the last all-passenger Series 10 was delivered to United Airlines on 22nd May 1981, a total of 122 of the type had been produced.

Douglas built nine Series 10CFs (Convertible Freighter), of which eight were delivered to Continental Airlines and one to United Airlines. The Series 10CF accepted by United Airlines on 20th September 1982 was the 2,000th jet aircraft delivered by McDonnell Douglas.

'Hot and High' Series 15

The development of the Series 15 was initiated by the Mexican carriers Aeromexico and Mexicana. Essentially the Series 15 is a Series 10 airframe fitted with the derated thrust engines of the Series 30. This combination gives the aircraft outstanding performance with maximum take-off loads from high altitude airports in hot climates like the carriers' Mexico City home base. Mexicana ordered five aircraft with the first being delivered on 15th June 1981. Only two were built for Aeromexico. The production run of seven aircraft was the lowest of all DC-10 series.

Long Range Series 30 and 40

The planned growth potential in the initial design soon led to the first long-range intercontinental version, initially named the Series 20. The aircraft, powered by Pratt & Whitney JT9D-20s, made its first flight on 28th February 1972. Northwest Orient Airlines was the launch customer of the Series 20, which was redesignated Series 40 at the request of the carrier. The range of this version is 5,350 statute miles (8,608km) The airline ordered 22 Series 40s.

The KSSU group (KLM, SAS, Swissair and UTA) was the launch customer of the Series 30.

This variant is powered by General Electric CF6-50s and had its maiden flight from Long Beach on 21st June 1972. The non-stop operational range came up to 5,860 miles (9,429km).

The heavier, long range, Series 30s and 40s required the installation of an additional central landing gear. The wingspan of both versions was increased by 10ft 0in (3.05m) over the medium range Series 10, providing space for the extra fuel capacity requirements as well as keeping the take-off and landing speeds consistent with contemporary long range aircraft.

Douglas later offered a further version of the Series 30, the so-called ER – Extended Range. This aircraft could be ordered with supplemental fuel tanks for additional range. A basic supplemental fuel cell with a capacity of 10,270lb (4,658kg) or an extended supplemental fuel cell holding 21,400lb (9,707kg) of fuel could be installed in the centre cargo compartment. These optional fuel packages were also available for the Series 40 aircraft.

The all-passenger Series 30 proved to be the most successful aircraft in the family. A total of 169 units left the Long Beach plant for delivery mainly to major international operators.

In April 1973, the first DC-10 Series 30CFs were delivered to Overseas National Airways and Trans International Airlines. With an arrangement for all passenger, all cargo or mixed passenger/cargo layouts, the Series 30CF was ideal for airlines operating in both fields. Douglas built 27 commercial Series 30CFs between 1973 and 1980.

A further version of the Series 40 was built for Japan Air Lines. Powered by Pratt & Whitney JT9D-59As, the aircraft has an increased operational range of up to approximately 5,750 miles (9,252km). JAL turned out to be the only customer and took delivery of the first of 20 ordered on 23rd November 1976.

The last commercial version built was the Series 30F. The all-freighter model was ordered by Federal Express in May 1984. A total of ten were delivered to the carrier.

After Douglas had been awarded the Advanced Tanker Cargo Aircraft contract by the US Air Force, production of the KC-10A Extender started and the first was delivered on 1st October 1981. Based on the Series 30CF, a total of 60 were built (see Chapter Five).

DC-10 versus L-1011

When the DC-10 production line closed in October 1988, a grand total of 446 aircraft of all variants had been produced:

Series 10	122	Series 30CF	27
Series 10CF	9	Series 30F	10
Series 15	7	Series 40	42
Series 30	169	KC-10A	60

With an initial hefty order book for the Lockheed L-1011 TriStar, the outlook for Douglas at the start of the production in 1970 had been gloomy. However, in the end the DC-10 was the winner in the sales battle with its arch-rival. The TriStar has always played second fiddle to the DC-10. Production of the Lockheed product stopped in October 1983 with a total of only 250 of the Series 1, 100, 200 and 500 aircraft built. The Douglas concept of growth potential, as exercised before with the DC-8 and DC-9 family of jetliners, had prevailed.

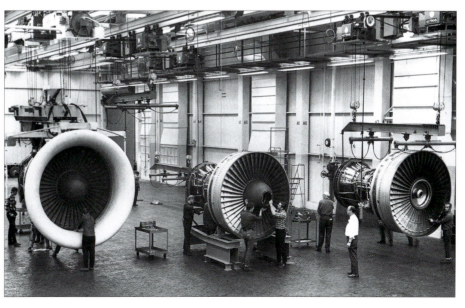

Photograph on the opposite page:

United Airlines did not follow the 'white-body' trend when it introduced its new colour scheme in January 1993. United Airlines

Photographs on this page:

During a ceremony on 29th July 1971 the first aircraft were delivered to American Airlines and United Airlines. McDonnell Douglas

Series 20 lettering on fuselage number 28. This was the first DC-10 long range version. Renamed the Series 40, it entered service with launch customer Northwest Orient Airlines. McDonnell Douglas

The Pratt & Whitney JT9D, the second engine available for the DC-10, was manufactured at the company's plant in East Hartford, Connecticut. United Technologies, Pratt & Whitney

Both Pratt & Whitney and General Electric used a modified US Air Force Boeing B-52 Stratofortress to test their new engines. Two of the bomber's P&W J-57 engines were replaced by a single high bypass ratio turbofan. Illustrated is a P&W JT9D on the flying test-bed. The Boeing Company

A fully assembled General Electric CF6-50 receives a final inspection before delivery to McDonnell Douglas. General Electric Engines

A spectacular sight is the transportation of a spare engine, the so-called 'fourth pod'. The assembly with the aerodynamic housing is seen on a Japan Air Lines DC-10-40. McDonnell Douglas

In the early 1970s, Douglas also planned to offer a twin-engined derivative, the so-called DC-10 Twin. In the aftermath of the 1973 Middle East War commercial aviation was faced with soaring fuel prices and a subsequent downturn in airline traffic which unfortunately led to the Twin project being terminated.

It is evident that McDonnell Douglas as well as Lockheed had envisaged higher production figures, but as the 1980s began, the recession, an increase in fuel prices, and the US airline industry deregulation all combined to stall commercial aircraft sales.

Engines

At the time of the C-5 Galaxy programme, which was awarded to Lockheed, both Pratt & Whitney (P&W) and General Electric (GE) were eager to obtain the engine contract for the super transport. General Electric built the TF39, developed from the GE1/6 turbofan demonstrator, for the C-5A.

Although Boeing had lost the contract, they pursued the development of a commercial derivative of their C-5 proposal which would ultimately become the 747. Boeing's project called for an engine with at least 43,000lb (191kN) thrust, more than twice that of the 18,000lb (80kN) thrust JT8D turbofans used on the DC-8 and Boeing 707. The engines were further required to be low noise and smokeless.

After General Electric had withdrawn from the 747 competition, P&W accepted the challenge to build the new engine, the JT9D, for the wide-body. The result was the 'high bypass ratio' turbofan engine. The bypass ratio is the proportion of airflow through the fan at the front of the engine and airflow through the engine core. A high bypass engine not only develops more power, it also is more fuel efficient and quieter. The large 8ft (2.4m) diameter fan, twice the size of the JT8D, together with a sophisticated combination of compressor stages and high and low speed compressors, made it possible to reach 43,500lb (193kN) thrust.

The JT9D was run for the first time on the test stand at the East Hartford, Connecticut, P&W plant in December 1966. For flight testing purposes P&W leased a Boeing B-52 Stratofortress bomber from the US Air Force. Two of the inboard P&W J57s were replaced by a single JT9D. The first flight of the test-bed aircraft took place in June 1968 and FAA engine certification followed in May 1969.

When PanAm Boeing 747 N736PA *Clipper Victor* took off from New York to London Heathrow on 22nd January 1970, it not only ʼed the first 747 commercial flight but also ʼrevenue service of the high bypass ratio turbofan engine.

On the basis of their joint studies with GE, P&W and Rolls-Royce, the three major engine

makers, Douglas and Lockheed evolved wide-body aircraft that were smaller than the 747 and were powered by three turbofan engines.

General Electric had started the development of the high bypass ratio CF-6 turbofan, a smaller derivative of the TF39 engine, while Rolls-Royce was working on the RB211.

Both the DC-10 and L-1011 were being studied with the new GE, P&W and R-R turbofans in mind. The multiple engine offerings were a break with the past when aircraft were designed around a single engine type. The airlines were now in a position to make their own decision and a fierce competition between the three engine manufacturers ensued.

The outcome is well known. Trans World Airlines (TWA), Eastern and Delta chose the Rolls-Royce RB211 for the L-1011s they ordered. It would remain the only engine available for the TriStar range.

After the decision of American, United followed suit and opted for the GE CF-6 turbofan for its DC-10s. P&W, with the JT9D turbofan, became the second manufacturer to supply engines for the DC-10. With only two customers for the JT9D, Northwest Airlines and Japan Air Lines, P&W would only play a minor role in the DC-10 programme. As had been the case with the P&W JT9D, the CF6 was flight tested on a US Air Force B-52, modified by the Edwards Flight Test Center team.

The roll out of the DC-10 at the Long Beach plant in July 1970 had a very special character. The DC-10 was the first commercial airliner ever to roll out under its own power. Behind a marching band of kilted Scottish bagpipers and drummers, the striking aircraft hove into view of thousands of airline officials, industry guests, McDonnell Douglas and GE employees, the governor of California and the US vice president, so honouring the heritage of the airframe manufacturer's two principal founders, Donald W Douglas and James S McDonnell.

Once production had started, engines were shipped from GE's Cincinnati plant, Ohio and P&W's East Hartford plant, Connecticut, to a subcontractor in San Diego for installation of controls and accessories. Thereafter, assembled engines were trucked to Long Beach for installation on the DC-10.

Following is a summary of the different engines which were available for the various DC-10 series.

Series	Engine	Take-off thrust
10	GE CF6-6D	40,000 lb (177kN)
10	GE CF6-6D1/D2	41,000 lb (182kN)
10	GE CF6-6D1A	41,500 lb (184kN)
10	GE CF6-6K/K2	41,500 lb (184kN)
15	GE CF6-50C2F	46,500 lb (206kN)
30	GE CF6-50C	51,000 lb (226kN)
30	GE CF6-50C1/C2	52,500 lb (233kN)
30	GE CF6-50C2B	54,000 lb (240kN)
40	P&W JT9D-20	45,700 lb (203kN)
40	P&W JT9D-59A	53,000 lb (235kN)
40	P&W JT9D-59B	54,500 lb (242kN)

The GE CF6-50C2 for the KC-10A carries the military designation F103-GE-100. The P&W JT9D-59B was certified for use on the DC-10, but no aircraft with this type of engine was ordered or delivered.

It is noteworthy that nearly every new member of each engine family introduced a higher performance in thrust and a lower specific fuel consumption. The reliability of the engines was demonstrated in 1987 when a CF6-50 on a Canadian Airlines International DC-10-30 made its first shop visit after 20,394 hours.

Because of the larger fan diameter of the P&W engines one can notice a difference in size and shape between the cowlings of the GE or P&W wing-mounted engines. The most remarkable difference is the 'coke bottle' look aft engine cowling of P&W powered aircraft, compared to the straight cowling profile of the GE aft engine.

The arrangement of the two wing-mounted engines and one mounted in the tail provided good weight-and-balance characteristics and resulted in an aircraft with lower weight and drag than that of any other tri-jet arrangement.

A dazzling view showing the removal of the tail mounted engine. With the proper ground support equipment, like the special hoist system, a complete engine change takes 12 hours.
Lufthansa Photo Archives

	Fan diameter	Engine length
GE CF6-6	86.4in (2.19m)	188.0in (4.8m)
GE CF6-50	86.4in (2.19m)	182.5in (4.6m)
P&W JT9D-59A	96.6in (2.43m)	131.9in (3.35m)

To fulfil the low noise requirement, all nacelles have inlet and fan ducts long enough to provide a large amount of surface area for sound-suppression material.

Ease of maintenance was an important factor in the design of the engine system installations. The large pylon-hinged nacelle doors expose the entire engine. The cowl doors and split thrust reverser allow easy access to the engine. For simplicity and reduced spare engine costs, these remain on the aircraft during an engine change. Not only for easy accessibility, but also to provide a cool environment for a prolonged life, accessory drive gear boxes are mounted externally on the fan case. A self-contained built-in platform for maintenance and inspection is located at the aft engine. With the proper ground support equipment available, a wing-mounted engine change takes eight hours. The tail engine change takes 12 hours.

The basic engine can be transported by highway truck without the need of a special permit. The DC-10 can transport a spare engine itself, the so-called 'fourth pod'. This option includes provisions incorporated in the inboard side of the port side wing to accept a pylon on which any engine used on the DC-10 can be installed. After installation on the pylon, the spare engine is surrounded and protected by an aerodynamic housing made of aluminium honeycomb covered with fibreglass. This feature is typical of the careful attention to detail given by Douglas and the engine builders.

The Cockpit
The cockpit design concept was based on simplicity, a low crew workload, growth capability, comfort and an adequate and efficient work space for the flight crew. Several factors played a role in achieving the design objectives. The proven cockpit features of the DC-8 and DC-9 formed a solid basis for further development. Douglas received important information from surveys held not only amongst pilots of the many airlines operating DC-8s and DC-9s, but also of those flying competitors' jet transports.

The cockpit design team's primary responsibility was to research and determine the best possible means of meeting the design objectives. The input from airline personnel helped the design team to create a working place offering maximum operational efficiency at a minimum 'total crew' workload level.

The team also ensured that the co-ordinated effort between the engineering and flight personnel was maintained throughout the design of the cockpit. During design, mock-ups and simulators were used to establish the basic grouping of instruments, controls and equipment. Layout of flight instruments and switches was arranged in such a way that each system was easily distinguishable from another, and to obtain a balanced arrangement of items, factors such as priority, frequency of use and space required, were taken into consideration.

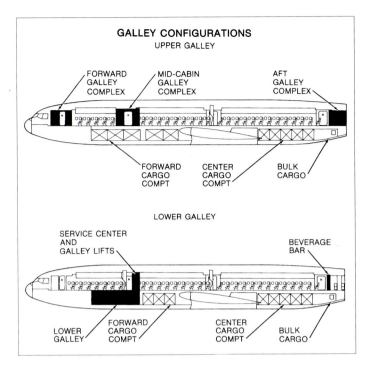

GALLEY CONFIGURATIONS
UPPER GALLEY

FORWARD GALLEY COMPLEX — MID-CABIN GALLEY COMPLEX — AFT GALLEY COMPLEX

FORWARD CARGO COMPT — CENTER CARGO COMPT — BULK CARGO

LOWER GALLEY

SERVICE CENTER AND GALLEY LIFTS — BEVERAGE BAR

LOWER GALLEY — FORWARD CARGO COMPT — CENTER CARGO COMPT — BULK CARGO

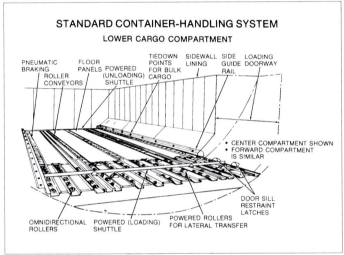

STANDARD CONTAINER-HANDLING SYSTEM
LOWER CARGO COMPARTMENT

PNEUMATIC BRAKING — FLOOR PANELS — POWERED (UNLOADING) SHUTTLE — TIEDOWN POINTS FOR BULK CARGO — SIDEWALL LINING — SIDE GUIDE RAIL — LOADING DOORWAY

ROLLER CONVEYORS

• CENTER COMPARTMENT SHOWN
• FORWARD COMPARTMENT IS SIMILAR

OMNIDIRECTIONAL ROLLERS — POWERED (LOADING) SHUTTLE — POWERED ROLLERS FOR LATERAL TRANSFER — DOOR SILL RESTRAINT LATCHES

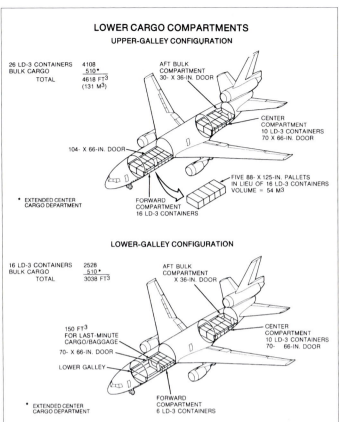

LOWER CARGO COMPARTMENTS
UPPER-GALLEY CONFIGURATION

26 LD-3 CONTAINERS 4108
BULK CARGO 510 *
TOTAL 4618 FT³
(131 M³)

AFT BULK COMPARTMENT 30- X 36-IN. DOOR

CENTER COMPARTMENT 10 LD-3 CONTAINERS 70 X 66-IN. DOOR

104- X 66-IN. DOOR

FIVE 88- X 125-IN. PALLETS IN LIEU OF 16 LD-3 CONTAINERS VOLUME = 54 M3

FORWARD COMPARTMENT 16 LD-3 CONTAINERS

* EXTENDED CENTER CARGO DEPARTMENT

LOWER-GALLEY CONFIGURATION

16 LD-3 CONTAINERS 2528
BULK CARGO 510 *
TOTAL 3038 FT³

AFT BULK COMPARTMENT X 36-IN. DOOR

CENTER COMPARTMENT 10 LD-3 CONTAINERS 70- 66-IN. DOOR

150 FT³ FOR LAST-MINUTE CARGO/BAGGAGE
70- X 66-IN. DOOR

LOWER GALLEY

FORWARD COMPARTMENT 6 LD-3 CONTAINERS

* EXTENDED CENTER CARGO DEPARTMENT

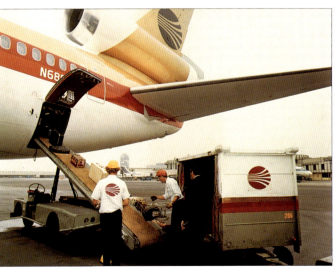

DC-10 galley configurations, upper and lower.

Lower cargo compartment details, for upper galley and lower galley configuration.

Schematic of the standard container handling system, lower cargo compartment.

The centre cargo compartment on all aircraft can be loaded with LD3 or LD6 containers. The one-man operation permits the loading or unloading of the forward and centre compartment within six minutes.

Because of its tapered shape, the aft cargo compartment only accommodates bulk cargo. It is also used for the shipment of pets and small animals. All McDonnell Douglas

Photographs on the opposite page:

McDonnell Douglas paid particular attention to the design of the instrument layout as seen from the captain's and first officer's perspective. Lufthansa Photo Archives

The DC-10 cockpit is one of the largest and roomiest in today's airliners and a comfortable working place for the three-man crew. Lufthansa Photo Archives

aft view, enabling each pilot to see the wingtips during taxying and close quarter manoeuvring. Since the forward vision cut-off is less than 57.4ft (17.5m) excellent forward-and-down vision is obtained during taxying. Upward forward vision is 39°.

A significant feature of the cockpit are the openable clearview windows. The DC-10 is the only aircraft of the early wide-body transports (DC-10, 747 and L-1011) to offer this feature, permitting a rapid egress in case of an emergency. Adequate vision is assured in case of hail or bird strike damage since the clearview windows may be opened in flight at speeds up to 286mph (460km/h). The openable windows also allow the cleaning of cockpit windshields without the need of ground support equipment.

On the comfort side, a heat-soaked cockpit can be cooled down through cross ventilation before the air conditioning system is in operation. Crew comfort is further enhanced by the cool air 'eyeball' diffusers located at each crew station. In order to eliminate wide temperature variations in the windshield and clearview window area, an additional 'air curtain' is supplied by the air conditioning system ducting.

State-of-the art crew seats for captain, first officer and flight engineer can be operated electrically and have a manual override system. In addition to the vertical and fore-and-aft travel functions of all three seats, the flight engineer's seat can be swivelled from the flight engineer's console to forward behind the engine control pedestal, a position normally taken for take-off and landing. The first observer seat behind the captain's position can be adjusted manually, fore-and-aft as well as vertically, and has a retractable footrest. A simple fold-up seat for a second observer is located at the cockpit's wall and occupies minimum space when not in use.

For easy access, an enlarged flightkit area is provided at the stations of the captain, first officer and flight engineer. Finally, the cockpit is furnished with a large crew coatroom and crew baggage area.

As one of the largest cockpits in jet transports, the spacious DC-10 cockpit provides uncrowded working conditions for the flight crew. Furthermore, the aerodynamic design of the nose of the fuselage and the V-shape windshield guarantee a minimum of airflow disturbance, resulting in extremely low cockpit noise levels. Through this cockpit design, Douglas achieved the envisaged efficient and comfortable workspace for the DC-10 flight crews.

The flight compartment overhead panel is positioned to provide easy access to all switches and controls with a minimum of reach. The low profile flight compartment pedestal and throttle quadrant design allows the flight engineer to view all of the engine instruments on the centre instrument panel from any of his normal seat positions.

Instead of the common 'round-dial' engine instruments, vertical-scale instruments could be installed. In contrast to the 'round' instruments, a single vertical-scale unit houses the instrumentation and displays for all engines for each of the parameters N1 (low pressure rotor, % rpm), N2 (high pressure rotor, % rpm), EGT (exhaust gas temperature) and FF (fuel flow). P&W-powered aircraft have an additional EPR (engine pressure ratio) read-out.

All communications equipment is centralised on the pedestal and allows a high degree of crew co-ordination at a minimum workload level. It also houses the captain's and first officer's navigation control/display units.

The flight engineer's station was designed for an efficient and safe operation of all systems under his surveillance. The arrangement of controls and instruments display functions directly and clearly and facilitate comprehension of the status of all systems continuously.

An important factor – pilot vision – has been well taken care of. The flat windshields panels and slightly curved clearview panels give unimpeded vision. The advantages of the flat windshields are a minimum amount of reflection and distortion, not achievable on curved windshields as used on the L-1011 and 747, maximum strength and optimal wiper efficiency.

The large side windows provide an excellent

The impressive maindeck of a DC-10 Convertible Freighter. While all passengers hand luggage bins are removed, side wall and overhead panels remain installed.

DC-10 cutaway showing one of the multiple variations of container configurations.
Both McDonnell Douglas

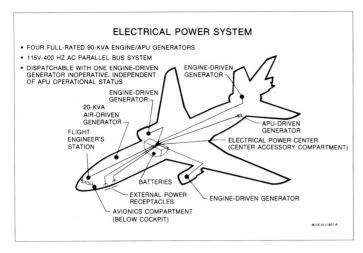

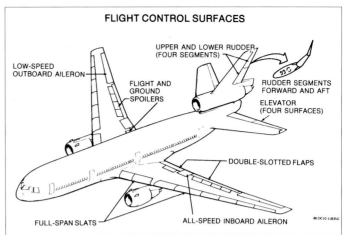

Electric power system. McDonnell Douglas

Flight control surfaces. McDonnell Douglas

Convertible Cabin

For the DC-10 interior configuration, Douglas wrote the word 'flexibility' in capital letters. Requirements from the various airlines differed greatly regarding the class configuration, seating arrangement and galley layout. Each airline had its own cabin design demands to be addressed by the aircraft manufacturer.

Douglas went to great lengths to satisfy the particular requirements of its airline customers. Although the L-1011 followed the same concept, Douglas was first in offering the lower galley configuration. On the planned high density short to medium range routes of American, United and other US carriers, the transport of cargo was of less importance, while removal of the galley from the main deck would have clear advantages. The below deck galley measures 22ft 3in (6.78m) in length, 12ft 6in (3.81m) in width and has a ceiling height of 6ft 1¾in (1.87m). With a working floor width of 5ft 2⅛in (1.58m) a spacious workplace for the flight attendants is provided. All food is prepared below deck and is carried to the cabin service centre by means of two galley lifts.

With only one service centre and a beverage bar in the main cabin, the number of seats could thus be increased. In a typical first and economy class mix, 28 and 301 passengers respectively may be accommodated. In the case of an all-economy layout, up to 380 seats may be installed. The lower galley configuration was not only available for the Series 10, but also for the Series 30 and 40.

Maximum flexibility was probably reached on the DC-10-30CFs of World Airways which were the first Series 30s with the lower galley option, while still offering the carriage of passengers and/or freight in varying combination. To give another example of the Series 30 layout, Condor Flugdienst of Germany operates its original three lower galley-equipped aircraft with a total of 370 economy passengers.

Douglas did not want to fall behind Boeing's 747 upper deck lounge idea. Several arrangements of a main deck cabin lounge were offered, including the 'Pub in the Sky' on Continental Airlines DC-10s. With increasing passenger traffic, these lounges soon disappeared to make way for much-needed passenger revenue seats.

The conventional main cabin galley arrangement was chosen by most carriers. Galley units are conveniently located to provide three service areas. In the 1970s, only first and economy class was offered by the airlines. With the introduction of business class, the main cabin galley arrangement would still provide one unit for each class, ensuring a separate and undisturbed service. Again, passenger seat configurations are numerous. From a typical 22 first, 45 business and 165 economy, they ranged up to a 380 all-economy seating arrangement.

With the flexibility of the total of passenger seats in mind, varied seating arrangements were offered. First class features a six abreast seating with large double seats and for business class an eight abreast configuration can be incorporated. By virtue of the inherent flexibility of the cabin, eight, nine or even ten abreast seating is available for economy class. In whatever configuration chosen, the wide cabin with its twin aisles provides a feeling of spaciousness in all classes.

The DC-10 has eight cabin doors of which the two port side forward doors are normally used for embarkation and disembarkation of passengers. Except for the overwing door, swift exiting is assured through the remaining three starboard doors.

The track-mounted doors open inward and then upward, being hidden in the cabin ceiling. Besides ease of operation by the cabin crew, this system provides protection from damage from ground servicing equipment, jetways and wind gusts. All doors have built-in emergency slides securing the evacuation of all passengers within 90 seconds, which is an aviation authority requirement.

In case of overwater operations the slides are of the combined slide/raft type. With a normal capacity of 30 (maximum 37) passengers for the rafts of the most forward and overwing

doors and 70 (maximum 87) passengers for the rafts of the remaining four doors, safe accommodation of all passengers and crew is guaranteed in case of an emergency ditching.

On entering the DC-10 through the large cabin doors, one immediately notices the spaciousness of the cabin and installations which heighten passenger comfort. All passenger versions of the DC-10 are equipped with overhead stowage compartments along the sidewalls of the cabin. Additional space for carry-on luggage can be obtained by the installation of centreline bins.

Brightness in the passenger cabin is provided by the 120 windows which each measure 11in x 16.14in (28cm x 41cm). Compared to conventional jet aircraft this means an increase of nearly 30% in glazed area. The lower and upper side wall and ceiling lighting, which each can be regulated separately in each cabin section, contribute to the pleasant environment at any time of the day.

An audio-visual entertainment system on board meets the required high standards of passenger comfort. In the early years the system consisted of pull-down or flip-over screens with movie projectors, later to be replaced by TV-monitors and video-players. With today's technology, some carriers have installed individual in-seat audio-video system in first and business class.

Not only passenger comfort was taken care of, extra crew comfort also could be provided. As is common today on nearly all wide-body aircraft operating extra-long range flights, separate crew rest areas with beds can be installed. Douglas offered various configurations of crew rest areas for the DC-10.

With many international carriers, the DC-10 replaced ageing DC-8s and 707s. However, with the decreasing passenger figures in the mid-1970s, the wide-body aircraft proved to be too large on certain routes. Again, Douglas showed the versatility of the DC-10. The Main Deck Baggage-Handling System (MDBS), provides the airlines with the flexibility to allow for seasonal variations in passenger and cargo mix. By placing the baggage-handling facilities in the main cabin, the lower cargo holds are available for cargo-only use during heavy

cargo but low passenger load-factor seasons. For installation in the rear of the main cabin, two different versions of the MDBS were offered. In the first version, baggage containers can be stored in an enclosed area that extends from the left sidewall of the cabin to about 43.3in. (1.1m) to the right of the centreline. The system offers two storage possibilities: 14 containers of 61.5 x 38.0 x 63.0in (1.56 x 0.97 x 1.60 m) for a total storage volume of 994ft^3 (28m^3) or seven of 125.0 x 38.0 x 64.0in (3.17 x 0.97 x 1.62m) with a volume of nearly 1,001ft^3 (28.3m^3). In this case, a row of double-seats could be installed on the right side of the cabin.

The second option features enclosures on both sides of the cabin, leaving a walk-through aisle from the passenger cabin to the rear galley complex and lavatories. In the basic version six containers of 61.5 x 30.2 x 64.0in (1.56 x 0.77 x 1.62m) can be transported on each side. The alternative version can transport eight containers of the same size on each side with a capacity of 960ft^3 (27.2m^3). With both designs offering different sizes of containers, carriers to equip the aircraft to their specific needs.

The Convertible Freighter (CF) version, available for all DC-10 series, was first ordered by Trans International and Overseas National and further enhanced the operator's flexibility. The main deck cargo loading area can handle as many as 30 88in x 108in (2.24m x 2.76m) cargo pallets, or up to 22 of the larger 88in x 125in (2.24m x 3.18m) size.

The pallets are loaded through the huge 140in x 102in (3.56m x 2.59m) main deck cargo door in the forward port side fuselage section. The Convertible Freighter offers the possibility of an all passenger-, all cargo-, or a mix of both configurations. The first European Series 30CF operator, Sabena, flew the aircraft with a four pallet and business/economy passenger class section, for instance.

With time as an important cost factor, the swiftness of converting the aircraft plays a major role. Depending on the experience of the crew making the change, conversion from the passenger to the cargo mode takes six to eight hours, from the cargo to the passenger mode eight to ten hours. DC-10, fulfilling all airline requirements!

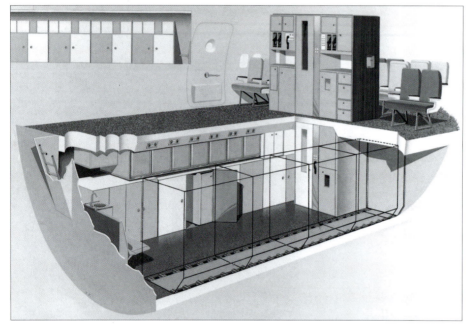

In a spacious business class configuration no passsenger is more than one seat from an aisle. The overhead centre bins provide extra room for passenger hand luggage. Lufthansa Photo Archives

Cutaway of the lower and main deck depicts the galley and mid-cabin service centre of lower galley-equipped DC-10s. Food and beverage trolleys are transported by means of two elevators. McDonnell Douglas

Intensive studies of DC-8 and DC-9 operators and airlines flying competing types allowed McDonnell Douglas to develop a superlative airliner – Condor DC-10-30 D-ADPO in its element. Originally Condor had a bare metal fuselage with yellow tail – see Chapter Three. Condor Flugdienst

Lower Compartments

All DC-10s have three baggage and cargo compartments in the lower fuselage. For these compartments there are two basic configurations. All aircraft with a below deck galley (as described above) have a standard forward, centre and aft compartment. Aircraft equipped with upper deck galleys provide extended forward and centre compartments with a smaller aft compartment.

The forward compartment on a lower galley equipped aircraft can accommodate six LD3 or three LD6 containers respectively, or bulk cargo. The cargo door of this version measures 70in x 66in (178cm x 168cm). In the main deck galley configuration, the volume in this compartment increases from 1,300ft³ (36.8m³) to 3,046ft³ (86.24m³). The forward cargo compartment in this configuration incorporates a wider door (104in - 264cm) permitting the handling of palletised cargo as well as the regular LD6 and LD3 containers or bulk cargo. A total of 16 LD3, or eight LD6 containers, or five 88in x 125in (2.24m x 3.18m) pallets can be loaded.

The centre compartment on aircraft with below deck galleys can handle eight LD3 or four LD6 containers, whereas the aircraft with upper deck galleys can handle ten LD3 or five LD6 containers. Bulk cargo can be accommodated in the centre compartments as well. In both versions, the size of the cargo door is identical: 70in x 66in (178cm x 168cm). The total internal centre compartment volume of the lower galley aircraft is 1,550ft³ (43.9m³) versus 1,935ft³ (54.8m³) of the upper galley aircraft

The volume of the bulk-only aft compartment on the lower and upper deck galley aircraft is 805ft³ (22.8m³) and 510ft³ (14.44m³). Aft compartment doors are 44in x 48in (112cm x 122cm) and 30in x 36in (76cm x 91cm) respectively.

To handle containers and pallets a sophisticated cargo handling system was developed for the DC-10. A powered handling system in the forward and the centre compartment moves containers laterally in or out of the door, and longitudinally within the compartment. The system is operated by only one person standing on the ground handling equipment located at the forward and centre cargo doors. If all ground equipment, container dolly and/or cargo pallet trains, are properly positioned, the compartments can each be loaded or unloaded in six minutes.

All cargo doors are hinged at the top and open outwards and upwards. They are opened and closed electrically and, if necessary, can be operated manually as well. For ease of loading and unloading the door sills are below the compartment floor. Omni-directional rollers are located at the doorway floor area to allow the lateral and longitudinal movement of the containers or pallets. Furthermore, the area is equipped with retractable powered friction rollers which move the containers or pallets through the doorway.

Five rows of roller conveyors, adequately spaced to support either LD3, LD6 containers or pallets, are installed in the cargo floor away from the door area. By means of powered loading and unloading shuttles the containers are moved from and toward the doorway area. Available as an option, aircraft could be equipped with electrically-powered directionally-reversible friction rollers, eliminating the loading and unloading shuttle bars.

In case of a power or component failure, the systems can be disengaged to permit manual loading and unloading. No matter what circumstances, operations are secured at all times.

Pure Freighters

The last commercial version of the DC-10 to be produced was the Series 30F, the pure freight version. Ordered by Federal Express, a total of ten were built and delivered to the world's largest door-to-door package and document carrier. These were among the last DC-10s to be built, with deliveries taking place between January 1986 and October 1988. FedEx also was the first carrier to have Series 10CF, Series 30 and 30CF converted to all-cargo aircraft.

The all-cargo configuration provides a freight carrying space in the cabin of 121ft (36.8m) in length and has a floor area of 2,200ft² (204m²). Total cargo volume of the freighter amounts to 17,096ft³ (484m³); 13,116ft³ (371m³) on the main deck and 3,980ft³ (112m³)on the lower deck. The lower deck cargo volume and capacity is the same as on the upper galley aircraft.

The DC-10-30 freighter, with GE CF6-50Cs, has a weight limited gross payload of 154,000lb (6,985kg). If equipped with GE CF6-50C2s the gross payload rises to 163,000lb (7,393kg). A converted DC-10-10 freighter with CF6-6Ds has a gross payload of 124,000lb (5,624kg). This is increased to 143,500lb (6,509kg) when fitted with GE CF6-6D1s or GE CF6-6Ks.

On the main deck the DC-10 freighter has a maximum standard pallet capability of 22 88in x 125in (2.24m x 3.18m), 20 96in x 125in (2.44m x 3.18m) or 29 88in x 108in (2.24m x 2.74m) pallets. The aircraft also offers the possibility of loading the large 96in x 196in (2.44m x 4.98m) or 96in x 238.5in (2.44m x 6.06m) pallets in combination with standard-size pallets.

An engine transport device can accommodate a DC-10 or MD-11 engine on the main deck. Pallets are loaded through the 140in x 102in (3.56m x 2.59m) forward cargo door.

Some of the major airlines meanwhile have sold their DC-10s and replaced the aircraft with MD-11s, Boeing 767s, 777s, Airbus A340s and other types. Although the majority will remain in service as passenger aircraft, a good number of used DC-10s are becoming freighters. The conversion package offered by McDonnell Douglas assures that also these aircraft will be making money for their new owners for many years to come.

The conversion includes the installation of a main deck cargo door and main deck pallet-handling system. A modified air-conditioning system and smoke detector systems are also installed. A cargo barrier net separates the freight section from the area behind the cockpit, which houses a galley, a toilet and seating for five passengers. In August 1997, a solid aluminium bulkhead was introduced in place of the net. Commissioned by McDonnell Douglas prior to the merger with Boeing, the bulkhead is produced and offered to DC-10 freighter operators by Tolo of Irvine, California. Not surprisingly, FedEx was the first operator to order the bulkheads, replacing nylon barrier nets.

If required, the main deck floor is modified and the centre wing floor supports are strengthened. If the aircraft has a lower deck galley complex, this also can be converted to a full-cargo compartment.

Performance improvement packages, engine upgrades, and cockpit standardisation can be incorporated during conversion to bring the freighter up to the latest standards.

The many converted DC-8 freighters, both 'short' and 'stretched' circling the globe are a good indication of the important role the DC-10, besides transporting passengers, will still be able to play. The innovative McDonnell Douglas MD-10 programme is an important pointer in that direction (described later).

Freighter conversions are not only carried out in the USA but also in Europe. Alenia subsidiary Aeronavali in Italy, has been a long time McDonnell Douglas partner and is performing such conversions.

State-of-the-art Systems

The DC-10 has been equipped with state-of-the-art systems to assure a safe, reliable operation and comfortable flight.

The electrical power system incorporates three generators. Each 90kVa capacity generator is driven by one of the three powerplants through a constant-speed drive.

All DC-10s have a self-contained 90kVa auxiliary power unit (APU) installed in an unpressurised section of the lower fuselage, aft of the cabin pressure bulkhead. The advantage of the APU is the supply of electrical power and compressed air for operation of the air conditioning systems and power to start the engines without being dependent on external power equipment for normal operation of the aircraft systems. The APU was designed and developed specifically for the DC-10 by Garrett AiResearch.

In the unlikely event of a loss of the primary power sources in flight, the DC-10 has two additional emergency power sources. First, the aircraft battery provides at least 30 minutes of system power for safe flight and landing. Secondly, there is an air driven generator, located in the forward starboard fuselage. When extended, this generator provides up to 20kVa long term emergency electrical power.

The hydraulic system consists of three separate, parallel, continuously operating closed circuit systems. Primary flight control surfaces are divided into segments and hydraulically powered in such a manner that loss of any one system does not significantly affect aircraft control during any phase of the flight including

approach and landing. This fail-safe philosophy played an important role in the design of the DC-10's systems.

The aircraft's pneumatic system processes and controls engine compressor bleed air so that it will be suitable for operation of the air conditioning system, wing ice protection system, cross-engine starting and various other air-using systems.

The sophisticated air conditioning system allows for temperature control in five different zones: cockpit, lower galley (if installed), forward, centre and aft cabin. Hot air from the pneumatic system distribution manifold is supplied to each of the three refrigeration units, so-called air cycle machines, where it is cooled and then distributed to the different zones.

Passenger comfort is greatly enhanced as the separate temperature control eliminates uncomfortable temperature variations which could result from unbalanced passenger loads between compartments. The APU has an exceptional cooling performance while the aircraft is on the ground.

Fresh air supplied to the passenger cabin is changed once every three minutes – an impressive ventilation rate. The air conditioning capacity of the DC-10's environmental control system would keep 72 three-bedroom homes at a comfortable temperature through both the hottest summer and the coldest winter.

The cabin pressure is maintained at sea level pressure conditions at flight altitudes up to 22,000ft (6,705m). Over 22,000 and up to 42,000ft (12,801m) the system creates a cabin altitude of less than 8,000ft (2,438m). Although manual control is provided, the system will automatically control cabin pressure throughout the flight once the destination airport elevation and its barometric settings are selected. Uncomfortable pressure changes are virtually eliminated by the advanced system.

The passenger oxygen system of the DC-10 is unique. Located at the passenger seats, the system consists of a chemical oxygen generator, a starting mechanism, supply hoses and regular passenger oxygen masks with reservoir bags. The lavatories and flight attendant stations are similarly equipped. Since the oxygen system is a self-contained unit, it completely eliminates the need for distribution lines, high-pressure oxygen cylinders and regulators. The system offers considerable weight reduction in comparison to conventional oxygen systems, and maintenance is reduced to a minimum.

The sophisticated pilot flight control and automatic flight control systems ensure the excellent handling characteristics of the DC-10. McDonnell Douglas' experience in commercial transport automatic approach systems and in manned space flight made it possible that a fully integrated flight guidance and control system could be developed. Providing all-weather landing performance, the system fulfilled the design goal, certification of the DC-10 for Category IIIa fail-operational automatic landings.

Fuel

Fuel for the DC-10-10 is contained in three integral tanks within the wing and outboard of the fuselage with a total fuel capacity of 145,810lb (66,139kg). The DC-10-30 and Series 40 are equipped with additional tanks in the wing centre section providing a fuel capacity of up to 245,579lb (111,394kg).

The tanks on the Series 10 hold enough fuel to run a motor car 329,085 miles (526,536km), more than 13 journeys around the equator, while the fuel of a Series 30 or 40 would be good for more than 21 trips around the equator!

The fuel system normally supplies fuel from the tank in each wing to the adjacent engine on that wing. The tank that delivers fuel to the aft engine is composed of the two inboard sections of both wings. In this way, the shortest tank-to-engine supply is ensured.

For fuel transfer purposes, two independent transfer systems are installed. Two adjacent fuel receptacles are installed in each wing. For normal fuelling operations the receptacles in the right wing are used. However, if necessary, the aircraft can be refuelled simultaneously on both sides.

Undercarriage

The main undercarriage units have four tyres and retract inboard where they are stored in a well beneath the cabin floor. Commonality being one of the DC-10 design characteristics, the main gear assembly can be installed on the right or the left wing. The main landing gear was designed and built by US supplier Howet Aerosystems.

The nose landing gear, and the centre gear on the Series 30s and 40s, retracts forward. The nose gear was a joint development of Abex Canada and Dowty Rotol of the UK. Although not a standard procedure, the crew of a Series 30 and 40 may opt for the centre gear to remain in the retracted position when operating at light gross weights.

The DC-10 disposes of dual hydraulic systems for its brakes and the nose wheel steering. Anti-skid control systems are incorporated in both brake systems. Aircraft of all series could be equipped with an automatic braking system. With selectable minimum, medium and maximum deceleration rates, the system greatly reduces the pilot workload and increases overall brake performance.

Continuing Profitability – the MD-10

If the official DC-10 launch date of 25th April 1968 was considered the most important date, 16th September 1996 may ultimately prove to be of equal importance in the aircraft's history. On this day McDonnell Douglas and freight and small package giant Federal Express Corporation announced the launch of the MD-10 programme. The project will convert a minimum of 60 FedEx DC-10s into advanced technology freighters and will occur in two phases.

The first phase will be the passenger-to-freighter conversion of DC-10-10 passenger aircraft acquired by FedEx from United and American. Dimension Aviation at Goodyear, Arizona, was selected by McDonnell Douglas as the principal centre for converting DC-10 jetliners for FedEx. The Goodyear facility is operated under the McDonnell Douglas' Federal Aviation Administration (FAA) repair station licence and accommodates work on as many as four DC-10s at one time. The first aircraft entered service in November 1997 and deliveries under contract between Douglas Aircraft Company (now Boeing) and Federal Express will continue on a regular basis into 2000.

Aeronavali in Italy, which already has completed many conversions, was selected to be the second source location for the Federal Express DC-10 conversion programme and Pemco of Dothan, Alabama, are also involved. Aeronavali will convert 13 DC-10s to freight configuration from 1997.

The freighter reconfiguration has been described above and applies to the MD-10 programme. Moreover, McDonnell Douglas has designed specialised tooling for fabricating and installing the cargo door to minimise the time the aircraft is out of service and to improve flexibility in production line rates.

The second phase includes the installation of the McDonnell Douglas designed Advanced Common Flightdeck (ACF) in the modified aircraft and other FedEx DC-10s, converting the three-crew cockpit into a two-crew 'glass' cockpit. The ACF is based on Honeywell's Versatile Integrated Avionics design, the VIA 2000. When the installation of this advanced technology is completed, the upgraded DC-10 freighter will receive the new designation MD-10.

Federal Express DC-10-30s will also be equipped with the Advanced Common Flight deck and receive the new MD-10 designation.
Federal Express Corporation

The majority of the new hardware and software for the ACF will be provided by Honeywell. Derived from the MD-11 flight deck (see Chapter Seven), the system features six 8in (20cm) flat panel, liquid crystal displays (LCD) and improved system control functions.

Behind the flight deck panels, triple VIA computers will integrate the LCD electronics and related software. Because the design will offer a high degree of flight deck commonality with the FedEx MD-11 fleet, flight crew training time for MD-11 pilots will be significantly reduced.

As a result of the ACF modification, an overall saving of about 1,000lb (453kg) from removed equipment is predicted. After all of all planned changes, the useful economic life of the aircraft will be extended by an expected 20 years.

Other major improvements during the ACF conversion will be the fitment of an advanced weather radar system with predictive windshear detection, a Category IIIb autoflight system, landing gear reliability improvements as well as aerodynamic drag reductions.

The operational reliability of the MD-10 will be further enhanced by Satellite Communications (SatComs), Global Positioning System (GPS) navigation capabilities, Future Air Navigation System (FANS) compatibility and an On-Board Maintenance Terminal.

(The MD-95 100-passenger airliner – which was renamed the Boeing 717 in January 1998 –features a similar set of advanced cockpit displays and systems which were also to be available for new McDonnell Douglas commercial aircraft. See Chapter Eight for notes on the Boeing take-over of McDonnell Douglas.)

The new ACF technology will offer significant cockpit and systems commonality across the entire family of aircraft. For airlines with more than one type of McDonnell Douglas aircraft in their fleet this will result in remarkable savings in crew training and operating costs. In June 1997, McDonnell Douglas signed a memorandum of understanding with SR Technics, Swissair's maintenance subsidiary, to install the ACF system in 25 DC-10-10s.

ACF installation in a flight test DC-10 will start in early 1998, with a first flight expected in the third quarter of 1998. A further two modified DC-10s will participate in the flight test programme of approximately 800 flying hours. FAA certification is scheduled for early 1999 and at that time the first MD-10s will join the FedEx fleet. SR Technics will then convert and deliver one equipped MD-10 every eight to ten weeks until 2002.

Once the last modified aircraft is delivered to the carrier, Federal Express will have a stable of like-new freighters. The MD-10 project is the largest aircraft modification program McDonnell Douglas has launched since the 1970s. It may well attract the interest of other airlines to upgrade their DC-10 workhorses with the same advanced technology.

	Series 10		Series 15		Series 30		Series 40	
Capacity								
Passengers:	250-380		250-380		250-380		250-380	
Cargo holds – lower galley aircraft:	3,017ft^3	85.4m^3	3,017ft^3	85.4m^3	3,017ft^3	85.4m^3	3,017ft^3	85.4m^3
– upper galley aircraft:	4,618ft^3	130.7m^3	4,618ft^3	130.7m^3	4,618ft^3	130.7m^3	4,618ft^3	130.7m^3
Dimensions								
Wingspan:	155ft 4in	47.35m	155ft 4in	47.35m	165ft 4in	50.40m	165ft 4in	50.4m
Length overall:	182ft. 3in	55.55m	182ft. 3in	55.55m	181ft 7in	55.35m	182ft 2⅛in	55.54m
Height overall:	58ft 1in.	17.70m	58ft 1in.	17.70m	58ft 1in	17.70m	58ft 1in.	17.7m
Wing area:	3.550ft^2	329.8m^2	3.550ft^2	329.8m^2	3,647ft^2	338.8m^2	3,647ft^2	338.8m^2
Sweepback:	35°	35°	35°	35°				
Landing gear								
Tread (main wheels):	35ft 0in	10.67m	35ft 0in	10.67m	35ft 0in	10.67m	35ft 0in	10.67m
Wheel base (fore and aft):	72ft 5in	22.07m	72ft 5in	22.07m	72ft 5in	22.07m	72ft 5in	22.07m
Engines	3 x GE CF6-6D		3 x GE CF6-50C2F		3 x GE CF6-50C2		3 x P&W JT9D-59A	
Take-off thrust:	40,000lb	177.9kN	46,500lb	206,8kN	52,500lb	233.5kN	53,000lb	235.7kN
Standard weights								
Gross weight:	443,000lb	200,940kg	458,000lb	207,746kg	575,000lb	260,820kg	558,000lb	253,061kg
Max take-off:	440,000lb	199,584kg	455,000lb	206,385kg	572,000lb	259,459kg	555,000lb	251,701kg
Landing weight:	363,500lb	164,854kg	363,500lb	164,854kg	403,000lb	182,766kg	403,000lb	182,766kg
Max zero fuel:	335,000lb	151,956kg	335,000lb	151,956kg	368,000lb	166,924kg	368,000lb	166,924kg
Empty weight:	244,193lb	110,764kg	248,496lb	112,716kg	267,191lb	121,197kg	272,368lb	123,544kg
Fuel capacity:	145,810lb	66,139kg	178,537lb	80,983kg	245,566lb	111,388kg	245,579lb	111,394kg
Weight limited payload:	98,807lb	41,189kg	86,504lb	39,328kg	100,809lb	45,726kg	95,632lb	43,378kg
Performance								
Level flight speed:	600+ mph	965km/h	600+ mph	965km/h	600+ mph	965km/h	600+ mph	965km/h
FAA take-off field length, standard weight:	8,900ft	2,625m	7,500ft.	2,212m	9,650ft	2,847m	9,550ft	2,817m
FAA landing field length, standard weight:	5,830ft	1,720m	5,830ft	1,720m	5,960ft	1,758m	5,840ft	1,723m
Range, 277 passenger and baggage, domestic reserves:	3,800 miles	6,114km	4,350 miles	7,000km	5,860 miles	9,429km	5,750 miles	9,252km

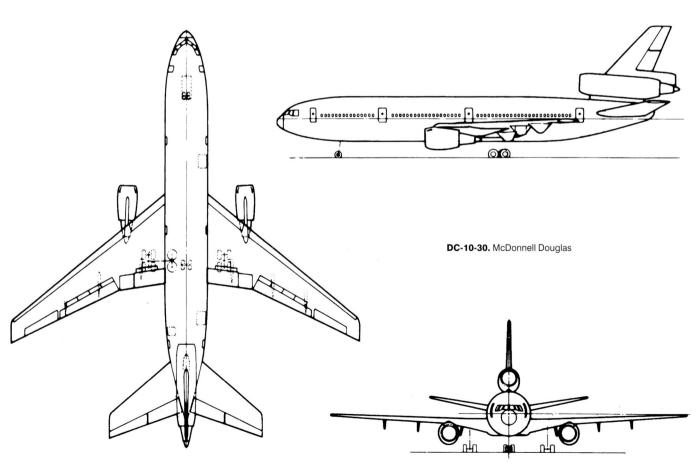

DC-10-30. McDonnell Douglas

Chapter Three

DC-10 Operators

Over 25 years have gone by since the first DC-10 was placed into service. During the production period McDonnell Douglas (McDD) delivered new aircraft to over 50 airline customers. Some of the original customers have meanwhile ceased to exist, some have sold their DC-10s after many years of service and replaced them by new-generation aircraft such as the MD-11, Boeing 747-400, 767-300, 777, Airbus A330 and A340. During the 1980s, the DC-10 was a favourite in the leasing business. Aircraft were used by smaller operators on a lease basis, and were in service from a few days, weeks or months, up to several years. Used DC-10s are increasingly being leased or acquired by existing or newly-founded passenger and freight carriers.

In this chapter, specific DC-10 operations by user airlines are defined. Airlines are given in alphabetical order by 'operating' name and abbreviation (if widely used to refer to the carrier). Major operators that ordered DC-10s, or announced their intention to operate them, but in the end failed to start operations are also detailed. Additionally, airlines that 'name' their aircraft are given in tabulated form.

Brief details of major accidents and write-offs sustained to DC-10s are also given. To help put operations into context, the types that DC-10s replaced with carriers and what type(s), if any, have – or are intended – to replace them are outlined. From a study of this chapter, it is interesting to note how many 'start-up' carriers have chosen the DC-10. No attempt has been made to list all of the individual aircraft operated by the larger users, as this material is readily available elsewhere. (See the Bibliography, page 4.)

With ever-changing 'corporate identities', all DC-10 liveries used by the operators over the years are described and every effort has been made to illustrate them. This includes 'one-off' and 'celebration' schemes that may have only been applied for a brief time. The rich variety of DC-10 colour schemes, and variants thereof,

DC-10-30 HB-IHF *Nidwalden* in Swissair's second paint scheme with additional '700th anniversary of the Swiss Confederation' sticker. Swissair

reflect the many uses to which airlines past and present have put the wide-bodied workhorse. The DC-10 has also become an ideal aircraft for airlines specialising in the supply of leased aircraft to other operations, both on short and long term assignments,

To keep this section as short as possible, some abbreviations are necessary, the principal one being the shortening of DC-10 designations. Wherever possible these are referred to as -10, -15, -30, -40 plus all the 'C', 'CF', 'ER' and 'F' combinations. Only DC-10s are referred to in this manner and it is felt that readers will have no problems with this. An index of IATA and relevant ICAO codes appears on page 99.

Aeronautica de Cancun, known as Aerocancun, operated former Mexicana DC-10-15 XA-TDI. Michel St Felix – Avimage

Aeroflot Russian International Airlines DC-10-30F N524MD, one of the western aircraft in the fleet. Nicky Scherrer – VIP Photoservice

AeroLyon's DC-10-30 F-BTDD at Toulouse-Blagnac Airport. Jean M Magendie

Amongst the wide-body aircraft operated by Aeromaritime was DC-10-30 F-BTDE, on lease from parent company UTA with 'Aéromaritime' title and and logo. Author's collection

Photographs on the opposite page:

Aeromexico's first DC-10-15, XA-AMM (later re-registered as N10038), sporting the carrier's second paint scheme. McDonnell Douglas

XA-DUG was the first DC-10 (a Series 30) to enter service with Aeromexico. McDonnell Douglas

Former Pakistan International Airlines and Canadian Airlines DC-10-30 XA-AMR was leased from Polaris from 1989 to 1994 and carried the current colours of the Mexican airline. Author's collection

Aeroperu DC-10-15 N10045 *Senor de Spain*, one of two aircraft leased from Mexicana. Fred Lerch

Aerocancun – Aeronautica de Cancun

The Mexican charter carrier was founded in 1989 and has operated a variety of MD-83s, A300-622Rs and A310s. Besides regional services to Brasilia, Buenos Aires, Guayaquil, and Puerto Alegre and others, international services to Cologne, Basle etc and destinations in the USA and Canada are conducted. The airline leased Skyjet -30 V2-LEH for a three month period in December 1995. This was operated in full Skyjet colour scheme and was used on high density charter routes from Mexico to Argentina and Brazil. In May 1996 Aerocancun obtained ex-Mexicana -15 N10045, becoming XA-TDI. The aircraft was operated in an all-white colour scheme with a black 'Aerocancun' title and Mexican flag applied to the upper fuselage. This lease was terminated in March 1997 and the aircraft was returned to the McDonnell Douglas Finance Corporation (MDFC).

Aeroflot Russian International Airlines

Formerly the Aeroflot international directorate, the new Aeroflot is one of many new airlines established after the collapse of the Soviet Union. Already operating western equipment – A310-308s and 767-3Y0(ER)s – ARIA took delivery of leased -30F (CF) N524MD in October 1995 for cargo services to the USA, Europe and the Far East. A twice-weekly -30 freighter service Frankfurt-Moscow-Seoul was started in November 1995.

The paint scheme is white with a light grey belly. A wide and narrow dark blue cheatline extends from the cockpit section to the rear of the aircraft. The winged hammer and sickle logo is located at the forward upper fuselage, followed by the name 'Aeroflot' in large cyrillic script and 'Russian International Airlines' in English in small lettering. The tail carries the flag of the State of Russia.

AeroLyon

The French charter carrier started operations with ChallengAir -30 OO-LRM in December 1996. Flights are conducted from Nantes, Lyon, Marseille, Paris and Toulouse to Abidjan, Bamako, Dakar, Lomé, Ouagadougou as well as Canadian and US destinations. In January 1997, -30 F-BTDD was acquired from AOM French Airlines, which features AeroLyon's own paint scheme. As is the case with Corsair, AeroLyon is a subsidiary of the French travel organisation Nouvelles Frontières.

The simple, yet attractive livery is based on a white fuselage with a turquoise 'Aero' and a purple 'Lyon' title placed on the forward fuselage. The purple company logo, consisting of the stylised letters 'A' and 'L' is displayed on the turquoise fin and on the wing engines.

Aéromaritime

Aéromaritime was a subsidiary of UTA (qv) and originally operated DC-6s and the four Aerospacelines Super Guppy outsize freighters for Airbus Industrie, the so-called Airbus Skylink. (In 1989 the Super Guppies were sold to Airbus

Inter Transport, a division of Airbus.) During 1988 and 1989 a fleet of 737s and 767s was acquired and two 747s were leased from the parent company to conduct international passenger charter flights to destinations in the Mediterranean, North Africa and the French overseas territories. Additional UTA -30s were leased when required. After the Air France–UTA merger operations were ceased and the 737s, 747s and 767s were transferred to the Air France fleet in 1992.

The DC-10s and 747s operated in the full UTA livery with the white stylised 'AM' logo of Aéromaritime on the tail fin. Small 'Aéromaritime' titles on the fuselage were also used.

Aeromexico

Aeromexico took delivery of its first -30 on 17th April 1974, to be followed by another of the type on 16th May 1974. Two more -30s were leased temporarily during the 1980s and early 1990s. Together with Mexicana, Aeromexico was the only airline to purchase the -15, two being delivered on 30th June and 12th November 1981. Basically a -10, the -15s were equipped with the -30's CF6-50C2s. This combination permitted so-called 'hot and high' operations with maximum payloads from the carrier's Mexico City homebase. Following the Aeromexico's bankruptcy in April 1988, the renamed Aerovias de Mexico restarted services in November that year under the Aeromexico trade name. European destinations – Madrid, Paris and Frankfurt – were dropped with the DC-10s employed on domestic routes and to New York and Miami. Following the introduction of the 757 and 767 in the fleet, the carrier stopped DC-10 operations. The only remaining DC-10, a -15, is withdrawn from use and stored at Mexico City.

The original colour scheme featured a highly polished metal fuselage with an orange cheatline and an orange upper tail section which depicted the 'hombre nguila', the famous Mexican birdman, in white. The name 'Aeromexico' appeared in red (Aero) and black (Mexico) on the upper forward fuselage and the rear engine. The second livery, introduced in the early 1980s, was a polished metal fuselage with a wide orange cheatline extending into the tail. White 'Aeromexico' lettering appeared on the orange cheatline and rear engine.

DC-10-30 OO-JOT in Air Europe's full colour scheme at Basle-Mulhouse Airport.
Nicky Scherrer – VIP Photoservice

ChallengAir DC-10-30 OO-JOT in the simple Air Europe 'Italy' livery during the first leasing period. Nicky Scherrer – VIP Photoservice

The colourful Air Florida paint scheme on N103TV, one of three DC-10-30CFs leased from Transamerica Airlines. Fred Lerch

Air Florida's first DC-10, Series 30CF N1035F still carried the basic livery of former lessee Icelandair Loftleidir. Nicky Scherrer – VIP Photoservice

After the takeover of UTA, Air France became a DC-10 operator. DC-10-30 F-BTDC in the simple yet attractive livery of the French airline. Nicky Scherrer –VIP Photoservice

Displaying the 'Guadeloupe Martinique' titles, Air Guadeloupe operated the Minerve DC-10-30 F-GGMZ. Fred Lerch

Briefly participating in the lucrative charter business, Air Hawaii used two DC-10-10s, N904WA illustrated. Author's collection

The current colour scheme features a polished fuselage with a wide orange and dark blue cheatline, dark blue tail with white birdman and 'Aeromexico' lettering on the tail engine.

XA-DUG	Ciudad de Mexico
XA-DUH	Castillo de Chapultepec
XA-RIY	Jose Marie Morelos
N10038	Anahuac
N1003N	Independencia

Aero Peru

Formerly the national airline of Peru, Aero Peru was transformed into a private enterprise in 1981. Besides serving domestic destinations, Aero Peru conducts scheduled flights from its home base Lima to Bogota, Buenos Aires, Caracas, Mexico City, Miami, Rio de Janeiro and Santiago. During 1981 and 1982 the airline leased two L-1011 TriStars from Lockheed for its international network but this proved to be unthrifty and the aircraft were returned. During 1993 and 1994 the carrier leased two -15s from Mexicana. Aero Peru also operated a Canadian Airlines International -30 on a short term lease from December 1994 through February 1995.

The paint scheme on the -15s was very similar to the present Aeromexico livery. It differed in the white upper fuselage, of course the name 'Aero Peru' on the rear engine and the logo on the tail section. Today, a member of the Aeromexico Group it operates with a fleet of six 727s and two 757s.

| N10045 | Senor de Spain |
| N1003L | Apu Kon Tiki Wira Cocha |

African Safari Airways – ASA

ASA was founded as a charter airline in 1967. With the acquisition of two DC-8-33s from KLM in 1973 the airline started its jet operation. The two 'short' DC-8s were replaced in 1982 by an ex-KLM DC-8-63. ASA today operates with only one aircraft (DC-10-30 PH-DTL, f/n 185) which was acquired from KLM in December 1992. The network covers flights from Basle, Cologne, Frankfurt, Hanover, Munich, and London to Mombasa–Kenya.

The airline is the first and only charter carrier worldwide to offer a three class cabin. Besides the 148 economy seats, 86 club class and 40 'Royal Safari' class seats are offered. There are no plans of increasing the fleet, and the DC-10 will remain the only aircraft with ASA.

The simple yet attractive livery consists of a light grey lower and white upper fuselage with one red, one dark blue and two light blue pinstripes along the fuselage. Large dark blue 'ASA' letters are located on the forward fuselage and the rear engine. To bring home the idea of a safari, zebra stripes are painted on the upper tail section underlined with a red pinstripe.

African West-Air – AWA

AWA was founded in 1992 and operated passenger flights with 757s leased from Air Holland when required. Additionally, -30 F-ODLX *Diamant* was leased from AOM French Airlines. The airline ceased operations during 1994.

DC-10 F-ODLX carried the basic AOM livery with 'AOM' lettering on the wing engines as well as on the tail fin. 'African West-Air' titles in green

French carrier Air Liberté operates three DC-10-30s. F-GPVD is seen at Frankfurt/Main Airport. Bernd Weber

Air Martinique's DC-10-30 F-GDJK remained on lease with the airline for only 16 months. It is presently in service with AOM French Airlines as F-GNDC. Fred Lerch

Air New Zealand operated a fleet of eight DC-10-30s. ZK-NZP, illustrated, crashed on Mount Erebus in November 1979. Fred Lerch

Air Outre Mer DC-10-30 F-ODLX *Diamant*. Fred Lerch

After the takeover of Minerve, Air Outre Mer changed its name to AOM French Airlines. DC-10-30 F-GKMY in the airline's new livery. Theo Handstede

AOM DC-10-30 F-GNEM carrying the 'Je veux rester à Orly Ouest!' titles, early 1996. Exavia

DC-10-30 N821L, was leased by Air Pacific. Nicky Scherrer – VIP Photoservice

DC-10-40 N133JC of Jet 24, operated for Air Panama. Author's collection

Photographs on the opposite page:

Martinair Holland carried out international flights for Air Seychelles with DC-10-30CF PH-MBN. Fred Lerch

Thailand's first DC-10, Series 30 HS-VGE carried the name 'Air Siam' in Thai on the starboard side and in English port side fuselage. The aircraft was originally ordered by Atlantis. Nicky Scherrer – VIP Photoservice

The first DC-10-30 delivered to Air Zaire, 9Q-CLI *Mont Ngaliema*, has been withdrawn from use since February 1995 and is stored at Tel Aviv, Israel. McDonnell Douglas

and 'Compagnie Aérienne Sénégalaise' titles in black were applied between the forward two doors, respectively above and under the passenger windows.

Air Afrique

Air Afrique took delivery of its first ever wide-body, -30, TU-TAL, on 28th February 1973. Two more -30s were to join the fleet, TU-TAM on 19th June 1975 and TU-TAN on 10th August 1979. The first entered service on the Paris-bound flights from Abidjan and Dakar. Later the DC-10s were also employed on high density flights within the extensive African network. The airline has extended its fleet of A300B4-203s,

A300-605Rs and A310-304s. First DC-10s to leave were TU-TAM and TU-TAN, joining AOM in November 1992 and February 1995.

Air Afrique ceased DC-10 operations on 29th February 1996. The last aircraft in service, *Libreville*, TU-TAL, was also sold to AOM. In February 1997, the African carrier made a brief DC-10 comeback by leasing Skyjet Belgium -15 V2-LER for the Hadj season. 'Air Afrique' titles were applied to the Skyjet scheme.

The Air Afrique colour scheme did not change on the DC-10s. Bright cheatlines of lime and green extended from the nose to the tail section. The stylised gazelle's head and globe decorated the tail section. Over the years, Swissair operated DC-10s for the African carrier. Small 'Air Afrique' titles were added to the full Swissair colour scheme.

TU-TAL	*Libreville*
TU-TAM	*Sriwanna*
TU-TAN	*Niamey*

Air Algerie

Laker Airways leased Series 10 G-AZZD *Western Belle* to Air Algerie for the period October through December 1977 for Hadj operations.

Air America

Air America intended to start charter operations in 1984 using DC-10s. Condor -30 D-ADPO was prepared to be leased to the carrier but was never delivered. The aircraft had basic Condor paint scheme with an 'Air America' title on the forward fuselage and a red and black 'A' logo on the tail. The airline never took to the skies.

Air Europe

Air Europe is a former member of the Airlines of Europe group, which failed in 1991, and is now associated with Italian flag carrier Alitalia. The carrier operates international charter flights from Milan-Malpensa with four 767-300ERs. ChallengAir -30 OO-JOT was leased to Air Europe 'Italy' in late 1994 and returned to the Belgian charter company in May 1995.

Plain black 'Air Europe' titles were applied on the white upper fuselage and tail fin. In early 1996 the same aircraft again operated on Air Europe flights to the Caribbean. This time, the aircraft received the full Air Europe livery. A multiple orange and red striping, together with the 'AE' initials, starting at the forward fuselage and continued up into the tail section. Black 'Air Europe' titles were placed on the cabin roof and tail fin. To underline the country of origin, the Italian flag was placed next to the 'Air Europe' fuselage title. Although the aircraft was returned to ChallengAir in February 1996, it was again in service for Air Europe in July the same year for the summer holiday traffic.

Air Florida

The Miami-based carrier initially operated a fleet of four DC-9s and 24 737s on its domestic network. Upon approval for scheduled flights to Amsterdam and Brussels -30 N1035F was leased from Seaboard World Airlines. In April 1981 London-Gatwick was also added to the transatlantic network and to cover the need for more aircraft three -30s (N101TV, N102TV and N103TV) were leased from Transamerica and returned in 1982. As a replacement, Air Florida leased World Airways -30 N109WA in March 1983. High operating costs and dwindling profits forced the carrier out of business and bankruptcy followed in July 1984.

The paint scheme of N1035F was quite simple with a wide and narrow blue cheatline on a white upper fuselage, blue 'Air Florida' title above the cheatline and blue 'AF' logo on the tail. The turquoise and light blue livery of the Transamerica aircraft was very attractive. 'Air Florida' titling was placed on the forward fuselage and on the tail engine, while the company logo decorated the fin.

Skyjet DC-10-30 V2-LEA was in service with Air Zaire for a short period during 1992. Fred Lerch

Series 30 I-DYNE *Dante Alghieri* was the second of eight DC-10s delivered to the Italian flag carrier, Alitalia. Today the aircraft is with Continental Air Lines. Alitalia

KLM DC-10-30 PH-DTI was leased to Philippine Airlines. In turn, the aircraft was sub-leased to Aloha Airlines as N801AL. Fred Lerch

Destroyed by fire at Chicago O'Hare Airport, American Trans Air DC-10-40, N184AT, was one of the charter carrier's two DC-10s. Fred Lerch

Air France

With the merger of UTA in October 1991, Air France took over the airline's six DC-10s. All aircraft were used on international services from the time of merger.

Before the UTA DC-10s were given the Air France colour scheme, the aircraft were operated in the UTA livery with an additional 'Compagnie Air France' title below the cockpit windows. Air France was one of the first airlines to paint their aircraft in an all-white colour scheme. Bold dark blue 'Air France' titles are located at the front above the passenger windows. The colours of the French flag, blue, white and red are represented in the fin. Four slanted dark blue lines, decreasing in width, and a red line adorn the white tail section, at the top of which the European Community flag is located.

It was evident that with the long haul fleet of Boeing 747s and ordered Airbus A340s there was no economic reason to keep DC-10s in the Air France fleet.

By 1995 five aircraft were sold off. Only one, the former F-BTDC, remains with the airline and is on lease to AOM French Airlines as F-GTDH.

Ariana Afghan Airlines' only DC-10-30, YA-LAS, was sold to British Caledonian in 1985. Author's collection

Arrow Air DC-10-10 N917JW departing Frankfurt/Main Airport in the dark blue cheatline scheme with red 'Arrow Air' titling. Fred Lerch

The other colour scheme of Arrow Air, using a red cheatline, was applied to DC-10-10 N904WA. Nicky Scherrer – VIP Photoservice

Frankfurt-based Atlantis never took delivery of its ordered aircraft. An artist's impression depicts the red and orange livery which was intended to be applied to the airline's DC-10-30s. McDonnell Douglas

Air Guadeloupe

During 1990 Air Guadeloupe leased from Minerve -30 F-GGMZ for charter operations. The quadruple cheatline of the Minerve livery was interrupted for the red 'Guadeloupe' and 'Martinique' title. A red 'Air Guadeloupe' title was placed on the port side of the tail engine while the tail fin showed the company's logo, an orange shining sun within a red circle. Since the aircraft was jointly operated with Air Martinique, the starboard carried their title on the tail engine and the Air Martinique logo on the fin. The airline presently operates with a fleet of DHC Twin Otters, Dornier Do 228s and AI(R) ATR 42s twin-turboprops.

Air Hawaii

The carrier operated two -10s, N904WA and N905WA, on charter flights to the American continent. The aircraft were leased in November 1985 and January 1986 respectively but were both returned to the lessor in February 1986. Operations lasted for only a short period and Air Hawaii ceased to exist in March 1986.

The livery consisted of a black 'Air Hawaii' title above the twin orange and green cheatlines which ended in the tail section, the orange stripe forming a stylised flower.

DC-10-30CF N105WA was leased by CIT to Russian carrier Avcom. Briefly registered as UN-10200, it was re-registered as RA-10200 and operated without any titles. Exavia

Balair DC-10-30 HB-IHK in the original paint scheme with black titles, on the fuselage and tail engine. The company's 'B' logo appears on the forward fuselage. Nicky Scherrer –VIP Photoservice

At Basle-Mulhouse, HB-IHK displays the revised colour scheme with red 'Balair' titles. Swissair

One of the three ex-Singapore Airlines DC-10-30s bought by Biman Bangladesh Airlines in 1983, S2-ACQ *City of Hazrat Shah Jalal (RA)*, showing the original paint scheme with the vertical extension of the twin cheatline. Nicky Scherrer – VIP Photoservice

Air Liberté

The French carrier operates charter flights to the Mediterranean, North Africa, Réunion, the Caribbean, North America and Asia. Operates scheduled domestic and international (eg London and New York) flights. In June 1996 Air Liberté signed a co-operation agreement with AOM to strengthen the position of both airlines especially on the domestic market against competing state-owned Air France Europe. Because of heavy losses, the airline was given a six month period in September 1996 to implement a survival plan or face bankruptcy. In November 1996, a French commercial court agreed to the take-over of Air Liberté by British Airways and French banking group Banque Rivaud. At the time of writing, Air Liberté operates three 737s, seven MD-83s and three -30s.

The fresh livery has the blue, white and red colours of the national flag represented in triple cheatlines starting at the lower nose and sweeping over the cabin roof with the 'Air Liberté' title in between. The same scheme is repeated on the tail fin. Small European Community flags are placed on all engines.

Air Martinique

Air Martinique jointly operated with Air Guadeloupe Minerve Series 30 F-GGMZ during 1991. 'Guadeloupe' and 'Martinique' titles were applied on the forward fuselage. The starboard side showed an 'Air Martinique' title on the tail engine and the company's logo on the tail fin.

In May 1992 the airline leased an ex-Linhas Aereas de Moçambique -30, F-GDJK. Twin red and white pinstripes were applied on the white fuselage. A small 'Martinique Guadeloupe' title appeared above the forward passenger windows and a large 'Air Martinique' title on the tail engine. The logo, a disc depicting the sun, water and the letter 'M', was placed on the fin. In September 1993 the aircraft was returned to the lessor, Equator Leasing Inc. Air Martinique today operates three Do 228s and two ATR42s.

Air New Zealand

Air New Zealand, the national airline of New Zealand, received its first -30 on 11th January 1973. Between 1973 and 1977 eight -30s were delivered for use on the international route network which included flights to Australia, the USA, Canada, the Far East and Europe. During a round flight in the Antarctic -30 ZK-NZP (f/n 182) was lost when it crashed on Mount Erebus on 28th November 1979.

With the introduction of the DC-10 the airline adapted a new livery. A combination of a turquoise and dark blue cheatline started at the nose and continued to the top of the tail which exposed a Maori symbol, known as a 'Koru'. A dark blue 'Air New Zealand' title was placed on the upper fuselage.

All but two aircraft were sold in 1981 and 1982; the remaining two were on a long lease to LAN Chile and were sold upon return to Air New Zealand in 1986. The carrier's DC-10s were replaced by 747s and 767s.

Air Outre Mer – AOM

Air Outre Mer started operations in May 1990 with a scheduled service from Paris to St Denis de la Réunion using DC-10s. In January 1992 the carrier took over Minerve and the name Air Outre Mer was changed to AOM French Airlines. The airline has an extensive scheduled passenger and charter network including: Réunion, French Polynesia, French West Indies, Ho Chi Minh City, Los Angeles, Paramaribo, Sydney and Tokyo. Ad hoc flights are also operated for Club Mediterranée. Aircraft are also frequently operated for other carriers. To compete better with state-owned Air France Europe in the domestic market, AOM commenced an alliance with Air Liberté (qv) in June 1996. The carrier presently operates a fleet of ten MD-83s and thirteen -30s.

A all-white fuselage and tail were the background for a blue 'Air Outre Mer' title and winged red and blue 'AOM' logo which appeared on the white engines as well. After the name change a huge 'AOM' logo replaced the 'Air Outre Mer' title on the forward fuselage.

Current Biman Bangladesh Airlines livery on S2-ACO, *City of Hazrat Shah Makhdoom (RA)*. The airline operates a fleet of four DC-10-30s. Fred Lerch

On lease to Birgenair, Finnair DC-10-30 OH-LHB in a basic livery without any titles. Reiner Geerdts

Former THY DC-10-10 TC-JAU Istanbul was transferred to charter subsidiary Bogaziçi BHT. The aircraft was named after the *City of Cengelköy*. Nicky Scherrer – VIP Photoservice

The attractive livery of British Airways on DC-10-30 *New Forest*, G-MULL. Fred Lerch

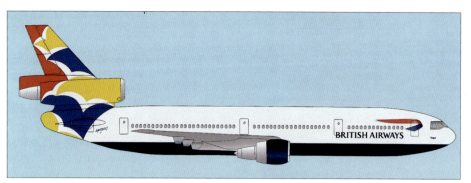

Computer-composed rendering of how a British Airways DC-10 would look in the colourful 'Wings' image by Danish artist Per Arnoldl. 'Vinger', the Danish name of the image, is placed on the forward fuselage. BA/Newell and Sorrell.

Once Britain's largest independent carrier, British Caledonian Airways operated a fleet of eight DC-10-30s. G-BHDH proudly carried the rampant lion. Adrian Meredith Photography

Third DC-10 to enter service with Cal Air was -10 G-GCAL. In 1971 the aircraft was acquired by Orbis – see Chapter Four. Author's collection

In the allocation battle at Paris airports, AOM underlined its wish to retain its present location by applying a 'Je veux rester à Orly Ouest!' (I wish to stay at Orly West!) legend on its aircraft in early 1996. In November 1997 F-GNDC carried a World Wildlife Fund livery of sea landscape and jungle with birds, a tiger and tortoise with 'WWF' on the tail engine.

F-ODLX   *Diamant*
F-ODLY   *Turquoise*
F-ODLZ   *Saphir*

Air Pacific

The flag carrier of Fiji leased a -30 from ILFC from 21st September 1983 until 28th December 1984. The present route network includes Suva, Tonga, Nadi, West Samoa, the Solomon Islands, Melbourne, Sydney, Brisbane, Auckland and Tokyo, although the DC-10 at that time was used on flights to Los Angeles, Honolulu and Bali. Presently Air Pacific operates a fleet of two Boeing 737s, one 747-200 and one 767-300ER.

The colourful livery had a yellow, an orange and a red broad diagonal band which swept over the cabin roof . A further dark blue band extends straight into the complete tail section and at its top was a stylised bird's head. The overall fuselage was white and in case of the DC-10 small dark blue 'Air Pacific – We Are Fiji' titles appeared on the forward fuselage.

Air Panama

The carrier used DC-10s for international operations on several occasions. From October 1984 until May 1985 -40 N133JC was leased from Jet Charter Service and operated in that company's Jet 24 colour scheme with a black and red 'Air Panama' title on the fuselage. A further Jet 24 -40, N144JC, remained with Air Panama until it was returned to Boeing in June 1985. A -10 was sub-leased from Arrow Air in September 1985 and returned the next month. The airline had a base fleet of up to three 727s and ceased operations in January 1990.

Air Seychelles

The national airline started international services with weekly scheduled flights to Frankfurt and London on 1st November 1983 with -30s chartered from British Caledonian Airways. For flights to Amsterdam, Frankfurt and Rome Martinair -30CF PH-MBN with 'Air Seychelles' stickers was used on a short-term lease. Today the airline operates with a 757-28A and a 767-2Q8(ER) on the international routes.

Air Siam

Air Siam started operating international flights

with a BAC 1-11 and a Boeing 707 in 1972. Equipment operated included a further 707, three 747s, an A300 and a -30 that had been built for Atlantis but the order was not taken up. Subsequently it was leased to Air Siam on 25th November 1974 until 10th November 1976 when it was returned to McDD. The aircraft was used on Air Siam's services to Los Angeles, Hong Kong and Honolulu. The airline ceased all operations in January 1977.

As the first DC-10 registered in Thailand, the title 'Thailand's First DC-10' was proudly displayed on the tail engine. The smart white and blue livery included the 'Air Siam' title in English on the port and in Thai on the starboard side. The blue tail displayed a bird logo.

Air Tchad

The carrier leased Air Zaire's -30 9Q-CLT *Mont Ngafula* in November 1975. The aircraft was operated in the Air Zaire livery and returned to the lessor in January 1976.

Air Zaire

The airline took delivery of its first wide-body aircraft, -30 9Q-CLI, on 8th June 1973. A second aircraft of the type followed on 26th June 1974, 9Q-CLT. Both aircraft were flying to the European destinations.

Despite the fact that the airline was transformed into a private company in 1978, the poor financial state of the airline required a major reorganisation. As part of this, 9Q-CLT was sold to British Caledonian Airways in 1985 and is still in service with British Airways. Skyjet Series 30 V2-LEA was leased for a short period during 1992.

Financial losses forced the carrier to cease operations in June 1995. Air Zaire was formally declared bankrupt by a Belgian court in October 1995. The last DC-10 has been stored with Israel Aircraft Industries, at Tel-Aviv since February 1995.

After the airline changed its name from Air Congo into Air Zaire in 1971, a new livery was adapted. The country's flag colours were represented in the yellow and green pinstripes above and below the red cabin window cheatline. The company's motif, a gold winged-leopard in a red circle, was displayed on the fin. The green rudder had an additional yellow-trimmed red band at the top. The company's name appeared in black letters on the upper fuselage. Skyjet aircraft displayed 'Air Zaire' alongside the 'Skyjet' title on the roof.

9Q-CLI   *Mont Ngaliema*
9Q-CLT   *Mont Ngafula*

Airstar International Airlines

The new carrier intended to commence charter flights from Boston and Last Vegas in January

1997. The company was 25% owned by Air Star of Zaire. In August 1996 Airstar International acquired former Shabair -10 9Q-CSS, re-registering it N902WA. It had been in storage since September 1994 and because of the high cost of bringing the aircraft back into service, all planned operations were cancelled. Although the aircraft was conditionally sold to Aero Controls Inc in October 1996, it was registered again to Airstar in February 1997 and sold to Chon Dal Inc in May 1997.

Alitalia

The Italian flag carrier was an early customer for the -30. A total of eight were ordered and delivered between February 1973 and May 1975. The -30s replaced the airline's DC-8-62 fleet and together with the Boeing 747 fleet served the worldwide network.

A decision was taken to standardise on a pure 747 fleet and all the DC-10s were sold between 1982 and 1986. Alitalia nevertheless remained a McDD wide-body aircraft customer when the carrier later decided to purchase a fleet of MD-11s.

Although Alitalia no longer operated DC-10s itself, the company's livery was applied on the starboard side of Continental -30 N68060 during 1995 and part of 1996, resulting from the co-operation between the two companies. The present long range fleet consists of three MD-11s, five MD-11Cs, ten Boeing 747s and twin-jet six 767s.

The livery represented the colours of the national flag. A broad dark green cheatline started as a wedge at the nose and partly swept up into the tail section to form the superimposed green and red company's 'A' logo. The white fuselage displayed a large 'Alitalia' title which, in a smaller form, was shown beside each cabin door.

I-DYNA   *Galileo Galilei*
I-DYNB   *Giotto di Bondone*
I-DYNC   *Luigi Pirandello*
I-DYND   *Enrico Fermi*
I-DYNE   *Dante Alghieri*
I-DYNI   *Michelangelo Buonarrotti*
I-DYNO   *Benvenuto Cellini*
I-DYNU   *Guglielmo Marconi*

Aloha Airlines

Aloha is Hawaii's largest inter-island carrier and operates a fleet of 22 Boeing 737s serving Hawaii, Kauai, Maui and Oahu. The only wide-body that Aloha Airlines operated was -30 N801AL, sub-leased from Philippine Airlines, from May through to November 1984.

The colour scheme displayed orange 'Aloha Pacific' titling and an orange and yellow flower above the twin cheatlines in the same colours, running along the fuselage to the top of the tail. An additional 'Aloha' title was placed diagonally on the leading edge of the fin.

American Airlines

American Airlines was the launch customer for the DC-10, placing an initial order for 25 -10s, with an option on 25 more. The first -10 was delivered on 29th July 1971 and the inaugural passenger flight from Los Angeles to Chicago took place on 5th August 1971.

The airline started transatlantic services in 1982 and three ex-Air New Zealand -30s were acquired to fulfil the need for long range capacity. Whereas the Series 10s were mainly used on domestic and trans-border services, the Series 30s were flown to destinations in Europe and the Far East.

The carrier has lost three of its DC-10s. The first, -10 N110AA, (f/n 22), crashed on take-off at Chicago O'Hare on 25th May 1979. N136AA (f/n 69), a -30, was written off after an aborted take-off at Dallas-Fort Worth on 21st May 1988. N139AA (f/n 105), another -30, was damaged beyond repair while landing at Dallas-Fort Worth on 14th April 1993.

Presently, the DC-10 fleet consists of 25 -10s and eight -30s. Currently nine -10s are on lease to Hawaiian Airlines and three -30s are subleased through FIN 3 of Ireland to Transaero. Two -10s have been placed in storage, or are not in service. Although the DC-10s were gradually being replaced by MD-11s and 767-323ERs, American sold seven MD-11s to Federal Express. Converted to MD-11Fs, they were delivered to the parcel and document carrier in 1996 and 1997.

A contract was closed in November 1996 between American's parent company, AMR, and Boeing foresees that only Boeing products will be ordered by the airline for the next 20 years. While it is planned to retain the Airbus A300-605R fleet, American intends to phase out all of its Fokker 100s, MD-82/83s, and the MD-11s and DC-10s.

On 2nd December 1996, American agreed with Federal Express Corporation to exchange 14 retired -10s and spares in return for Stage 3 hushkits for 30 of its 727s, American started delivery the same month and the exchange was completed at the end of 1997. Other facets of the transaction between the two carriers include American's right to sell to FedEx its remaining -10 fleet between December 1997 and the end of 2003 coupled with American's opportunity to acquire additional hushkits for the 40-50 727s which will remain in the fleet beyond the end of 1999.

The American Airlines livery dates back to 1969. A triple blue, white and red cheatline is applied on the natural metal fuselage with a large red 'American' title on the cabin roof.

The DC-10 is called the 'Luxury Liner' in American service and this title is shown below the forward entry door. The company logo, a red and a blue letter 'A' together with the blue scissor eagle, is displayed on the tail fin.

Note: The American Airlines colour scheme is illustrated on the front cover of this book.

American Trans Air – ATA

The carrier operates an extensive network of domestic and international charter passenger and cargo services. It also performs scheduled passenger services from its Indianapolis base, New York and Chicago Midway hubs to destinations within the USA. The first DC-10 ATA operated, Series 10 N183AT *City of Indianapolis*, started transatlantic services in February 1983. Another DC-10, a former Northwest -40, was acquired from Boeing in June 1984. This aircraft, N184AT (f/n 36) was destroyed by fire at Chicago O'Hare on 10th August 1986.

During 1985 the airline bought nine TriStars from Delta and sold the remaining DC-10 in December of that year. By 1995 the L-1011 fleet had grown to 17 units. The current fleet consists of 727s, 757s and L-1011s.

The smart livery consisted of a triple cheatline in gold, white and dark blue running from nose to tail. Large dark blue 'American Trans Air' titles are displayed across the white upper fuselage. A 'runway' in blue and two taxiways in gold form the 'ATA' logo which is placed on the tail fin and alongside the fuselage title.

ARCA Colombia – Aerovias Colombianas

The Colombian cargo airline operates a fleet of three DC-8 freighters from Bogota and Cali to destinations in South and North America, especially Miami. In July 1994, ARCA acquired -10 N104WA from Global Aircraft Sales Inc. The passenger aircraft was originally delivered to Laker Airways in 1974 and was converted in 1996 to a -10F.

Ariana Afghan Airlines

As a replacement for an ageing Boeing 720, Ariana received on 21st September 1979 its one and only -30. The aircraft was used on flights to Frankfurt, Paris and London.

Following the Soviet occupation in December 1979, the airline ceased all European operations. Soviet aircraft were added to the fleet and the DC-10 was sold to British Caledonian on 21st March 1985.

A light and royal blue cheatline separated by a narrow white window line along the whole fuselage marked the attractive livery. The same scheme was repeated on the fin to form the letter 'A', encompassing the company's bird logo. The white roof displayed the 'Ariana Afghan' titles in English and Afghan.

Arrow Air

Starting 1981, scheduled passenger and worldwide charter services were flown with DC-8s. Contract services for the US forces were also carried out, but following the crash of one of the

carrier's DC-8-63s near Gander, Newfoundland, Canada, on 12th December 1985 the US government contracts were cancelled. To meet the growing demand on the transatlantic routes a total of five -10s were leased from International Air Leases during 1983 and 1984. The carrier to stopped all passenger services in 1986 and today operates worldwide cargo flights with a fleet of six DC-8Fs and three TriStar freighters – Arrow was the first to operate the L-1011F.

Using the same scheme, a red or blue broad cheatline along the fuselage ended up in the tail fin to form a large letter 'A' on the DC-10. Both versions displayed bold red 'Arrow Air' titles on the white cabin roof.

Atlantis

The Frankfurt-based German charter operator was already a Douglas customer, having taken delivery of new DC-8-63s and DC-9-32s from the manufacturer. An order for two -30s was placed, but the airline ceased operations on 20th October 1972. Fuselage number 90 was sold to Air Zaire and delivered on 8th June 1973, while f/n 125 became the only DC-10 in Air Siam's fleet on 25th November 1974.

Avcom Aviation Commercial

In December 1994 Avcom obtained former World Airways -30CF N105WA on lease from CIT Leasing to conduct international cargo services. Originally registered UN-10200, the aircraft was re-registered and operated as RA-10200. The lease was cancelled in September 1995 and the aircraft was returned to CIT as N105WA on 1st October. Since April 1996 TAESA of Mexico has operated this aircraft on behalf of STAF, Argentina.

The livery consisted of a dark blue cheatline along the completely white fuselage, trimmed on either side by red pinstripes. The aircraft was operated without any titles.

Balair

The charter subsidiary of Swissair received new -30 HB-IHK on 31st January 1979. At the time it was the only wide-body aircraft in the fleet. It was mainly used for services to North and Central America, the Caribbean and the Far East, but was also operated on flights to destinations in the Mediterranean and the Canaries.

The first and second liveries were almost identical with a red window cheatline on a white upper fuselage and a red tail with the white Swiss cross. The first paint scheme had black 'Balair' titles on the fuselage and the tail engine and the company's red 'B' logo on the forward fuselage. The latter was omitted in the second paint scheme and the 'Balair' titles changed to a red colour.

After use with Laker Airways, former *Californian Belle* was leased to British Caledonian Airways. G-BJZE was one of two DC-10-10s operated by the charter subsidiary British Caledonian Charter Ltd. Author's collection

DC-10-30 G-BHDH *Loch Torridon* showing Caledonian Airways' beautiful paint scheme. Fred Lerch

Caledonian Airways DC-10-30 G-BWIN *Loch Awe*, showing the partial colour scheme of former operator, Leisure Air. Exavia

Caledonian DC-10-30 OO-LRM, on lease from ChallengAir, with black titling on white fuselage. The tail fin carries the golden lion rampant on a blue crest. Exavia

In 1992 the wide-body fleet consisted of four Airbus A310s and the decision was taken to sell the DC-10 which left the fleet in June of that year. Balair merged with CTA under the name Balaircta in 1993. This company was integrated into Swissair and Crossair in November 1995.

Biman Bangladesh Airlines

The airline became a DC-10 operator when it bought three -30s from Singapore Airlines in 1983. Another of the type was acquired new from McDD on 30th December 1988 – f/n 445 was the next to the last DC-10 built. The DC-10s replaced the airline's 707s. International services are operated to Brussels, Frankfurt, London, Paris, Rome, New York, Abu Dhabi, Dubai, Doha, Jeddah, Muscat, Riyadh, Kathmandu, Karachi, Bombay, Calcutta, Bangkok, Hong Kong, Kuala Lumpur, Singapore, and Tokyo amongst others. In July 1993 a -30 was leased from McDD and returned in January 1994. A further aircraft was leased from McDD in August 1993. This was returned in September 1996, bringing the DC-10 fleet up to the present strength of four units.

In the first livery, the red and green colours of the national flag were reflected in the twin cheatlines which extended to the top of the fin, interrupted only by a white stork motif in a red circle. In the present livery, the twin cheatlines continue to the end of the fuselage and two twin red and green bands are placed at the top and bottom of the fin. The black titles appear in English on the port side whilst the starboard side displays the titles in Bengali.

S2-ACO	City of Hazrat Shah Makhdoom (RA)
S2-ACP	City of Dhaka
S2-ACQ	City of Hazrat Shah Jalal (RA)
S2-ACR	The New Era

Birgenair

The Turkish charter group operated with a 737-3M8, a 757-225 and a 767-269ER. The carrier leased -30 OH-LHB from Finnair for the 1994 summer holiday season. This sported a basic

Finnair paint scheme without any titles. The only aircraft owned by the carrier, 757 TC-GEN crashed shortly after take-off from Puerto Plata, Dominica on 6th February 1996. Following the disaster the airline stopped all operations.

Bogaziçi Hava Tasimaciligi – BHT

In December 1987 BHT, a subsidiary of THY Turk Hava Yollari, received on lease two -10s which had been withdrawn from service by THY earlier in the year. The aircraft were used for international passenger charters to Europe and the USA. TC-JAU was returned to THY in February 1989 and subsequently sold to Federal Express as N68058 in November 1989. The other DC-10, TC-JAY, remained with the carrier until it stopped operations during 1989 and this aircraft was also acquired by Federal Express.

An all white fuselage formed the background for a thin dark blue striping along the fuselage and the bold dark blue 'Bogaziçi BHT' title above the passenger windows. The tail fin showed the company logo, three horizontal wide stripes flowing out into six smaller ones.

TC-JAU   *Cengelköy*
TC-JAY   *Yeniköy*

British Airways

While all the Lockheed TriStars have been retired from service and sold, BA still operates all eight former BCAL -30s, of which one was on lease to the charter subsidiary Caledonian Airways until February 1997. This aircraft, G-NUIK, is currently operated by Flying Colours Airlines. Unfortunately, British Airways did not accept the orders and delivery positions, inherited from the take-over of British Caledonian, for three MD-11s and the aircraft in question were sold to American Airlines. Today, British Airways mainly uses the DC-10s on flights to the USA but also destinations in the Middle East and Africa are served.

BA did not follow the idea of an overall white fuselage presently used by many carriers but selected a distinctive livery. The top of the fuselage is pearl grey with midnight blue 'British Airways' lettering at the front. The midnight blue belly has a symbolized dark red 'Speedwing' which extends as a cheatline to the rear of the aircraft. The colours of the Union Flag appear on the rear engine while the white crown highlights the dark blue tail. All BA DC-10s in this paint scheme are named after well known British forests.

On 10th June 1997, the airline unveiled its new 'sky high art' livery. It features a softer, rounder typeface 'British Airways' title and a new three-dimensional 'Speedmarque' on the forward, pearl white, fuselage. The belly and engined feature a brightened dark blue.

Fifteen world images, which adorn the tail sections, were revealed at the time of the launch of the new image. It is BA's intention to

Photographs on the opposite page:

Canadian Pacific DC-10-30 C-FCRE *Empress of Canada* interim livery and English title on the port side fuselage. Canadian Airlines International

The starboard side of the fuselage of DC-10-30 C-FCRE displaying the French title 'Canadien Pacifique'. Fred Lerch

A Potomac DC-10-30 was used for a Canadian advertisement campaign in 1993, displaying signatures of company employees. Author's collection

Since late 1995, C-FCRE *Spirit of Canadian* has permanently featured the signatures of very important customers, frequent travellers and company employees. Author's collection

Photographs on this page:

The present Canadian Airlines attractive livery on DC-10-30(ER) C-GCPH *Empress of Lima*. Canadian Airlines International

At Amsterdam Schiphol Airport, DC-10-30 C-GCPD showing the special livery of CP Air for Expo 86 in Montreal. Fred Lerch

Sporting one of the most striking colour schemes of its day, CP Air DC-10-30(ER) C-GCPE *Empress of Alberta* over the Rocky Mountains. Canadian Airlines International

Capitol Air was one of the first airlines applying huge titles on the fuselage, plus the 'Sky Saver' logos. Author's collection

At Toronto International Airport, Caribbean Airways DC-10-10, G-BBSZ, on lease from Laker Airways. Nicky Scherrer – VIP Photoservice

ChallengAir aircraft have a basic white fuselage for easy conversion to the requirements of its regular lessees. DC-10-30 OO-JOT with the carrier's own title and logo. Fred Lerch

Condor's first DC-10-30, D-ADFO, in the airline's second 'off-white' livery. Condor Flugdienst

Photographs on the opposite page:

Adapting to the parent company's paint scheme, Condor DC-10s received an all-white fuselage in early 1990. Condor Flugdienst

Continental Airlines' second DC-10-30, N12061, in the original gold, red and white paint scheme. McDonnell Douglas

Continental DC-10-30 N1462 at Newark in the current livery, against the impressive backdrop of the Manhattan skyline. Continental Airlines

add 12 world images to the portfolio each year until the millennium, creating a total of at least 50 by then. The fleet will be painted over the next three years, however none of the DC-10s had acquired the controversial livery at the time of writing.'

G-BEBL	Forest of Dean
G-BEBM	Sherwood Forest
G-BHDI	Forest of Ae
G-BHDJ	Glen Cap Forest
G-BHDH	Benmore Forest
G-DCIO	Epping Forest
G-NIUK	Cairn Edward Forest
G-MULL	New Forest

British Caledonian Airways – BCAL

British Caledonian Airways, Britain's largest independent carrier, was awarded the routes to South America, West and Central Africa in 1976. Following this government's decision, the airline was looking for a large capacity aircraft and decided to purchase -30s. Between March 1977 and April 1981, eight were delivered. Long range passenger services were extended to North America, Africa, the Middle and Far East.

In 1988, after financial difficulties, the airline was taken over by one of its strongest competitors, British Airways. The fleet of nine DC-10s was transferred to the new owner.

The livery was extremely attractive; a golden cheatline started below the nose and was joined by a dark blue cheatline behind the cockpit windows. Bold black 'British Caledonian' titles and the Union Flag were placed on the upper white fuselage. The most remarkable part of the paint scheme was the dark blue tail

with the gold lion rampant. The company was often referred to as BCAL, this lettering together with a shield appeared on the wing-mounted engines.

G-BEBL	*Sir Alexander Fleming - The Scottish Challenger*
G-BEBM	*Robert Burns - The Scottish Bard*
G-BFGI	*David Livingstone - The Scottish Explorer*
G-BGAT	*James Watt - The Scottish Engineer*
G-BHDH	*Sir Walter Scott*
G-BHDI	*Robert the Bruce - The Scottish Warrior*
G-BHDJ	*James S McDonnell - The Scottish American Aviation Pioneer*
G-DCIO	*Flora McDonald*
G-MULL	*Ian Ritchie - The Caledonian Airline Executive*

British Caledonian Air Charter

British Caledonian Air Charter was the charter subsidiary of BCAL. Two -10s (both ex-Laker Airways) were leased from Mitsui and Company Inc on 22nd February 1982. The company was renamed Cal Air (qv) in 1983. The only difference in the livery with the BCAL aircraft was the black 'British Caledonian Charter' or 'BCA Charter' lettering on the fuselage.

Cal Air International

Originally named British Caledonian Air Charter (qv), Cal Air started services in 1983. A third -10 was bought and added to the fleet of two in February 1986. (This DC-10 was the second aircraft built and remained with McDD for flight testing purposes. It was first delivered to Laker on 3rd June 1977, registered as G-BELO, and was bought by American Trans Air on 21st February 1983.) The Cal Air network included charter flights from Europe to the USA.

Following the take-over of British Caledonian by British Airways in 1988 Cal Air was disposed of and went on to become a wholly-owned subsidiary of the Rank Group. At the end of that year Cal Air was renamed Novair (qv).

The aircraft featured an all-white fuselage with a wide red band starting underneath the nose running up diagonally to the top of the rear fuselage section, interrupted by large white and blue 'Cal Air' lettering. The large rampant lion was still present, however it was painted red on the white tail.

Caledonian Airways

After the acquisition of British Caledonian by British Airways, charter activities of BCAL and BA's wholly-owned subsidiary British Airtours were consolidated. British Airtours was founded as a charter division in 1969 and later renamed Caledonian Airways. In December 1994 Caledonian was acquired by UK tour company Inspirations Holidays. Mainstay of the fleet are A320s and TriStars. A BA -30, G-NIUK, was added to the fleet in April 1993 for charter flights to the Caribbean. An extensive charter network is operated from Gatwick and other British cities to the USA, Canada, Thailand, Kenya and the Mediterranean. The airline also operates winter charter flights to Munich, Salzburg, Geneva and Zurich.

In addition to G-NIUK, Caledonian operated another BA -30, G-BHDH, from April 1993 until October 1995. On different occasions DC-10s were leased from other operators, eg AOM and ChallengAir. To further fulfil long range requirements, former Leisure Air -30 N831LA was leased from GE Capital Aviation as G-BWIN in December 1995. This joined the new Laker Airways DC-10 fleet in July 1996.

Caledonian replaced G-BWIN with former PAL -30 G-GOKT in May 1996. G-NIUK returned to BA in February 1997 and was replaced by ChallengAir -30 OO-LRM from June 1997 until February 1998. The airline acquired a former Biman Bangladesh -30, S2-ADB, in August 1997, which became G-LYON.

Aircraft have a very attractive paint scheme, a pale grey upper and deep blue lower fuselage, a gold pinstripe on the lower section, and bold 'Caledonian' titles above the windows between door No.1 and No.2. The blue tail sports the golden rampant heraldic lion.

G-BHDH   *Loch Torridon*
G-BWIN   *Loch Awe*
G-NIUK   *Loch Loyal*
G-GOKT   *Loch Roag*

One of the recent 'new' DC-10 operators, DAS Air Cargo with ex-Sabena -30CF OO-SLA. Exavia

Delta Air Lines DC-10-10 N902WA, in the airline's former, very attractive, colour scheme. MAP

Dominicana leased Taesa DC-10-30 XA-SYE to take part in the lucrative charter business to and from the Dominican Republic. Exavia

Former Alitalia I-DYNB *Giotto di Bonbone* Series 30 N391EA was one of three DC-10s bought and operated by Eastern Air Lines. Fred Lerch

Before delivery, Ecuatoriana DC-10-30 in the basic colours and registration (HB-IHA) of the former owner, Swissair. Fred Lerch

Once in operation, a colourful livery was applied to Ecuatoriana's only DC-10, HC-BKO. Author's collection

Ecuatoriana DC-10-30, HC-BKO, in the livery introduced in 1996. Aviation Photography of Miami

Photographs on the opposite page:

A short-time DC-10 operator, Express One used DC-10-30 F-OKBB for transatlantic services. Author's collection

DC-10-30F N306FE *John Peter Jr* was the first Series 30 freighter built and first of ten units delivered to Federal Express. McDonnell Douglas

DC-10-30F N313FE *Brandon Parks* in the current, and very striking, colour scheme of the world's largest express transportation company – FedEx. Federal Express Corporation

Finnair DC-10-30 OH-LHB displaying the cartoon characters livery introduced during 1995. Author's collection

Canadian Airlines International – Canadian / Canadien

After the merger of Canadian Pacific (qv) and Pacific Western Airlines in 1987 the airline's name was changed to Canadian Airlines International. Until November 1996 the following European destinations were served: Frankfurt, London, Paris and Rome. Due to reorganisation, Frankfurt and Paris were dropped from the network, while London flights were increased. Flights to Rome continue in co-operation with Alitalia. South American destinations include Mexico City, Rio de Janeiro, Buenos Aires, São Paulo and Santiago. Always a stronghold of the company, extensive scheduled flights across the Pacific are also flown.

On 15th January 1990 Wardair (qv), also a DC-10 operator, was taken over by Canadian Airlines International. However, the two -30s operated by the charter carrier were sold to the GPA Group prior to the merger.

Awaiting a new livery, the 'CP Air' titles on the lower fuselage were first replaced by 'Canadian Pacific' / 'Canadien Pacifique' and then later by 'Canadian' / 'Canadien' titles. A new interim livery was applied to C-FCRE with a large 'Canadian Pacific' title on the upper port side and a 'Canadien Pacifique' on the upper starboard side of the fuselage. The bright upper fuselage was divided from the blue lower fuselage by a grey and a red cheatline. Red horizontal lines were also applied to the blue-coloured wing-mounted engines. The broad stripes in the company logo represent the five continents being served by the airline and this motif was prominently displayed on the dark blue tail.

The final Canadian paint scheme as used today only differs slightly from the interim one. The company logo and broad striping on the tail fin have been extended to the top of the engine assembly and the red striping on the wing mounted engines was omitted. The problem of showing the new 'Canadian' name in English as well as in French was overcome by using the company's arrowhead logo instead of the third 'a', resulting in the title 'Canadi>n'.

In 1993, while on a C-check at Canadian's Vancouver facilities, a -30 aircraft belonging to Potomac was used for a publicity campaign featuring the signatures of company employees. This aircraft, N6150Z, had been bought by Potomac from Canadian in 1991. Canadian leased the aircraft in October 1993 and it is in service under its former registration, C-FCRD. This paint scheme was only used as a static display and never took to the air. With the addition of signatures of VIP customers and frequent travellers, the concept was permanently introduced in 1995. The two DC-10s receiving the 'signature treatment' were C-FCRD and 'E. The English and French names on these two are placed on the port and starboard grey cheatlines respectively.

Besides serving the international network, the DC-10s are also used on trans-Canada and

trans-border US operations. At the time of writing, the long haul fleet consists of ten -30s, of which five are ER-versions, three 747-475s and one 747-4F6 and nine 767-375ERs.

C-FCRD	*Pride of Canadian /*
	La fierté de Canadien
C-FCRE	*Spirit of Canadian /*
	L'esprit de Canadien

Canadian Pacific Airlines – CP Air

Canada's second largest airline received its first -30 on 27th March 1979 and by 1982 a total of eight were in the fleet. The aircraft were used on scheduled services to Amsterdam and the Far East, as well as on transatlantic charters. Through a lease agreement with United the carrier received three -10s in 1983, in exchange for three -30s. The aircraft, N1834U, '36U and '37U remained with CP Air until mid-1987. A decision to standardise on the DC-10 as the airline's only long range type was made in 1986 and the four 747s were exchanged for four Series 30s from Pakistan International. In 1987 the airline was taken over by Pacific Western Airlines and continued operations under the new name Canadian Airlines International (qv). At the time of the merger the -30 fleet comprised 12 aircraft of which five were converted -30ERs.

The bright orange and red livery together with a partly polished fuselage was a smart combination which made the CP Air aircraft stand out at any airport. On the occasion of the world exhibition in Montreal, a white 'Expo 1986' title was applied on the tail engine and an orange shaded '86' placed underneath the forward passenger windows. In line with CP Air's other long range aircraft -10 N1836U was appropriately christened *Empress of Expo 86*.

N1836U	*Empress of Santiago,*
	renamed *Empress of Expo 86*
C-GCPC	*Empress of Quebec,*
	renamed *Empress of Amsterdam*
C-GCPD	*Empress of British Columbia,*
	renamed *Empress of Sydney*
C-GCPE	*Empress of Ontario,*
	renamed *Empress of Alberta*
C-GCPF	*Empress of Alberta,*
	renamed *Empress of Santiago,*
	then *Empress of Buenos Aires*
C-GCPG	*Empress of Fiji*
C-GCPH	*Empress of Lima*
C-GCPI	*Empress of Auckland,*
	renamed *Empress of Honolulu*
C-GCPJ	*Empress of Rome*
C-FCRA	*Empress of Hong Kong*
C-FCRB	*Empress of Tokyo*
C-FCRD	*Empress of Lisbon*
C-FCRE	*Empress of Canada*

Capitol International Airways – Capitol Air

The carrier started operations in 1968 with a new DC-8-63CF. Another of the type was delivered the following year. An array of DC-8 series 55s, -61s, -62s and -63s in all passenger, convertible freighter and pure freighter versions were bought or leased. In 1981 Capitol International Airways changed name to Capitol Air. Worldwide freight and passenger charters as well as services for the USAF's Military Airlift Command were conducted. In 1982 a -10 was bought and two leased from International Air Leases Inc. The three aircraft remained with the carrier until May, July and August 1983 respectively. An Airbus A300B4 was also leased from the German charter airline Hapag-Lloyd from June until October 1984. The company ceased to exist at the end of 1984.

The huge red and blue 'Capitol' lettering on the forward white fuselage was based on the national flag, the stars and stripes. To underscore the low charter fares, an additional '$ky $aver' title was applied on the tail engine.

Caribbean Airways International

Known as the 'National Airline of Barbados' the carrier leased aircraft from contract carriers when required. In the early 1980s the airline leased Boeing 707s and DC-10s from Laker Airways. Flights between Europe, the West Indies and Mexico as well as flights from Barbados to the USA and Canada were operated.

Aircraft had a basic Laker colour scheme with the Barbados flag and black 'Caribbean Airways' titles on the upper fuselage and golden 'Caribbean' titles on the tail fin.

After the demise of Laker in 1982, a -30 was leased from BCAL for flights linking the West Indies and Brussels. In 1984 Ghana Airways operated for Caribbean Airways -30 9G-ANA on short term lease. Martinair Holland conducted flights for Caribbean with DC-10s PH-MBN and 'BT. During 1987 the airline leased a Boeing 747-123 from Cargolux of Luxemburg. Operating under the call-sign Caribjet, the carrier conducted international charter flights in 1994 and 1995 using Birgenair 757s and 767s. The company suspended operations in May 1995.

ChallengAir

The company was founded as a charter operator in 1994 and commenced services with two leased DC-10-30s. Aircraft are regularly subleased to other carriers, eg Tarom and Corsair. At the end of 1997 one aircraft went to Continental while the other example is operated by Caledonian. The livery is simple with 'ChallengAir' titles in blue and red, with a 'CA' corporate logo on a white fuselage. The same 'CA' logo reappears on the tail section. The aircraft were also operated without 'ChallengAir' titles.

Challenge Air Cargo

CAC was founded in 1985, a wholly owned subsidiary of Challenge Air Transport, from which it separated in 1986. Based at Miami, Florida, USA, the carrier operates an extensive scheduled and charter cargo network to Central and South America. The fleet currently consists of three Boeing 757-23A/PFs and a single Boeing 707-330C freighter. Gemini Air Cargo operates cargo flights with a DC-10-30F on behalf of CAC. In December 1997 CAC announced that it would be the launch customer for the Aeronavali freighter conversion of the -40, with two due for delivery in 1998 and options on another three. The aircraft will be leased from Omega Air and are former Japan Air Lines examples.

China Airlines

China Airlines placed an order for a -30, f/n 214, but the order was not taken up. The aircraft went to BCAL on 23rd February 1977.

Condor

Condor Flugdienst is the wholly-owned charter subsidiary of German flag carrier Lufthansa. In 1971 Condor became the first charter airline world-wide to put the Boeing 747 into service. By 1972 two were used on short and long range destinations. Their use on tourist routes proved to be uneconomical and Condor decided to switch to the DC-10. Two -30s were delivered in 1979, replacing the 747s. In January 1981 a third -30 joined the two sisterships. As one of the largest charter operators in the world, Condor has an extensive network within Europe and operates internationally to the Far East, the Caribbean and the Americas. In December 1997, the German anti-trust commission granted Condor and tour organiser NUR (Neckermann) to set up a joint enterprise.

When Lufthansa phased out its last DC-10s at the end of 1994, Condor acquired D-ADJO and D-ADLO from the parent with delivery in 1995. The present fleet is four 737s, 18 757s, nine 767s and three DC-10s. As the launch customer, Condor ordered 12 stretched 757-300s (plus 12 options) in September 1996. The two former Lufthansa DC-10s were sold to Aviation Investors in May 1997 and left the fleet during November 1997. The remaining three -30s will be gradually phased out when the first six Boeing 757-300s are delivered in early 1999.

Originally the livery consisted of a natural metal fuselage with dark blue 'Condor' titles – see page 20. With the arrival of the Airbus A310, which has a composite material belly, all aircraft obtained a light grey paint scheme, called 'off-white'. In the early 1990s another change took place when the livery was adapted to that of the parent company and a white fuselage with light grey lower belly was introduced. From the beginning the tail section has been yellow and shows the dark blue stylised condor within a dark blue circle. This company logo is repeated underneath the cockpit windows and on the wing-mounted engines.

A long time McDonnell Douglas customer, Finnair once had a fleet of five DC-10-30s, OH-LHA illustrated. Finnair

DC-10-30 PK-GIB, the second of the type delivered to Garuda Indonesia Airways, in the early paint scheme. Garuda Indonesia

The sixth and final Series 30 for Garuda Indonesia, PK-GIF in today's livery at Frankfurt/Main Airport. Author's collection

Former Lufthansa DC-10-30 D-ADAO, the first converted Series 30F for Gemini Air Cargo becoming N601GC. Aviation Photography of Miami

Continental Airlines – Continental Micronesia

The first -10 arrived with Continental Airlines of the USA on 14th April 1972 and the first order was completed when the eighth aircraft was delivered in May 1973. Continental was the first carrier to order the -10CF and a total of eight was added to the fleet. For international services two new -30s were acquired in 1980. The airline operated under Chapter 11 bankruptcy protection twice, from September 1983 until February 1987 and from December 1990 until May 1993. Scheduled domestic and international services to Canada, Mexico, Europe, the South Pacific and the Far East are offered.

Subsidiary Continental Micronesia operates flights from Guam and Honolulu using leased 727s and DC-10s from the parent company.

As well as 747s and 767s, the wide-body fleet currently includes six -10s and 31 -30s. On 10th June 1997 Continental announced an order for five 777s, in addition to five already on order, and 30 767-400ERs to replace the DC-10 fleet. Like American Airlines and Delta Air Lines, Continental will purchase from Boeing the carrier's requirements for new jet aircraft (other than regional jets) over the next 20 years.

Gemini Air Cargo Series 30F N600GC, formerly Lufthansa D-ADMO, leaving Basle for Chicago on its first commercial flight in the new livery on 20th April 1996. Andreas Lang

Ghana Airways DC-10-30 9G-ANA in the airline's attractive and colourful livery. Nicky Scherrer – VIP Photoservice

On a long term lease from Skyjet Belgium, Ghana Airways' second DC-10-30 9G-PHN *The Royal Oak*, wearing simplified livery. Flite-Line-Photos

Hawaiian Air operates an ever-changing fleet of leased American Airlines' DC-10s – Series 10, N148AA illustrated. Nicky Scherrer – VIP Photoservice

Iberia DC-10-30 EC-CBN *Costa Brava* was the first of the type acquired by the Spanish flag carrier in 1973. McDonnell Douglas

The current 'sunny' livery of Iberia on DC-10-30 EC-DEA *Rias Gallegas.* McDonnell Douglas

Icelandair Loftleidir DC-10-30CF N1035F at a wintry Reykjavik Airport. Icelandair

Japan Airlines and Northwest Airlines were the only customers to order the Pratt & Whitney powered DC-10-40. JAL's JA8530 was the first of 20 aircraft delivered to the Japanese carrier. McDonnell Douglas

Approaching Tokyo-Narita Airport, DC-10-40, JA8535, in the somewhat dull livery introduced in 1989. Japan Airlines

DC-10-40 JA8450 showing off JAL's toll-free reservations number on the fuselage, October 1996. Exavia

On 1st March 1978, -30 N68045 (f/n 44) was damaged beyond repair after an aborted take-off at Los Angeles International, California.

The white, red and gold colour scheme remained until May 1993 when a new livery was introduced. A white and light grey fuselage is separated by a gold pinstripe. The new company 'globe' logo is displayed on the dark blue tail fin. On Continental Micronesia aircraft, an additional 'Micronesia' title is added alongside the 'Continental' title on the white cabin roof.

Through the co-operation with Alitalia, one Continental -30, N68060, obtained a mixed livery in 1995. It displayed the Continental colour scheme on the port side and that of Alitalia on the starboard side until mid-1996.

N12061	*Richard M Adams*
N68046	*The Hawaiian Islands*
N68048	*Employee Owner Ship 1*
N68060	*Robert F Six*
N68065	*Robert D Gallaway*

Corsair

Formed as Corse Air International in 1981, Corsair has an extensive network of scheduled and charter flights from France to destinations within Europe, Africa, North America, the Far East and the French overseas territories. Operating mainly with 737s and 747s, the airline subleased -30 OO-LRM from ChallengAir in July 1995 for use on its flights from Lyon to Saint Denis, Port-au-Prince and Pointe-a-Pitre.

The lease was terminated from March until June 1996. During this time, the aircraft was used by Garuda for Hadj pilgrimage flights. From March 1996 until mid-September 1997 Corsair leased a further -30, OO-JOT, from ChallengAir. This aircraft was also operated in the full Corsair colour scheme.

With the establishment of the new name Corsair, a new paint scheme was introduced in 1991 – a fully white fuselage with large dark blue titles on the forward section and an artist's expression of sun and water in blue, white and green on the tail fin.

Cubana

To support the long range Ilyushin IL-62M fleet Cubana chartered -30s from Air Outre Mer. This procedure has continued with AOM French Airlines. Twice-weekly Havana-London-Gatwick services were started in October 1996 with a leased AOM French Airlines DC-10. In both cases, the aircraft were operated in the standard Air Outre Mer and AOM colour scheme with additional 'Cubana' titles on the forward fuselage.

DAS Air Cargo

Dairo Air Services was founded in 1986 and started cargo operations from Entebbe, Uganda, with two 707 freighters. In 1995 the carrier acquired a -30CF which originally was the first of its type in Europe when in was delivered to Sabena as OO-SLA in September 1973. Series 30CF 5X-JOE transports flowers for the famous flower trading-centre in Aalsmeer, Netherlands, between Nairobi and Amsterdam.

The UK-based carrier also conducts cargo flights from London to Dubai and Abu Dhabi. Besides the -30CF, three 707Cs are operated. A second -30 was acquired in March 1997 and its conversion to freighter was completed in November 1997. This aircraft is also used for the transport of flowers.

A triple red, yellow and black cheatline is applied on the all white fuselage. A large red 'DAS Air Cargo' title is placed on the roof and, in the case of 5X-JOE, a red 'EAF' (East African Flowers) title on the rear engine. The second aircraft, N400JR, has a 'TFA' (Tele-Flower Auctions) title on the tail engine. The company's logo, a lion with a winged globe is applied on the tail fin and wing-mounted engines.

Delta Air Lines

With an order for 25 TriStars it seemed rather strange that Delta ordered five -10s from McDD. This decision was taken to avoid fleet problems

Japan Air Lines' charter subsidiary Japan Air Charter also operates with Series 40s, on lease from the parent company. The aircraft carry a basic JAL colour scheme. Japan Airlines

'Super Resort Express' titles and paint scheme, with Unicef logos, were applied to Japan Air Charter aircraft in 1994. Neville Parnell

One of the carrier's two DC-10-30s, Japan Air System JA8551. Author's collection

Japan Air System introduced a cartoon character paint scheme in 1995, under the heading 'JAS Peter Pan Flight'. Neville Parnell

Starting operations in 1975, Japan Asia used a revised, basic Japan Air Lines colour scheme. Fred Lerch

Following parent company JAL, Japan Asia adapted a new livery in 1989. DC-10-40 JA8531 at Hong Kong. Fred Lerch

While on lease from JAL Series 40 JA8545 had a simple 'quick change' paint scheme. Exavia

Jet Charter Service operated two DC-10-40s, including N133JC, under the 'Jet 24' name. Fred Lerch

On the occasion of the Olympic games in 1986, the title 'Official Olympic Carrier' was applied to JAT aircraft. Fred Lerch

Photographs on the opposite page:

Jugoslovenski Aerotransport's first DC-10-30 YU-AMA *Nikola Tesla* was delivered in December 1978. McDonnell Douglas

Back in service since March 1996, JAT DC-10 YU-AMB *City of Belgrade* in the airline's interim livery. Nicky Scherrer – VIP Photoservice

World Airways' subsidiary Key Airlines operated charter flights with DC-10-10 N917JW. Fred Lerch

KLM Royal Dutch Airlines was the second airline to place the DC-10-30 into passenger service. The fleet was named after famous composers, PH-DTF being *Giuseppe Verdi*. McDonnell Douglas

in case of late delivery of the L-1011s. Before delivery from the manufacturer Delta sold all five units to United Airlines, but leased them back from that carrier for a period of 2½ years. During their service with Delta the aircraft flew with United registrations, N1833U to '37U.

With the take-over of Western Airlines in 1987, Delta again received DC-10s. The L-1011 fleet being up to 35, there was no need for another type of wide-body and by the end of 1988 all nine -10s had been sold.

Although no longer a DC-10 operator, Delta became a McDD wide-body customer by ordering 15 MD-11s. In March 1997 the airline announced a long term loyalty contract with Boeing to purchase airliners only from the Seattle-based manufacturer for the next 20 years.

The DC-10s featured Delta's attractive livery which remained unchanged for a long period of time until the introduction of a new colour scheme in March 1997. The name 'delta' originating from the Mississippi river delta, the company's logo is a dark blue and red delta. This logo appeared on the forward fuselage and on the tail section. The lower part of the fuselage was natural metal, the upper part was white with a wide dark blue line over the windows and a red pinstripe above the latter. The sloping 'Delta' lettering appeared on the upper forward fuselage and on the rear engine.

Dominicana de Aviacion

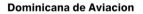

Dominicana operates schedules to Aruba, Caracas, Miami, New York, Port-au-Prince and San Juan as well as charters to the Caribbean. Dominicana already operated a DC-10 in 1984 when a -40 was leased from Jet Charter Service/Jet 24 from June until October. The carrier

The attractive light blue upper fuselage paint scheme of Korean Air stands out amongst the increasing trend towards 'white-body' aircraft. The carrier ceased DC-10 operations in December 1995. Fred Lerch

Korean Air Lines DC-10-30 HL7315, in the first livery, was the second of three new aircraft delivered to the airline. McDonnell Douglas

One of the first DC-10s to be operated in Russia, Kras Air Series 30 N525MD, shown with the temporary 'rampant lion' logo. Author's collection

Kras Air's second aircraft, Series 30 N533MD in the final paint scheme. Exavia

Photographs on the opposite page:

After the Gulf War, British Airways DC-10-30 G-NIUK was on a three month lease to Kuwait Airways. Nicky Scherrer – VIP Photoservice

Laker Airways was the first European carrier to operate DC-10s. Series 10 G-AZZC *Eastern Belle* was delivered on 26th October 1972. McDonnell Douglas

The new Laker Airways DC-10 Super 30 N832LA *Endeavour* at Fort Lauderdale, Florida. Aviation Photography of Miami

Laker's fourth DC-10, Series 10 N946LL, carries the tail colour scheme as used in the 1970s. Flite-Line-Photos

currently uses equipment on lease from other airlines, mostly from TAESA, Mexico and AvAtlantic, USA. TAESA -30 XA-SYE was one aircraft involved. In the early phase of operation it was completely white with red 'Dominicana' titles on the upper fuselage. Later the aircraft obtained the TAESA colour scheme with additional red 'Dominicana' titles. With the DC-10, charter flights between the Dominican Republic and Germany were staged until July 1996 when the aircraft returned to TAESA.

Eastern Airlines

Eastern Airlines began their one and only transatlantic operation on 15th July 1985. After Air Florida had ceased operations, Eastern was allowed to fly the Miami to London-Gatwick route. Although a major TriStar operator, Eastern acquired three ex-Alitalia -30s for this purpose. With heavy losses accumulating, the airline abandoned the transatlantic operations altogether in October 1986. The three DC-10s ended up with Continental. After financial problems Eastern filed under Chapter 11 and stopped operations on 18th January 1991.

Although simple, the livery was eye-catching with light and dark blue cheatlines along the polished metal fuselage, extending to the top of the tail with dark blue lettering and falcon emblem above the cabin windows.

Ecuatoriana

Compania Ecuatoriana de Aviacion, operating under the name Ecuatoriana, was formed in 1974 as the national carrier of Ecuador. Scheduled passenger services were operated from Quito and Guayaquil to New York, Chicago, Los Angeles, Caracas, Panama City, Cali, Mexico City, Lima, San Jose, Buenos Aires, Bogota and Santiago with a fleet of two Boeing 707s

and one -30. Freight services were also conducted to New York, Miami and Panama City.

The -30 (f/n 57) was the first of the type to be delivered to Swissair. The Swiss carrier operated *St Gallen*, HB-IHA, until September 1983 when it was delivered to Ecuatoriana. When it left Zurich for Ecuador as HC-BKO it still carried the brown and black Swissair cheatlines with added 'Ecuatoriana' titles on the fuselage and the black and white 'E' logo on the tail.

The full livery introduced by the airline probably was one the most colourful, yet daring, of paint schemes. A yellow, a green and a blue band came down from the top of the fuselage and met with a magenta, an orange and a red band coming up from the belly. The six cheatlines continued along the fuselage and swept up the tail section ending just below the company's 'E' logo. Simple 'Ecuatoriana' titling was located on the forward fuselage.

Ecuatoriana suspended all operations on 28th September 1993 and the DC-10 was stored at Latacunga. Through the partnership with VASP the long intended restart took place in early in 1996. HC-BKO was withdrawn from storage and received a VASP-like paint scheme with two-tone blue cheatlines and a huge blue 'Ecuatoriana' title across the white fuselage. (This aircraft was re-registered as PP-SFB in May 1996.) Scheduled services from Quito and Guayaquil to New York, Miami, Los Angeles, Rio de Janeiro and Buenos Aires are operated.

Egypt Air

Egypt Air ordered two -30s and one -30ER for services on its international network. Although all three aircraft were built, none of the orders were taken up by the airline. Subsequently aircraft f/n 345 was delivered to Finnair on 11th August 1981, aircraft f/n 348 to Zambia Airways on 20th July 1984. Aircraft f/n 434 was taken up by Thai Airways International and was accepted by the airline on 1st December 1987.

Excalibur Airways

This British carrier was founded in 1992 and conducted charter flights from Manchester and London-Gatwick. During 1995 the airline operated with a fleet of four leased Airbus A320-200s. However, in November of that year all aircraft were returned to the leasing company GE Capital Aviation Services. For charter flights to Florida, Excalibur leased Skyjet -30, V2-LEH, from 30th May until 26th June 1996. Excalibur intended to acquire two -30s, to be registered G-SPNA and G-SPNB, but ceased operations on 26th June 1996.

Express One International

Formerly known as Jet East International Airlines, Express One operates as a supplemental carrier with a fleet of 20 Boeing 727 freighters. For transatlantic passenger charter flights three -30s were leased by the airline and operations to Frankfurt started in 1993. The carrier voluntarily grounded its fleet in June 1995 and filed for bankruptcy protection. By this time transatlantic services had come to a stop and all the DC-10s were returned to lessors.

A deep blue cheatline, trimmed on either side by narrow red lines, extended from the front to the rear encompassing the whole tail section. 'Express One' titling appeared on the upper fuselage, 'Express' in white letters with a blue trim and 'One' in bold red letters.

Federal Express Corporation

Federal Express Corporation, generally known as FedEx, is the world's largest parcel and document carrier. Not surprisingly, Memphis, Tennessee, where FedEx has its headquarters, retained its position of the world's busiest cargo hub again in 1997. During 1980, FedEx acquired the first three ex-Continental Series 10CFs for use on the long range network which includes the European hub, Paris.

FedEx is the only carrier to have ordered the Series 30F and a total of ten were delivered by McDD between January 1986 and October 1988. Over the years the DC-10 fleet has vastly expanded and at the time of writing stands at 64: 29 -10s (to become freighters), five -10Fs, eight -10CFs, 16 -30Fs and six -30CFs. The carrier's code changed from FM to FX in July 1996.

Another 'first' is the MD-11F of which a fleet of 24 is operated. This number includes the first seven MD-11s which FedEx has taken over from American Airlines during 1996 and 1997 and were converted to MD-11Fs. Other widebodies operated are 22 Airbus A300-600s and 37 A310 freighters. Four 747Fs (SCD) are part of the FedEx wide-body fleet but these aircraft are currently leased to Atlas Air.

Series 10CF N68055 (f/n 191) was destroyed by a cargo fire after a diversionary landing at Stewart International, Newburgh, New York on 5th September 1996.

In September 1996 FedEx announced the purchase of 36 -10s from United Air Lines with deliveries and passenger-to-freighter conversions starting in early 1997. In return FedEx will deliver hushkits, developed jointly by FedEx and Pratt & Whitney for United's 727 fleet. A similar agreement was reached with American Airlines in December 1996 which includes the delivery of 17 -10s. As part of this transaction, American acquired the right to sell its remaining -10s to FedEx over the next seven years, while FedEx granted American options on additional hushkits. Most of the aircraft purchased from American will be stored by FedEx and brought into service as needed.

FedEx is the world's largest operator of the DC-10 and will have 87 by the end of 1997. Following the reconfiguration of the freighters, the former United and American aircraft, together with other sisterships, will be converted to MD-10 status. The first MD-10 is expected to join the FedEx fleet in mid-1999.

The original eye-catching purple and white livery with a white and orange cheatline and large white 'Federal' and orange 'Express' titles stayed 1994 with the introduction of the current scheme. This has a huge 'FedEx' title in purple and orange on the forward white fuselage and a 'Federal Express' title underneath. The 'Fedex' title is also applied on all three engines. The tail section and rear part of the fuselage is kept in purple. A 'The World On Time' title is placed under the forward entry doors.

N301FE	Tara Lynn
N302FE	Brian Jr
N303FE	Amanda Marie
N304FE	Alison
N305FE	John David, renamed Lamar
N306FE	John Peter Jr
N307FE	Erin Lee
N308FE	Ann
N309FE	Stacey
N310FE	John Shelby
N311FE	Abe
N312FE	Angela
N313FE	Brandon Parks
N314FE	Caitlin Ann
N315FE	Kevin
N316FE	Brandon
N317FE	Madison
N322FE	King Frank
N392FE	Axton
N10060	Haylee
N40061	Garrett
N68049	Dusty
N68050	Merideth Allison
N68051	Todd
N68052	Janette Louise
N68053	Chayne
N68054	Lisa Marie, renamed Dani Elena
N68055	Chandra Renee
N68056	Valerie Ann
N68059	Maryrea

Finnair

The Finnish carrier received its first Series 30, OH-LHA *Iso-Antti*, on 27th January 1975, the second followed on 6th May that year. A further two -30s were acquired in 1981 and 1983 and the airline leased another in 1988. These replaced the airline's DC-8s in use on the international network which presently includes Toronto, New York, Los Angeles, Bangkok, Singapore, Tokyo and Beijing. Finnair ceased DC-10 operations in June 1996 and today operates four MD-11s on its long range network.

The white and blue livery originates from the colours of the national flag which, in a slanted form, is displayed on the tail fin. The company's logo, a stylised letter 'F' in a blue circle, is placed below the cockpit windows. A publicity campaign for Japanese tourists included a paint scheme with 'Moomin' cartoon characters which was applied on -30 OH-LHB in 1995.

The first DC-10 to be leased by LAN Chile was Series 30 CC-CJN *Santiago* from Pan American. Author's collection

Leisure Air operated with four DC-10s – Series 30 N831LA at Amsterdam Schiphol Airport. Fred Lerch

LAM's only DC-10-30 F-GDJK *Maputo*, in the carrier's original livery. Nicky Scherrer – VIP Photoservice

Before F-GDJK left the fleet of Linhas Aéreas de Mocambique, the aircraft featured a new livery. Author's collection

Flying Colours Airlines

In May 1997 this British charter airline started operations with a fleet of four Boeing 757s to Orlando, Florida, destinations in the Mediterranean on behalf of Sunset Holidays, Priority Holidays and Club 18-30. The former British Airways contract for long range charters with Caledonian Airways was taken over by the carrier in April 1997. As a BA franchise partner, Flying Colours flies to the Grand Cayman, Nassau, San Juan and Tampa, using BA -30 G-NIUK. In November 1997, Flying Colours' parent company, Airline Management Ltd (AML) and British Airways agreed to extend the charter operations to Jamaica, Mexico and Tobago.

Garuda Indonesian Airways / Garuda Indonesia

The airline started operations with two -30s in 1976. The last of six aircraft ordered was taken into service in August 1979. With an extensive international network to destinations such as Amsterdam, Frankfurt, Paris, London, Jeddah, Colombo, Sydney and Tokyo, DC-10s are used alongside 747-200s and -400s and, since 1993,

LOT Series 30, operating in a part Malaysian colour scheme, at Warsaw Airport. LOT

The first DC-10 in service with Lineas Aéreas Paraguayas was Series 30 N602DC.
Nicky Scherrer – VIP Photoservice

DC-10-30 D-ADCO in Lufthansa's present white fuselage livery. Lufthansa

Photographs on the opposite page:

DC-10-30 9M-MAS was first of the type delivered to Malaysian Airline System. McDonnell Douglas

A slightly revised paint scheme with 'Malaysian' title on DC-10-30 9M-MAV. Author's collection

Malaysia DC-10-30 9M-MAX in the present livery, introduced in 1989. Theo Handstede

World Airways DC-10-30CF N105WA while on lease to Malaysia for 'MASkargo' operations.
Fred Lerch

MD-11s. As far as McDD products are concerned, Garuda currently operates with five DC-10s, three MD-11s and MD-11ERs.

Garuda Indonesia lost one of its DC-10s when PK-GIE (f/n 284) was destroyed after an abortive take-off from Fukuoka, Japan on a scheduled flight to Denpasar and Jakarta on 13th June 1996.

The original paint scheme showed two cheatlines in crimson and bright red on a white background along the fuselage and in the tail section. The red 'Garuda' title appeared on engine number two while the 'Indonesian Airways' title was placed over the red cheatlines. In 1985 a new livery was introduced, it presents an all white fuselage and dark blue tail which carries a bird motif consisting of the bird's head and five winged stripes, gradually turning from blue to turquoise. The same symbol is repeated alongside the 'Garuda Indonesia' title on the fuselage.

PK-GIA	Irian Jaya
PK-GIB	Bali
PK-GIC	Java
PK-GID	Sumatra
PK-GIE	Kalimantan
PK-GIF	Sulawesi

Gemini Air Cargo

Gemini Air Cargo was founded in 1995 and began by operating freight services for other airlines. During its first year the carrier commenced twice-weekly Swisscargo, the Swissair cargo division, flights from Basle to Chicago and Atlanta. Further customers included Alitalia, British Airways, Fast Air, Finnair and KLM. In September 1996 the carrier started a once-a-week Swisscargo service from Basle via Dakar to São Paulo and in November 1996 a twice-a-week cargo service from Geneva to Dubai, Madras and Singapore. Currently Gemini itself also operates a six times weekly service from New York-JFK to Seoul, Korea. After a series of proving flights, Gemini started a Washington DC-Columbus-Chicago-New York JFK-Anchorage-Macau-Anchorage-New York-JFK route on 22nd October 1996.

The carrier presently operates with seven ex-Lufthansa converted -30Fs and at the time of writing, the carrier also operates one DC-10 each for ChallengAir Cargo (Miami to Latin America), FedEx (New York to Miami, Santiago and São Paulo) and Qantas (transpacific cargo flights from Los Angeles). In November 1997, a further DC-10, originally delivered to Wardair, was acquired. After conversion to freighter it will join the fleet in April 1998.

The aircraft were first operated in a livery without any official titles. The all-white fuselage showed a small brown and white crate with white 'air cargo' title within a dark blue square. The crate was also placed on the tail fin. The 'DC-10-30F' title was applied on the tail engine. First aircraft to receive the permanent paint scheme was N600GC. A dark blue 'Gemini'

Martinair Holland was the second European airline to order the DC-10-30CF. PH-MBN *Anthony Ruys* was lost at Faro, Portugal on 21st December 1992. Nicky Scherrer – VIP Photoservice

Martinair Holland DC-10-30 PH-MBG *Kohoutek* was renamed *J Henry Dunant* when flights were performed for the International Red Cross. Nicky Scherrer – VIP Photoservice

PH-MBN *Anthony Ruys* also performed flights for the International Red Cross. The aircraft sported the red cross at the forward and rear fuselage. Fred Lerch

First airline to receive the DC-10-15 was Mexicana. N1003L in the first white and gold paint scheme. Fred Lerch

and yellow 'Air Cargo' title is displayed on the white fuselage. The dark blue tail section shows the engine's white 'DC-10-30F' title and the Gemini Air Cargo logo on the fin. This attractive logo consists of a crate circling a globe which is encompassed by a dark blue letter 'G' and a white ring with a dark blue 'Gemini Air Cargo' title.

N600GC	*Christopher*
N601GC	*Molly*
N602GC	*Doris*, renamed *Wendy*
N603GC	*Leslie*
N604GC	*Christa*
N605GC	*Kari*
N606GC	*Ryann*

Ghana Airways

A new DC-10 was delivered to the airline on 25th February 1983. The -30, 9G-ANA, is the only owned wide-body aircraft in the fleet and is used on the airline's long distance flights to Dusseldorf, Johannesburg, London, Rome and New York.

The DC-10 carries the colours of the national flag, red, yellow and green on the triple cheatline while the Ghanaian flag itself is placed on the tail fin. All three engines display the emblem of the company and black 'Ghana Airways' titles appear above the cheatlines on the white upper fuselage.

KLM operated DC-10s on behalf of Ghana Airways on multiple occasions. Small 'Ghana Airways' titles were added to the regular KLM paint scheme.

In May 1996 Ghana Airways leased Skyjet DC-10-30, *The Royal Oak*, OO-PHN. The aircraft sports an all-white fuselage with black 'Ghana Airways' titles and was registered as 9G-PHN in early 1997. The tail section paint scheme is the same as that carried on 9G-ANA. During February 1997, Ghana also operated the Skyjet sistership, Series 15 V2-LER.

Further to the DC-10, the airline operated a MD-11 on lease from World Airways from October 1994 until the end of March 1995.

Harlequin Air

See Japan Air System.

Hawaiian Airlines – Hawaiian Air

Hawaiian Air flies scheduled passenger services to the Hawaiian Islands, the South Pacific Islands as well as to Los Angeles, San Francisco and Seattle.

In 1983 the airline obtained its first wide-body transports, L-1011s. Beginning in 1994 these aircraft were replaced by DC-10--10s on lease from American Airlines. Because of financial problems, the carrier entered Chapter 11 protection in September 1993 until 1995. Presently Hawaiian operates a fleet of ten -10s and 13 DC-9-51s.

A full-length light purple and red cheatline is separated by a white pinstripe on the highly polished fuselage which also displays the deep purple 'Hawaiian' title. The fin is decorated with a stylised red, white, purple and black orchid.

N119AA	Oahu - the gathering place
N122AA	Kauai - the garden island
N146AA	Niihau - the forbidden island
N152AA	Hawaii - the orchid island
N153AA	Maui - the valley isle

Iberia – Lineas Aéreas de España

Iberia took delivery of a total of nine -30s as replacement for the DC-8 fleet. The first aircraft, EC-CBN (f/n 87) was accepted by the airline 20th March 1973. Unfortunately this aircraft was lost when it crashed on final approach at Boston Logan Airport on 17th December the same year. It was the first DC-10 to be involved in an accident.

During 1996 Iberia placed the first of four Airbus A340s ordered into service. Together with seven 747s and the four A340s, four DC-10s form the long haul fleet of the carrier and services are operated to destinations in North, Central and South America, Africa, the Middle and Far East.

The DC-10s carried the simple paint scheme, consisting of a red cheatline on a white upper fuselage with a red 'Iberia' title and an 'IB-globe' on the tail fin, until the introduction of the present striking livery in the early 1980s. An all-white fuselage forms the background for a triple dark red, bright red and yellow cheatline which starts at the top of the cabin roof and continue to the tail section. A white 'Iberia', alongside a golden 'Lineas Aéreas de España' title, is displayed on the dark and bright red cheatline. The fin is highlighted by a stylised 'IB' in dark red and yellow, the top of the letter 'I' incorporating the golden Spanish crown.

EC-CBN	Costa Brava
EC-CBO	Costa del Sol
EC-CBP	Costa Dorada
EC-CEZ	Costa del Azahar
EC-CLB	Costa Blanca
EC-CSJ	Costa de la Luz
EC-CSK	Cornisa Cantabrica
EC-DEA	Rias Gallegas
EC-DHZ	Costas Canarias

Icelandair – Loftleidir

To supplement its fleet of four DC-8-63s the airline leased -30CF N1035F from Seaboard World Airlines for long range passenger charters during the period of January 1979 through to March 1980. The aircraft was jointly operated with Air Bahama. While Air Bahama ceased operations in 1981, Icelandair today is a successful airline operating with Fokker 50, 737-400 and 757-200 equipment.

A wide and narrow light blue cheatline ran along the whole fuselage on a white upper fuselage. The name 'Icelandic' was followed by a small company's logo and the name 'Icelandair' above the cheatline. A large blue logo was placed on the tail fin.

Japan Air Lines / Japan Airlines – JAL

The first -40 was delivered to JAL on 9th April 1976. Another 19 of the type were put into service, the last one on 5th March 1983. JAL and Northwest Orient were the only two airlines to order Pratt & Whitney powerplants. However, JAL opted for the uprated JT9D-59A version. Within the DC-10 fleet, JAL uses the designation 'D' for domestic and 'I' for international versions. The I-version has a maximum take-off weight (MTOW) of 554,991lb (251,744kg), but the D-version's MTOW has been decreased to 444,993lb (201,849kg) by completely removing the centre landing gear, in order to reduce landing fee costs when the aircraft is used only on domestic routes.

Initially the DC-10s served the whole JAL network but were replaced by 747s and MD-11s on international services. The aircraft now are primarily used on domestic routes and some Asian destinations. JAL remained a McDD customer with an order of ten MD-11s. As the parent company of Japan Asia and Japan Air Charter (JAZ), JAL currently leases four DC-10s to each of its subsidiaries.

On 27th August 1997 the airline announced a bulk sales agreement with NI Aircraft Leasing Corporation (NIALCO), a subsidiary of major Japanese trading company Nissho Iwai, who will buy the 20 -40s in the JAL Group fleet over the next nine years. The first two aircraft will be handed over in March 1998. After that between one and four aircraft a year will be delivered up to 2005, when the last three aircraft will leave the JAL fleet. The aircraft will subsequently be sold to the Ten Forty Corporation which will offer the aircraft for sale or lease. In November 1997 Ten Forty selected Aeronavali to convert all 20 aircraft to freighters.

The original livery showed a red and black cheatline, the tail emblem consisting of a rising sun formed by the spread wings of a red crane, called the 'Tsuru', with white 'JAL' letters. The present livery, introduced in 1989, features a white fuselage with a red and grey cheatline on the forward section with large 'JAL' lettering while the tail emblem remained the same.

Starting a six month promotion campaign in August 1996, the airline applied its domestic and international toll-free reservations telephone numbers to several aircraft. Also -40 JA8540 carried these large numbers on its fuselage.

Japan Air Charter – JAZ

JAZ was founded in 1990 as a wholly-owned charter subsidiary of Japan Airlines. The present fleet consists of four DC-10s and two 747s. As with Japan Asia, more equipment can be leased from the parent when required.

The JAZ colour scheme is based on the current JAL livery. A special paintscheme with 'Super Resort Express' titles and large flowers and birds on the tail was introduced by JAL during 1994. The JAL Super Resort Express service is operated between Japan and Honolulu, Guam, Saipan, Brisbane, Cairns, amongst others, using DC-10 and 747 equipment.

Japan Air System – JAS

Having obtained a permit to operate international flights, TOA Domestic Airlines changed its name to Japan Air System on 1st April 1988. Two new -30ERs were ordered. JA8550 was delivered on 30th March 1988 and sistership JA8551 on 29th July 1988, they were amongst the last DC-10s built. The aircraft are used for charters to Hawaii and Singapore. JA8551 was in service with Korean Air Lines from July 1988 until June 1989 to supplement the latter carrier's DC-10 fleet. Further aircraft in the airline's wide-body fleet are 34 A300B2s and 'B4s and two 777s, with an additional five 777s on order.

One DC-10 (JA8550) was transferred to Harlequin Air in December 1997. It features a white fuselage and a wine red tail with harlequin logo. The subsidiary took over Japan Air System's charter operations and also operate domestic JAS flights from its Fukuoka base, with DC-9s.

The attractive livery has a yellow-orange-red-blue cheatline along the fuselage which is reversed on the tail section. In 1995 JAS painted cartoon characters on -30 JA8551 to be used on charter flights to Honolulu under the 'JAS Peter Pan Flight' banner.

Japan Asia Airways – JAA

In order to be able to operate flights to Taiwan, the Republic of China, Japan Asia was formed in 1975 as a wholly-owned subsidiary of Japan Airlines. JAL faced the same problem as the

European carriers who wanted to serve both the People's Republic of China and Taiwan, Republic of China. For political reasons this was prohibited by the government in Peking. Presently, daily services are operated to Taipei and Kaohsiung using four DC-10s and four 747s. Additional aircraft are leased from Japan Airlines when required.

Except for the tail emblem, the previous and present liveries are similar to that of JAL. A variation of the present colour scheme was applied to JA8535 and JA8545. A large 'JA' title was placed at the start of the red and grey cheatline and the white tail section showed a diagonal 'JAA' title. Furthermore, a small 'UNICEF' title and emblem appeared above the rear passenger windows.

Jet 24 – International Charter Service

The company was founded in 1979 and operated international passenger and cargo flights using leased DC-8, 707, 747 and DC-10 aircraft. Jet Charter Service bought two ex-Northwest Orient -40s from Boeing in 1984 but these were returned in June 1985. A lease agreement between the two companies was reached and both aircraft remained with the carrier until October 1985.

During their time with Jet 24, the aircraft, N133JC and N144JC, were also leased to Dominicana and Air Panama. The carrier ceased all operations in 1988.

The aircraft had a white upper and dark blue lower fuselage with an additional red cheatline on the lower part. Large Jet 24 titles were displayed on the tail fin.

Photographs on opposite page:

The second Mexicana livery displayed a colourful tail section. Series 15 N1003W on approach to Mexico City. G Schütz

Mexicana DC-10-15 N1003W in the third and last livery before being retired at the end of 1994. Reiner Geerdts

The original Minerve paint scheme on DC-10-30 F-GGMZ. Nicky Scherrer – VIP Photoservice

Minerve DC-10-30 F-GKMY in the beautiful burgundy livery from the merger into AOM. Author's collection

Photographs on this page:

Monarch operates former Zambia Airways DC-10-30 G-DMCA. Exavia

National DC-10-30 N60NA *Barbara*. McDD

DC-10-30 5N-ANN was the first aircraft delivered to the Nigerian flag carrier. McDonnell Douglas

5N-ANN showing the Nigeria's interim paint scheme of the mid-1990s. Fred Lerch

Jugoslovenski Aerotransport – JAT

The Yugoslavian flag carrier received the first Series -30 on 8th December 1978 with another of the type following on 14th May 1979. Two more -30s were leased in 1988 and 1989. Sabena -30CF OO-SLA was leased from June until November 1986 and from June 1987 until November 1989. Furthermore, JAT has leased DC-10 equipment from Air Afrique, Finnair and World Airways. The aircraft were used on international flights to North America, the Middle and Far East and Australia. One aircraft was returned to the leasing company in 1991 and two were returned during 1992.

The blue, white and red cheatline on a white upper fuselage represented the colours of the national flag. The 'JAT' logo appeared on the blue tail fin and red 'Jugoslovenski Aerotransport' titles were placed on the forward fuselage. An additional 'Official Olympic Carrier' title was shown on the lower forward fuselage in 1987.

Due to the war in the former Yugoslavia, the airline stopped all long haul international operations and the remaining DC-10, YU-AMB *Edvard Rusijan*, was stored at Belgrade. In March 1996 the aircraft was reactivated and placed into service on European routes. The airline resumed international long range services with the DC-10 in December 1997 on the Belgrade-Beijing route. Renamed *Belgrade*, it now featured an all white fuselage with a 'JAT Yugoslav Airlines' title on the port side and a 'Jugoslovenski Aerotransport JAT' title on the starboard side. The tail section shows the company's new logo in blue, white and red.

In November 1997 the colour scheme was revised. Huge 'JAT' titles at the forward fuselage replaced the smaller titling beside the airline's name.

YU-AMA   *Nikola Tesla*
YU-AMB   *Edvard Rusijan*,
                renamed *Belgrade*

Kenya Airways

KLM Royal Dutch Airlines performed flights on behalf of the national airline of Kenya in the mid-1980s with DC-10-30s PH-DTB, 'C and 'E. Lufthansa -30 D-ADJO was on a short-term lease to the Kenyan carrier in May of 1994. The airline presently operates with a fleet of Fokker 50s, Boeing 737s and Airbus A310-300s.

Key Airlines

This carrier, founded in 1962, was a subsidiary of World Airways and operated contract and *ad hoc* passenger flights within the USA with a fleet of ten 727s. During 1989 and 1990 a -10 was leased which operated under the registrations N917JW and N40KA. The company suspended operations on 10th May 1993.

A quadruple white, red, white and blue lining

Above, left: **The Green Bay Packers were flown to the 1997 Super Bowl in -30 N232NW.** Exavia

Top, right: **Northwest's DC-10s received stickers to mark their role in the development of the Pacific market in 1997, -40 N148US illustrated.** Flite-Line-Photos

In 1989 Northwest introduced a new distinctive livery, depicted on N143US. Northwest Airlines

Before planned delivery to Okada Air, -10 5N-OGI was stored at Marana, Arizona. Fred Lerch

After the name change to Novair, DC-10-10 G-GCAL sported revised Cal Air livery. Author's collection

Photographs on the opposite page:

Northwest Orient was the launch customer of the DC-10-40, illustrated is N156US. Northwest Airlines

N161US showing the 'Northwest' title following the company's name change to Northwest Airlines in 1986. Northwest Airlines

Northwest DC-10-40 N144JC being readied to take the New England Patriots aboard, 1997. Northwest Airlines

started at the nose and ended at top of the fin, separating the light grey upper and white lower fuselage and tail section. Blue and white 'Key Air' titles on the forward fuselage completed the smart livery.

KLM Royal Dutch Airlines

KLM – Koninklijke Luchtvaart Maatschappij – is the world's oldest airline and has operated all the Douglas products since the DC-2 over the years. Together with SAS, Swissair and UTA, KLM was the launch customer for the -30. The so-called KSSU group announced the selection of the -30 as their next generation aircraft at the Paris Air Show on 7th June 1969. The first of eleven ordered arrived at Schiphol Airport on 17th December 1972 and the last was delivered in March 1975.

Five DC-10s were leased to VIASA, Philippine Airlines and Garuda. The remaining examples were used on KLM's long range worldwide network. Moreover, KLM leased a -30CF from Martinair Holland from October 1989 through April 1992. This aircraft, PH-MBT, was sold to the Royal Netherlands Air Force in June 1992. The Dutch carrier conducted DC-10 flights for Ghana Airways on multiple occasions. The aircraft used sported the full KLM livery with small 'Ghana Airways' titles added to the fuselage.

With the introduction of the MD-11 into the airline's fleet, KLM stopped its DC-10 operations in 1994. Currently KLM operates ten MD-11s, of which one aircraft is leased to VASP through the manufacturer.

The DC-10s carried the still current attractive livery of the airline. A deep blue window line separated the prominent light blue cabin roof from a white cheatline below the windows. The KLM logo, existing of the letters 'KLM' and a stylised crown, appeared in white on the forward cabin roof. The company logo, this time in light and deep blue, was also displayed on the white tail section and on the inboard and outboard cowlings of the wing mounted engines. The fleet was named after famous composers. The composer's name and the 'Royal Dutch Airlines' title were shown at the front of the white cheatline, while the title 'The Flying Dutchman' was located in front of the last cabin door. Since 1993 the 'Seal of Partnership' was applied on the cabin roof to underline the co-operation with Northwest Airlines.

DC-10-30CF N1033F *Holidayliner Enterprise* was one of four of the type delivered to Overseas National Airways. McDonnell Douglas

Capitol Air DC-10-10 N905WA on a short term lease to Pacific East Air. Author's collection

AP-AXC, the first DC-10-30 delivered to Pakistan International Airlines. McDonnell Douglas

PIA's -30 AP-AXD in the second, slightly revised, livery without the double row of stars.
Nicky Scherrer – VIP Photoservice

PH-DTA	*Johann Sebastian Bach*
PH-DTB	*Ludwig von Beethoven*
PH-DTC	*Frederic Francois Chopin*
PH-DTD	*Maurice Ravel*
PH-DTE	*Wolfgang Amadeus Mozart*
PH-DTF	*Giuseppe Verdi*
PH-DTL	*Edward Hagerup Grieg*
PH-MBT	*George Gershwin*

Korean Air Lines / Korean Air

Three new -30s were delivered to the airline between February and April 1975. In February 1977 the carrier acquired another -30, an ex-Air Siam aircraft. A further aircraft, a -30CF, was bought from Overseas National in August the following year, bringing the DC-10 fleet up to five units. The DC-10 fleet was mostly used on Asian routes as well as on flights to the Middle East and Libya.

The airline lost its first DC-10, HL7339 (f/n 237), in Anchorage on 23rd December 1983 when a take-off was performed, in thick fog, resulting in a collision with a light aircraft. From July 1988 until June 1989, a leased Japan Air System -30 was added to the fleet. On 27 July 1989 DC-10 HL7328, f/n 125, crashed 3¾ miles (6km) short of the runway while attempting to land in foggy weather at Tripoli, Libya.

The end of over 20 years of DC-10 operations came when the remaining original three were sold to Boeing at the end of 1995. The carrier's large wide-body fleet presently consists of two MD-11s, three MD-11Fs, 31 Airbus A300s and 42 Boeing 747s.

The first livery used on the aircraft was a simple use of a blue cheatline and a red pinstripe on a white upper fuselage which also carried the title 'Korean Air Lines' in Korean and English. The tail section showed the company's logo, a red circle with a stylised bird.

Relieving the monotony of 'white bodies', Korean Air Lines presented a new livery in 1984. A light blue upper fuselage with a silver cheatline and light grey underside form the remarkable paint scheme. The company's new logo, known as the 'Taeguk', is on the tail section and also forms the 'O' in the 'Korean Air' title on the forward fuselage.

Kras Air – Krasnoyarsk Airlines

Kras Air, formerly the Aeroflot Krasnoyarsk-Yemilianovo division, started passenger and freight services in 1993 using former Aeroflot aircraft. The first western aircraft, ex-KLM -30 PH-DTA was leased from McDD. Registered N525MD, it was delivered to the airline in July 1995. Sistership PH-DTD was also leased to Kras Air and delivered to the carrier in April 1996 as N533MD. Flights between Moscow and Los Angeles and New York JFK commenced in December 1995 using DC-10s. Kras Air ceased DC-10 operations in August 1996 when both aircraft were returned to McDD.

The airline's livery features a light blue and two dark blue cheatlines on a white fuselage, starting at the front and widening up into the rear tail-section. 'Kras Air' lettering and the Russian flag on the fuselage complement the colour scheme. The first aircraft showed a dark blue shield with a white lion on the fin, however this was later omitted.

Kuwait Airways

At the end of the Gulf War Kuwait Airways was faced with the problem that some of its aircraft had been destroyed and some seized by Iraqi forces. Resuming services and awaiting delivery of new aircraft ordered, Kuwait Airways leased aircraft from other carriers.

Lufthansa DC-10-30 D-ADGO and British Airways G-NIUK were on a short term lease to the airline beginning in June 1992. While the Lufthansa aircraft operated in the airline's full colour scheme, G-NIUK carried the basic British Airways paint scheme, without titles and crown, but with 'Kuwait Airways' titles in English and Arabic applied on the forward fuselage.

Laker Airways (UK)

Laker accepted its first -10, from McDD on 26th October 1972 and was the first European airline to start services with the type on 21st November 1972. Another four -10s were to follow and awaiting approval for Sir Fred Laker's planned 'Skytrain' service between London and New York, some of the aircraft were leased to other carriers. The first 'Skytrain' service was not to take place until 26th September 1977 when a Series 10 took off from Gatwick to New York. During 1978 the airline received permission to operate the Los Angeles route as a 'Skytrain' service and to satisfy the need of non-stop operations a total of five -30s were ordered.

After five years of rapid expansion, the 'no frills' carrier collapsed, alleging it had been forced out of business by unfair price tactics of British and US rivals and stopped all operations in February 1982. The -10s were quickly disposed of, and the -30s were all returned to the manufacturer.

The livery consisted of a red and black cheatline from nose to tail separating the grey belly and the white top. The same red and black lines with white 'Laker' title appeared on the fin. Laker's stylised bird logo and the Union flag were placed on the forward upper fuselage. To underline the USA-UK connection, the 'Skytrain' title on the upper fuselage incorporated the flags of both countries.

G-AZZC	*Eastern Belle*
G-AZZD	*Western Belle*
G-BELO	*Southern Belle*
G-BBSZ	*Canterbury Belle*
G-BGXH	*Florida Belle*
G-GFAL	*Northern Belle*
G-GSKY	*Californian Belle*

Laker Airways (USA)

Laker Airways (Bahamas), Sir Freddie Laker's new enterprise, was founded in 1992. The airline operated charter flights from Freeport and Fort Lauderdale with two Boeing 727s. Founded in 1995, sister company Laker Airways started operations in 1996 and received its first -30 in February of that year. The fleet originally consisted of three DC-10-30s, N831LA, N832LA and N833LA. The first DC-10 flight took place on 28th March from Orlando, Florida to London-Gatwick. The present network includes scheduled passenger flights from Miami, Orlando and Fort Lauderdale to London-Gatwick and Manchester, Prestwick and Copenhagen.

The paintscheme with a red and black cheatline on an all-white fuselage is reminiscent of the original Laker colours. The company's stylised bird logo has been slightly changed and appears on the tail fin. A fourth DC-10,-10 N946LL (to be registered N834LA) joined the fleet in May 1997. This aircraft sports the full old Laker colour scheme of the 1970s. The aircraft are named after the US NASA Space Shuttles.

N831LA	*Columbia*
N832LA	*Endeavour*
N833LA	*Discovery*
N834LA	*Atlantis*

LAN Chile – Linea Aérea Nacional de Chile

The first wide-body aircraft for the Chilean carrier was -30, G-BGXF, on lease from Laker Airways from January until March 1981. In June 1981 the Chilean carrier leased another -30, N81NA, from PanAmerican World Airways as CC-CJN. The aircraft was returned in June 1982 when LAN Chile took delivery of two former Air New Zealand -30s, CC-CJS *Santiago* and CC-CJT *Valpariso*.

The aircraft were used on the flights to New York and Miami and to the European destinations Frankfurt, Rome and Madrid. The airline took delivery of its first two 767ERs in 1986 and the DC-10s were returned to Air New Zealand in March and July of that year.

The striking livery is based on the colours of the national flag with a triple blue, red and white cheatline running from under the nose, along the fuselage to the top of the fin. The 'LAN Chile' title is placed in white on the tail section and appears in red on the white roof alongside a white star in a blue and red circle.

Lauda Air

For long range charter operations Niki Lauda's airline ordered a -30CF, scheduled to be registered as OE-ILD. The aircraft, fuselage number 339, was built but the order was not taken up and after completion it was delivered to FedEx on 7th September 1984, becoming N305FE, *John David*

Parked at Long Beach, Pakistan International Series 30 AP-AYM in the revised colour scheme introduced in 1976. McDonnell Douglas

Pan American World Airways DC-10-10 N63NA *Clipper Eclipse* **N63NA displaying the airline's famous livery.** Fred Lerch

KLM DC-10-30 PH-DTK was leased to Philippine Airlines from April 1975 until February 1985. Illustrated at Zurich, the aircraft displays the first livery. Nicky Scherrer – VIP Photoservice

Photographs on the opposite page:

Philippines DC-10-30 RP-C2003 in the latest paint scheme. Philippine Airlines

VARIG DC-10-30 PP-VMW has been in service with PLUNA, Uruguay since July 1994. Luftfahrt-Journal

PLUNA's only DC-10, PP-VMW, displaying the revised paint scheme introduced in April 1996. Author's collection

One of five DC-10s operated by Premiair, Series 10 SE-DHU, now registered OY-CNU and named *Bamse.* PremiAir

Leisure Air

This charter airline was founded in 1992 operating a fleet of five A320s, two 757s and two -10s. The DC-10s were used for European charter flights and were frequent visitors at Amsterdam-Schiphol. The two Series 10s, N1826U and N1827U were leased from United Airlines. Another two aircraft, -30s N831LA and N832LA, were leased from Polaris Aircraft Leasing Corporation during 1994 and returned to the lessor in October of that year. Financial problems forced the airline to cease operations in January 1995 and the operating certificate was withdrawn by the FAA the following month.

The paint scheme consisted of a black lower and white upper fuselage, both colours flowing up into the tail section, with a parallel red narrow line. The titles 'Leisure Air' and 'SunTrips' and three stars were carried on the upper fuselage. The tail fin showed the large letters 'L' and 'A', the latter enclosing a star.

Linhas Aéreas de Moçambique – LAM

LAM leased the former Air New Zealand -30, ZK-NZR, from 18th December 1982 from the International Lease Finance Corporation (ILFC). It was returned to the new owner, Equator Leasing Inc, in May 1992. The aircraft was registered in France as F-GDJK. With the arrival of a 767-2B1(ER) in the fleet, the DC-10 was withdrawn from use and temporarily stored at Le Bourget, Paris before being leased to Air Martinique. A further wide-body currently operated is a Lockheed TriStar 500, on lease from TAP.

During the nearly ten years of service, the DC-10 *Maputo*, named after the country's capital, had two different paint schemes. The first scheme had a basic white fuselage with light grey belly, a red and blue pinstripe cheatline below the windows with the airline's full name over the windows between the third and fourth door. All three engines were dark blue with large 'LAM' lettering. The upper tail section showed a white stylised bird on a red background. A wide red cheatline sweeping up into the complete tail assembly and a narrow black cheatline above the former marked the later livery. 'LAM' lettering appeared on the forward fuselage and engine Nos.1 and 3, while the airline's full name in small letters was now placed above the passenger windows between the second and third door.

Lineas Aéreas Paraguayas – Air Paraguay

LAP started operations as the national airline of Paraguay in 1963. For international services three 707s and two DC-8s were used. To supplement the fleet, -30 N602DC was leased in June 1992 and was returned to the leasing company, the GPA Group Ltd, in March 1994. In 1993, leased VARIG -30 PP-VMX joined the

fleet and was returned in January 1994. Air France -30 F-BTDB, was with LAP on a short term lease from July until October 1993. This aircraft was operated with LAP titles and logo. Today the carrier has a fleet of two 737-200s, three A320-200s and two A310-300s jointly operated with SAETA Air Ecuador. N602DC carried the same paint scheme as the 707s and DC-8s, a full white fuselage with red cheatline and the airline's name above the passenger windows. The national colours, red, white and blue were displayed on the stabilizer and a small company logo was placed on the tail fin.

LOT – Polskie Linie Lotnicze

LOT presently operates with a fleet of four 767s on its international network. Before all the aircraft of this type were delivered to the airline, DC-10-30s were leased from Finnair as well as from Malaysia Airlines in 1993, 1994 and 1995.

The Malaysia Airlines' aircraft was operated in the basic colour scheme of that carrier but featured the 'LOT' and 'Polish Airlines' titles on the upper fuselage and the LOT company logo on the dark blue fin.

Lufthansa

Deutsche Lufthansa AG originally placed an order for nine -30s. The first aircraft, D-ADAO, was delivered to the German flag carrier on 12th November 1973 with the remaining aircraft joining the fleet during 1974 and 1975. An additional two -30s were ordered and the last aircraft arrived 9th December 1977. The DC-10s replaced the ageing fleet of 707s and services were started when the first aircraft took off from Frankfurt to Tokyo on 14th January 1974. The aircraft were utilized on the extensive international network.

In June 1992 the first DC-10 was taken out of service when D-ADCO was temporarily stored at Marana, Arizona, on 24th January 1994. It was then the world's highest hour DC-10, having accumulated 87.749 hours and 18.861 cycles. The end of the DC-10 era came on 1st December 1994 when D-ADLO returned from its last flight, Toronto-Frankfurt. During more than 20 years of operation, the fleet had logged 910.000 hours, a total of 550 million flight kilometres, and performed 200,000 take-offs and landings. More importantly, 42 million passengers travelled in absolute safety and comfort on board the wide-body workhorses.

Long distance services are now performed with a fleet of 16 A340-200s and -300s and 30 747-200s and -400s. At the 1996 Farnborough Airshow Lufthansa subsidiary Lufthansa Cargo announced an order of five MD-11Fs, with an option on seven more. The MD-11 freighters will be delivered in 1998 and will replace the carrier's five DC-8-73Fs and one 747-230F. With the MD-11F, a McDD product will be represented again in the Lufthansa corporate fleet.

Photographs on the opposite page:

Wearing the basic Airtours International colour scheme introduced in December 1996, Premiair DC-10-10 OY-CNU. Flite-Line-Photos

Sabena DC-10-30CF OO-SLA, was the first convertible freighter delivered in Europe. Sabena

A Sabena DC-10 in the revised livery of 1984. Sabena

DC-10-30, OO-SLG, in the 1994 paint scheme, parked at the new Zaventem Airport terminal. Sabena

Photographs on this page:

'Flying together with Swissair' titling, as shown on OO-SLH, marks the partnership with the Swiss carrier. Exavia

The last DC-10 in Sabena's fleet, OO-SLG carried the Disney colour scheme until the end of April 1997. This marked the end of over 23 years of uninterrupted DC-10 operations by the Belgian flag carrier. Buena Vista International Belgium

Scanair DC-10-10 SE-DHS Baloo at Stockholm Arlanda Airport. Scandinavian Airlines System

A dark blue window cheatline separating the white cabin roof from the highly polished lower fuselage marked the first livery. A large 'Lufthansa' title was placed above the passenger windows. The dark blue tail displayed the company logo, a stylised blue crane in a yellow circle, and this motif was repeated on the engines and the nose section. (See rear cover.)

A design change took place in 1989 when a white fuselage with light grey lower belly was adapted. On the same occasion the company logo received a darker shade of yellow.

D-ADAO	Düsseldorf, renamed *Leverkussen*
D-ADBO	*Berlin*, renamed *Bochum*
D-ADCO	*Frankfurt*, renamed *Augsburg*
D-ADDO	*Hamburg*, renamed *Köln*, renamed *Duisburg*
D-ADFO	*München*, renamed *Furth*
D-ADGO	*Bonn*
D-ADHO	*Hannover*
D-ADJO	*Essen*
D-ADKO	*Stuttgart*
D-ADLO	*Nürnberg*
D-ADMO	*Dortmund*

Malaysian Airline System / Malaysia Airlines

The first -30 was delivered to the airline in August 1976. Two more were ordered and the initial fleet was completed in 1981. During 1990 another three -30s were acquired. The aircraft were operated on international services in the Far East, Europe, Australia and the USA. Additional -30CFs have been leased frequently from World Airways to operate cargo flights and in these cases the 'MASkargo' title was displayed on the cabin roof.

The remaining four -30s in the fleet were transferred to World Airways and Malaysia suspended DC-10 operations in April 1996. In August 1997 two aircraft, 9M-MAS and 'V, were withdrawn from use and stored. MAS regularly

operates MD-11 passenger and freighter aircraft, on lease from World Airways, and took delivery of A330s in 1995, scheduled to be a replacement for the DC-10.

The original livery consisted of two red cheatlines over and below the windows with the 'Malaysian Airline System' title on the roof. The white stylised Malaysian 'Kalantan Kite' motif appeared on the red tail fin. Based on the first livery, an interim experimental paint scheme with double red cheatlines, of which the lower one extended into the now all-red tail section, was introduced in 1981. As was the case with the first livery, the national and islamic flags were placed on the upper fuselage, together with the new large 'Malaysian' and small 'Airline System' titles.

The present paint scheme, introduced in October 1987, features an all-white upper half with a twin red and blue cheatline which widens at the tail section. The name 'Malaysia' appears on the upper fuselage, while the 'Kalantan Kite' motive is retained on the fin. To promote the country's tourist industry additional 'Visit Malaysia Year' titles have been regularly placed on the fuselage. To commemorate the inauguration of the Kuala Lumpur–Los Angeles service in 1986, a large sticker in red, white and blue, featuring a 'Kuala Lumpur–Los Angeles 86' title with the Malaysian and US flags was applied to the rear fuselage.

Mandala Airlines

Martinair Holland -30CF PH-MBN *Anthony Ruys*, was on lease to the Indonesian carrier from October to December 1977. It was used for Hadj operations and was flown in full Martinair Holland livery.

Photographs on the opposite page:

SAS DC-10-30 SE-DFD *Dag Viking* in the 'Viking' colour scheme. Fred Lerch

Displaying the second SAS livery, DC-10-30 N5463Y *Leif Viking*. Scandinavian Airlines System

Scibe Airlift Zaire sub-leased DC-10-10 N102UA from United Aviation Services. Author's collection

Artist's impression of a DC-10-30CF of Seaboard World. McDonnell Douglas

Photographs on this page:

Shabair of Zaire operated DC-10-10 9Q-CSS. Author's collection

Skyjet DC-10-30 OO-PHN with additional Shabair title. Author's collection

To commemorate the inauguration of SIA's California flights, stylised stars and stripes and a 'California Here We Come' banner were applied – 9V-SDA illustrated. Fred Lerch

DC-10-30 9V-SDA was the first of six delivered to Singapore Airlines. McDonnell Douglas

Martinair

Martinair of Holland received its first DC-10, a Series 30CF, on 13th November 1973. Another three convertible freighters were ordered and delivered in 1975, 1976 and 1978 respectively. The aircraft were used for worldwide passenger and cargo charter flights and scheduled passenger services to the USA and Canada. Martinair Holland frequently operated flights with DC-10s for other carriers, eg Hadj flights.

The carrier lost one of the DC-10s, PH-MBN (f/n 218) while landing at Faro, Portugal on 21st December 1992. DC-10 operations came to an end in 1994 and the aircraft were replaced by four MD-11CFs. A further MD-11F was delivered in September 1996 while another is on order. The last two DC-10s, PH-MBP and 'T, were sold to the Royal Netherlands Air Force, becoming KDC-10s – see Chapter Five.

'Martinair Holland' titles were placed above the red cheatline on a white upper fuselage. The company's logo appeared on the fin and a 'Martinair' title on the tail engine. A smaller logo and title were repeated on the wing engines.

PH-MBG was leased to the International Red Cross for relief flights and was appropriately named *J Henry Dunant*, the Swiss founder of the IRC. Food, medical supplies and tents were transported to the earthquake shaken countries Algeria and Yemen. A red cross, in combination with the red cheatline, was applied on the forward fuselage. PH-MBN was also operated for the IRC. For better identification, the red cross was placed on the forward, as well as on the rear, fuselage.

PH-MBG   *Kohoutek*, later *J Henry Dunant*
PH-MBN   *Anthony Ruys*
PH-MBP   *Hong Kong*
PH-MBT   *Holland*

Photographs on the opposite page:

Skyjet Brazil -30 PP-AJM, the first to leave the Lufthansa DC-10 fleet. Lufthansa Technik

Skyjet Belgium DC-10-15 V2-LER is the first Series 15 operated in Europe. Exavia

Spantax DC-10-30CF EC-DSF in the early paint scheme and DC-10-30 EC-DUG, in the carrier's second livery. Both Fred Lerch

Photographs on this page:

STAF Cargo DC-10-30CF XA-TDC at Miami, Florida. Aviation Photography of Miami

Sun Country DC-10-40 N144JC in the striking original colour scheme. Fred Lerch

The new Sun Country scheme of 1995 on DC-10-15 N151SY. Aviation Photography of Miami

Swissair DC-10-30 HB-IHH *Basel-Stadt* in the company's early livery. Author's collection

Tribute to a great workhorse: Series 30 HB-IHI *Fribourg* with 'Farewell DC-10' titles. Fred Lerch

TAESA DC-10-30, XA-SYE at London-Gatwick Airport. Flite-Line-Photos

Scibe Airlift Zaire Series 30 F-GHOI on sub-lease to Taino Airlines. Fred Lerch

Mexicana

Mexicana, the oldest airline in North America, became a private company on 22nd August 1989 and a reorganisation took place which included extensive changes of the network and fleet planning. With Aeromexico as an associate partner schedules and network were amalgamated. Mexicana took delivery of the first -15, the 'hot-rod' version, on 15th June 1981. Four more -15s followed, with the last one delivered on 13th January 1983.

Three of the -15s are now operated by Sun Country Airlines and two by Skyjet Belgium. The airline today operates a fleet of Fokker 100s, Airbus A320s and Boeing 727s and 757s.

The first livery of Mexicana's DC-10s consisted of a white upper fuselage, golden cheatline, accentuated by black striping and black 'Mexicana' titles on the forward upper fuselage and engine No.2. The stylised black eagle on the tail ends in the form of the initial 'M'. Cowlings of engine Nos.1 and 3 were painted the same golden colour as the cheatline.

In the early 1990s a white fuselage with large 'Mexicana' titles below the passengers windows was adapted. The artistic yellow and blue, pink and blue or green and blue scheme extending from the top of the fin to the bottom of the fuselage incorporated the white company eagle logo.

Before the DC-10s were withdrawn from service in 1994 yet another colour scheme was applied. It featured a white upper fuselage with the 'Mexicana' title and a dark blue rear and tail assembly with the white logo on the fin.

N907WA	*Olmeca*
N1003L	*Azteca*
N10045	*Maya*, renamed *Mazaltepec*
XA-MEW	*Iztaccihuatl*
XA-MEX	*Popocatepetl*

Minerve

The airline was founded in 1975 and operated worldwide charters, also serving the French colonies in the Pacific and the West Indies. Three -30s were the wide-bodies in the fleet at the time of the merger into AOM Air Outre Mer on 1st January 1992. Together with some other aircraft, the DC-10s were transferred to the AOM fleet.

During the years of operations two different paint schemes were applied. A large red 'Minerve' title and four cheatlines in burgundy, white, blue and red on a white fuselage form the first colour scheme. The quadruple lines were also on engine Nos.1 and 3. The tail displayed the white goddess Minerve in a red and blue circle with an additional 'Minerve' title on the tail engine. In the second livery, the colours of the quadruple cheatlines changed to burgundy, white, black and burgundy. Burgundy titles as well as the white goddess in a burgundy and black circle completed the paint scheme.

Monarch Airlines

British charter carrier Monarch started operations in 1968 with a Bristol Britannia turboprop from its base at London-Luton to Madrid, after which charter operations were expanded to other Mediterranean destinations. Charter flights to the USA commenced in 1988.

The present network includes destinations in the Mediterranean, Egypt, East Africa, the Caribbean, the USA and Asia. Furthermore, ski charter flights are carried out to Munich, Switzerland and Austria in winter. Today the fleet consists of Boeing 737s and 757s, Airbus A320s and A300-600s. In March 1997 Monarch became the first British airline to order A330 twin-jets for its long range charter operations.

In March 1996 the airline acquired Series 30 G-DMCA. This aircraft was delivered new to Zambia Airways in 1984 and remained with that carrier until it ceased operations in 1994. The aircraft is presently used on the London-Gatwick and Manchester routes to Orlando, Florida and Montego Bay, Jamaica and the Far East.

The livery has striking broad yellow and black cheatlines on a white fuselage. A black 'Monarch' title is placed on the forward fuselage and the tail fin displays the crowned 'M' company logo.

National Airlines

The airline received the first of eleven -10s ordered on 1st November 1970. These aircraft were used on the extensive domestic network. In 1970 transatlantic services were started to Amsterdam, Frankfurt, London, Paris and Zurich. To operate the long distance flights National ordered four -30s of which two were delivered in June 1973. The other two aircraft followed in June 1975. In January 1980 the carrier merged with PanAm and the DC-10s were integrated in the latter airline's fleet. (A fifth -30, N84NA, was ordered but was delivered to PanAm after the merger in August 1980.)

The bright livery showed a black 'National' title and twin cheatlines in orange and yellow on a white upper fuselage. The attractive 'sun king' motive in the same colours was displayed on the tail. A special feature was the christening of the aircraft with names of their stewardesses and these appeared at the forward entry doors. Some aircraft later carried the names of famous entertainers.

N60NA	*Barbara*, renamed *Suzanne*
N61NA	*Dorothy*, renamed *Dinah*
N62NA	*Frances*, renamed *Cecile*
N63NA	*Phyllis*
N64NA	*Geraldine*, renamed *Jerry Lewis*
N65NA	*Eileen*
N66NA	*Shirley*
N67NA	*Joyce*
N68NA	*Sylvia*, renamed *Janie*
N69NA	*Betty*
N70NA	*Wisty*
N80NA	*Tammy*, renamed *Bing Crosby*
N81NA	*Renee*
N82NA	*Marienne*, renamed *Bob Hope*, renamed *Sammy Davis Jr*
N83NA	*Timmi*

Nigeria Airways

For international services to Amsterdam, Jeddah, London, Paris, Rome and New York, the airline received the first -30, 5N-ANN *Yankari*, on 14th October 1976. Before being used on the international network, the aircraft was first employed on pilgrim flights to Mecca.

Another Series 30, 5N-ANR was added to the long range fleet on 18th October 1977. This aircraft (f/n 243) was destroyed by fire following a touch-and-go accident at Ilorin, Nigeria on 10th January 1987. A third Series 30, N3042W, was delivered on 25th July 1989 – this was the last DC-10 to leave the McDD production line. (On lease from Japan Leasing Corporation, it was originally to receive the registration 5N-AUI.) Financial problems forced the airline to reduce costs and to suspend unprofitable routes. In December 1993 N3042W was returned to the leasing company, which at present leaves the airline with only one DC-10 in its fleet.

Being the national carrier, the colours of the national flag were reflected in the original livery.

The white upper fuselage had two green cheatlines with green 'Nigeria Airways' titling, the lower fuselage finish was natural metal. The company logo, a flying elephant, combined with the green and white national flag was carried on the tail fin. This was later replaced by a large green letter 'N' encompassing a white circle with a green falcon.

In the mid-1990s, a livery based on a white paint scheme with two dark green lower lines, one widening up at the rear belly, the other flowing up and encompassing the tail section was introduced. A golden pinstripe ran parallel with the upper green line from the nose to the top of the fin. 'Nigeria Airways' titles appeared on the fuselage and on engine number two. A large gold and white falcon decorated the tail. This motif was repeated on the forward fuselage and the wing engines. However the company opted to return to the more conservative former paint scheme.

Northwest Orient – Northwest Airlines

Northwest Orient was the first airline to order the -40, with the Pratt & Whitney JT9D-20s. The first aircraft was accepted on 10th November 1972 and altogether 22 -40s were delivered. In 1988 the name was changed to Northwest Airlines. Besides operating a dense domestic network, the airline serves destinations in the Far East, Canada, the Caribbean and, since 1979, in Europe.

During 1991 and 1992 Northwest bought eight -30s from Swissair and a further four of the type in 1995. Ex-Malaysia Airlines -30 9M-MAT was acquired in February 1996. In August 1996 the airline again expanded the DC-10 fleet by acquiring three ex-Korean Air -30s from Boeing. Sixteen -30s, together with 21 -40s and 41 747-100s, -200s and -400s form the present long range fleet.

The Northwest Orient livery displayed a broad white band, encompassing the cockpit section, and a dark blue band across the bare metal fuselage. The company logo and 'Northwest Orient' title were placed on the forward section of the white band. The complete tail section was red. After the name change in 1988, the 'Orient' part of the title was omitted.

With the introduction of the 747-400 in 1989, a new paint scheme was adopted. A black stripe separates the grey and white fuselage which top as well as the tail section are red. The new logo, the letter 'N' with a 'northwest' pointer in a white circle, is displayed on the upper fin. Since 1993 the 'Seal of Partnership' is applied alongside the large white 'Northwest' title to emphasize the partnership with KLM.

The National Football League season of US professional football culminated in the Super Bowl XXXI game in New Orleans, Louisiana on 26th January 1997 between the Green Bay Packers from Green Bay, Wisconsin, and the New England Patriots from Foxboro, Massachussetts. The Super Bowl weekend can be

considered the biggest and most important sports event in the USA. Northwest carried both teams on charter flights from their homebases to New Orleans, using DC-10s. The -40 aircraft transporting the Patriots, N144JC carried a 'Go Patriots!' title; the Packers' aircraft, N232NW, a -30, featured a 'Go Packers!' title. The helmets of the teams were placed beside the tiles, as was the 'Stars and Stripes' banner.

On 15th July 1947 Northwest Airlines commenced the first polar route service with a Douglas DC-4. The flight routing was from Seattle to Manila with stops at Anchorage, Tokyo, Seoul and Shanghai. At that time the name of the company was changed to Northwest Orient Airlines. Celebrating fifty years of trans-Pacific services in 1997, Northwest selected a 747-400 for a special paint scheme. With the title 'Worldplane' and special artwork, the 747 also carried a '50 Years Bridging the Pacific' sticker on the forward fuselage. This included a yellow stylised 'bridge' placed over red '50 Years' lettering while the title 'Bridging the Pacific' was shown in blue. The DC-10 fleet, which played a major role in the development of the airline's Pacific market, also obtained the commemorative stickers.

Novair International Airways

The Rank Organisation became the owner of Cal Air after the take-over of BCAL by British Airways in 1988. Since British Airways charter subsidiary was named Caledonian Airways it was agreed that in order to avoid confusion Cal Air would be renamed. Under the new name Novair the airline continued charter operations with the existing fleet of DC-10s and 737s. Services were offered from Gatwick, Manchester, Birmingham, Glasgow and Newcastle to North America and the Mediterranean. With additional new 737s on order, Novair operations came to a final halt in May 1990 due to ever decreasing passenger figures.

The basic Cal Air scheme was retained with large blue and white 'Novair' titles inserted. The impressive red rampant lion on the tail fin was replaced by a large blue and white star.

Okada Air

The Nigerian carrier operates a fleet of 20 BAC 1-11s and three 727s on its domestic network, linking cities as Lagos, Port Harcourt, Kano and Kaduna. For international passenger charter and freight flights a 707-355C and a 747-146 were used. Destinations are London, Frankfurt and Zurich amongst others. Okada Air also operates subcharters for other carriers. The carrier bought a -10 which was scheduled to join the fleet in March 1993. The aircraft had been painted in the airline's livery, two dark blue cheatlines on the white upper fuselage. The lower part was been kept in natural metal finish. The titles 'Okada Air' were located on the

Photographs on the opposite page:

Tarom operated DC-10-30 OO-JOT on lease from ChallengAir, Belgium. Nicky Scherrer – VIP Photoservice

Thai Airways International started DC-10 services with leased aircraft including Air Afrique DC-10-30 TU-TAM. Nicky Scherrer – VIP Photo Service

Colourful livery of unsuccessful The Hawaii Express on DC-10-10 N905WA. Nicky Scherrer – VIP Photoservice

Transaero DC-10-30 N141AA with the preliminary small dark blue title. Flite-Line-Photos

DC-10-30 N140AA displaying the larger white-outlined dark blue title of Transaero. Flite-Line-Photos

Photographs on this page:

Aircraft 96, N101TV, was the first DC-10-30CF for Trans International Airlines. McDonnell Douglas

DC-10-30CF N101TV in interim Transamerica livery with 'Trans International' titles. Fred Lerch

N101TV in the full Transamerica livery. Fred Lerch

Short-lived charter carrier Transtar operated with leased DC-10-10 N102UA. Nicky Scherrer – VIP Photoservice

fuselage and the tail engine. The head of a chieftain was placed on the dark blue upper tail. The aircraft, 5N-OGI, was not delivered to the airline and ended up on lease to Shabair from August 1993 as 9Q-CSS.

Omni Air Express – Omni Air International

Founded in 1984 as Continental Air Transport, the company's name was changed to Omni Air Express the following year. Over the years the airline has operated as a supplemental carrier with a fleet of one Learjet, one 727-90 'combi' and 727-222 freighters. In August 1997, Omni Air Express acquired thee former American Airlines -10s, two of the aircraft being used for scheduled passenger charter operations. The third aircraft, formerly N147AA (f/n 18) will be dismantled for spare parts by the carrier.

The name of the passenger charter division is Omni Air International. This title is displayed in burgundy on the white upper fuselage. The company logo, consisting of burgundy 'OAI' lettering, a light grey aircraft silhouette and vapour trail is placed on the tail engine. At the time of writing, no specifics on forthcoming DC-10 operations and route network were available. See page 98.

Overseas National Airways – ONA

ONA was one of the first -30CF operators and received the first aircraft on 21st April 1973, just two days after the first -30CF had been accepted by Trans International Airlines. Another four of the same type were acquired. The aircraft were mainly used for long haul cargo services and transatlantic passenger charters.

The first aircraft, N1031F (f/n 81) was written off in a landing accident and was damaged beyond repair at Istanbul on 2nd January 1976. The second aircraft, N1032F (f/n 109) was destroyed by fire on 12th November 1975 after a bird-strike during take-off at JFK International Airport in New York. N1033F (f/n 237) went to Korean Air Lines who bought the aircraft from ONA in August 1978. N1034F was bought by Spantax in December 1978. The sole remaining aircraft of ONA's DC-10 fleet, N1035F, after having served with various airlines, found a safe home with Federal Express in May 1984 as N304FE *Alison*. Overseas National Airways ceased to exist in September 1978.

A dark blue cheatline on the white upper fuselage started at the nose and continued in the tail section. The 'Overseas National Airways' title was applied on the roof while a blue 'ONA' title appeared on the white engine No.2. The blue tail fin carried the company's logo, a white aircraft on a globe encompassed by a white ship's steering wheel.

N1031F	*Holidayliner America*
N1032F	*Holidayliner Freedom*
N1033F	*Holidayliner Enterprise*
N1034F	*Holidayliner Liberty*

Pacific East Air

The carrier started passenger charter flights to Hawaii with a DC-8-61 and a -62 in 1982. Capitol Air -10 N905WA, was sub-leased from 17th November until 17th December 1982. This had a narrow red cheatline, starting at the top of the cockpit windows, on an all-white fuselage. A large 'Pacific East Air' title was applied on the lower forward fuselage and a diagonal 'Pacific East' title to the tail fin. Operations continued with two leased DC-8-62s until the company ceased to exist in 1984.

Pakistan International Airlines – PIA

The airline received the first wide-body aircraft in the fleet when three new -30s were delivered in 1974. A fourth aircraft was accepted by the carrier in August 1976. The DC-10 fleet was reduced by one aircraft when AP-AXE (f/n 172) was lost in a hangar fire at Karachi on 2nd February 1981. To restore the fleet to its previous level, an ex-Alitalia -30 was bought in May 1983. Alongside the 707s and 747s, the DC-10s were used on the international route network. After an agreement was reached with CP Air in 1985 to exchange the entire fleet for four 747s from the Canadian carrier, the DC-10 era with PIA came to an end in 1986.

The first livery consisted of a green cheatline which commenced at the nose and flowed into the green tail section which displayed two rows of white stars above and below the white 'PIA' title. The 'Pakistan International' title and the nation's flag were placed on the upper white fuselage. A slightly changed livery, without the row of stars, was applied in 1975. In 1976 a new paint scheme was adopted. The fuselage now had a golden and a broad green cheatline and, instead of the national flag, a sabre styling alongside the 'Pakistan International' title. The two rows of stars on the fin of the former livery were permanently omitted.

PanAmerican World Airways – PAA

Until the takeover of National Airlines in January 1980, PanAm had been a mainly Boeing operator. A total of 16 DC-10s, eleven -10s and five -30s, were added to the PanAm fleet. The DC-10s sported the PanAm livery: a polished belly, white fuselage with light blue cheatline and black lettering and the famous PanAm globe on the tail section. It should be noted that some aircraft featured a completely white fuselage with the blue cheatline.

Although all of the ex-National DC-10s were operated by PanAm, a decision for fleet standardisation ended their employment. The sale of 15 aircraft to American Airlines started on 1st November 1983 and was completed by 22nd July 1984. The last -30 (f/n 328) had been delivered to PanAm after the merger and was the

only one to be sold to United Airlines, on 29th April 1985. Once the pride and glory of the US airline industry PanAm ceased operations on 4th December 1991. PanAm 'The New Airline' restarted operations from Miami, Florida, with a fleet of three A300B4-203s in 1996.

N60NA	*Clipper Meteor*
N61NA	*Clipper Evening Star*
N62NA	*Clipper Morning Star*
N63NA	*Clipper Eclipse*
N64NA	*Clipper Shooting Star*
N65NA	*Clipper National Eagle*
N66NA	*Clipper Sirius*
N67NA	*Clipper Star of Hope*
N68NA	*Clipper Star of Gazer*
N69NA	*Clipper Star Light*
N70NA	*Clipper Star King*
N80NA	*Clipper Star of the Union*
N81NA	*Clipper Atmosphere*
N82NA	*Clipper Aurora*
N83NA	*Clipper Celestial Empire*

Philippine Airlines / Philippines

Philippine Airlines started DC-10 operations with two -30s leased from KLM in 1974, replacing DC-8s on flights to Amsterdam, Frankfurt and Rome. Two new -30s were delivered in 1976 and 1980 respectively. In 1986 747s started replacing the DC-10s. Philippines ceased DC-10 operations on 14th March 1996 when the last aircraft, RP-C2114, was returned to Polaris. Awaiting delivery of new A330s and A340s in 1997, besides its long range fleet of 747s, the carrier currently also operates two MD-11s, on lease from World Airways.

The first colour scheme had a twin cheatline in blue and red all along the fuselage with blue 'Philippine Airlines' title on the white roof. The colours of the national flag, red, white and blue, were represented in a stylised form on the tail fin. In 1987 a new pure white livery with dark blue 'Philippines' titles was introduced. Additionally the blue section on the fin was highlighted by a superimposed yellow rising sun.

PLUNA – Primeras Lineas Uruguayas de Navegacion Aérea

The national airline of Uruguay operates with a fleet of three 737s, one 707 and one -30. This aircraft, PP-VMW, leased from VARIG since July 1974, operates the sole overseas route, Montevideo-Madrid. The first livery showed the dark blue title 'PLUNA' on the white and natural metal fuselage. The bird logo, within a white circle, was applied on the dark blue fin whilst the 'Uruguay' title was placed on the tail engine. The scheme introduced in 1996 has a small country flag and 'Uruguay' title followed by a large 'PLUNA' title on the white upper fuselage. The belly is kept in natural metal finish. The dark blue of the tail section extends across the rear top fuselage. A restyled yellow bird logo is applied on the tail fin.

THY was the second European airline to operate DC-10-10s. TC-JAV *Ankara* was the Ermenonville crash aircraft. McDonnell Douglas

Series 10 TC-JAU *Istanbul*, re-registered N68058, showing experimental 'Turkish Air' paint scheme. Nicky Scherrer – VIP Photoservice

United Airlines Series 10 N1805U in the original livery. Nicky Scherrer – VIP Photoservice

The later United four-star treatment on the fuselage and tail engine on DC-10-10 N1818U. United Airlines

Introduced in 1974, the second United Airlines paint scheme would last almost 20 years.
McDonnell Douglas

DC-10-10 N1823U with the larger United logo and title adapted later on the second livery.
United Airlines

A United Airlines Worldwide Cargo DC-10-30F on finals for Los Angeles International Airport.
K Ziehl, Luftfahrt-Journal

UTA DC-10-30 F-BTDD in the carrier's original and impressive livery. Fred Lerch

VARIG Series 30 PP-VMZ in the airline's full white colour scheme. Author's collection

Series 30F PP-VMU, one of two DC-10 freighters operated by VARIG. Fred Lerch

After the football world championship, DC-10-30 PP-VMD obtained a special paint scheme. Author's collection

Premiair

Premiair was founded in 1994 after the merger of Scanair and Conair and operates inclusive tour and charter flights using Conair A300s and A320s as well as six -10s of which two aircraft are presently sub-leased to Sun Country. During 1996 the carrier became a subsidiary of Simon Spies Holding and Airtours plc, UK. From its home base Copenhagen and the Oslo and Stockholm hubs, flights to France, Greece, Italy, Spain, Thailand and the UK are conducted. To further fulfil its long range requirements, Premiair leased a TAESA -30 for a three year period early in January 1997.

Before the merger, Premiair aircraft were flown in a simple livery. The white fuselage displays the title 'Premiair', with an orange and blue dot on the letters 'i' respectively, on the cabin roof and on the port and starboard engines. An orange sun with a blue shade is shown on the white tail fin.

In December 1996 the first Premiair aircraft took on the basic livery of Airtours International. The attractive paint scheme consists of a white upper fuselage with large blue 'Premiair' titles. The deep blue of the lower fuselage sweeps up encompassing the complete tail with a thin turquoise blue pinstripe flowing from the front

Series 30F PP-VMU was the first freighter to wear the new VARIG colour scheme with the eye-catching 'Cargo' title. Manfred Kaspczak

VARIG DC-10-30 PP-VMA at Zurich, March 1997, featuring the airline's new livery, introduced in October 1996. Rolf Wallner

VASP DC-10-30 PP-SOM leased from Potomac Capital Investment Corporation. Fred Lerch

VASPEX, the cargo division of VASP, operates DC-10-30CF N107WA on lease from World Airways. Vicky Mills

up to the tail engine. This pinstripe is also applied on the deep blue wing engines. The red, turquoise and yellow logo appears on the tail fin.

OY-CNT	Dumbo
OY-CNU	Bamse
OY-CNY	Snoopy
SE-DHS	Baloo

Qantas

Martinair Holland conducted cargo flights for the Australian carrier from 21st December 1987 until 16th February 1988. The aircraft was operated in full Martinair Holland livery without any titles. In November 1997, Gemini Air Cargo started to operate transpacific cargo flights from Los Angeles for the Australian carrier.

Sabena

The airline was the first European carrier to introduce the -30CF, taking delivery of the first aircraft on 18th September 1973. Another four aircraft of the type were ordered and by 1980 Sabena operated all five -30CFs.

Initially the aircraft were used on routes to destinations in the Far East and Africa. After the introduction of the 747s, they were put into service on routes to the USA and Canada as well.

Although the -30CFs originally owned by Sabena have all been sold off, the airline leased two Lufthansa -30s in 1994 to supplement the other wide-bodies in the fleet. OO-SLH (previously D-ADHO) stayed in service with Sabena until November 1996. The lease of sistership OO-SLG (formerly D-ADGO) was terminated in April 1997. The airline's present long range fleet consists of a mixture of A340s and 747s, augmented by A330s during 1997.

The Royal Air Force leased Sabena -30CF OO-SLC from 28th January until 5th March 1991. The DC-10 was used for troop and material transport from London-Stansted to Dubai, United Arab Emirates, during the Gulf War.

The livery introduced in 1973 had a deep blue window cheatline running from the nose to the tail with a dark blue pinstripe on either side. This scheme also appeared on the tail engine in the form of a wedge. A large stylised letter 'S' in a white circle adorned the tail fin. 'Sabena' title alongside the Belgian flag and a 'Belgian World Airlines' title were displayed towards the centre on a white cabin roof. This paint scheme was slightly revised in 1984 with a light blue colour replacing the dark blue on the cheatline, pinstripes and tail section. The 'Sabena' title in bold letters, the Belgian flag and the subtitle 'Belgian World Airlines' were now placed on the forward fuselage.

Late in 1994 the DC-10s also obtained the all-new livery based on a completely white scheme. A huge 'Sabena' title in a very light shade of blue is accompanied by a small dark blue 'Sabena' title on the fuselage. Changes in the tail section include the restyled letter 'S' in a dark blue circle on the fin and the display of the Belgian and European Community flags on the engine. To enforce the partnership with Swissair, 'Flying together with Swissair' titles were applied on the rear fuselage at the end of 1995. During 1996 all Sabena aircraft obtained a Belgian cartoon character sticker, placed below the cockpit windows. In the case of the DC-10s, the characters come from the 'Boule and Bill' cartoons. Also, an Olympic carrier sticker was applied next to the forward entry door.

On 27th March 1997, Buena Vista International, the marketing and distribution division of Walt Disney Studios, and Belgacom, the Belgian communications company, presented a flying communications platform for the European premiere of 101 Dalmatians, Disney's latest animated film production. In co-operation with Sabena, -30 OO-SLG received a special livery featuring five huge dalmatians on both sides of the fuselage. Red 'Disney's 101 Dalmatians' stickers were applied on the upper fuselage while Belgacom's title and logo appeared on the forward fuselage and the wing engines. Further partners in the project were 3M Belgium Commercial Graphic and air transport advertising company, Air Concept.

The last DC-10 in Sabena's fleet, flown on the airline's Brussels-Chicago route, carried this livery until the end of April when the leasing contract expired. This marked the end of over 23 years of uninterrupted DC-10 operations by the Belgian flag carrier.

Saudia – Saudi Arabian Airlines

Overseas National Airways -30CF N1031F was on a short term lease to the Saudi Arabian carrier when the aircraft was damaged beyond repair after over-running the runway at Istanbul on 2nd January 1976. The lease had started in November 1975. The airline became a direct McDD customer with an order for four MD-11 freighters and 29 MD-90-30s. The first MD-11F, an MD-90, a 747-400 and a 777-200 were delivered to the carrier during a ceremony at Everett on 22nd December 1997. Additionally, two passenger MD-11s will enter service with the Saudi VIP division.

Scanair

Scanair, the charter subsidiary of SAS, operated charter and inclusive-tour flights with eight DC-8-63s until the change over to DC-10 equipment. The network included destinations in the Mediterranean, the Canary Islands, North Africa, Germany, Switzerland, Austria, the UK and France. The first DC-10 in the fleet was a SAS -30 on lease to Scanair from October 1986 until March 1987. In 1988 the DC-8s were replaced by a fleet of six -10s on lease from UASI, the United Airlines leasing division. On 1st January 1994 the carrier merged with Conair and operates as Premiair.

An all white fuselage displayed a blue 'Scanair' title, diagonal orange striping below the forward passenger windows and the flags of Denmark, Norway and Sweden at the rear. To underline the holiday character, a large orange sun was placed on the white tail fin. Later the additional orange title 'Sun Jet' was added on the tail engine.

SE-DHS	Baloo
SE-DHT	Dumbo
SE-DHU	Bamse
SE-DHY	Snoopy
SE-DHZ	Moby Dick

Scandinavian Airlines System – SAS

The three-nation SAS received its first Series 30 on 1st October 1974. Another five were delivered new to the airline by McDD. The DC-10 fleet reached its peak in 1989 when eleven -30s were in operation.

The aircraft were used on international flights to North and South America, the Middle and Far East and Africa. By the end of 1991 all of the DC-10s had been disposed of and replaced by a fleet of 767-283s and -383s.

The early paint scheme consisted of a dark blue window cheatline with a viking's head, starting at the front of the upper white fuselage which also displayed a dark blue 'Scandinavian' title. As was common with many airlines in the early days of DC-10 operations, the lower part of the fuselage was highly polished metal. The three national flags appeared on the tail engine with a dark blue 'SAS' logo on the fin above. The livery introduced in 1983 has a pure white fuselage as a background for the dark blue 'Scandinavian' title, which is outlined in gold, the stripings in the national colours of Denmark, Norway and Sweden and the flags of the three countries. The dark blue 'SAS' logo is displayed on the tail.

LN-RKA	Olav Viking
LN-RKB	Haakon Viking
LN-RKC	Leif Viking
LN-RKD	Bjarne Viking
SE-DFD	Dag Viking
SE-DFE	Sverker Viking
SE-DFF	Solve Viking
SE-DFG	Yngve Viking
SE-DFH	Rurik Viking
OY-KDA	Gorm Viking
OY-KDB	Frode Viking
OY-KDC	Godfred Viking

Scibe Airlift Zaire – SBZ

Charter passenger and cargo flights are conducted by the carrier. The present fleet consists of two 727s in a 130 economy seat configuration. A single 707 freighter is stored at Tel-Aviv. In 1990 a subsidiary in Belgium was founded under the name European Airlift. This company used equipment from the parent company until it suspended operations in 1993. A Series 10, N102UA, was leased in October 1992 and subleased to European Airlift for holiday charter flights. Amongst others charter flights from Frankfurt, Germany, to the Dominican Republic were operated. The aircraft was returned to its lessor early 1993.

Triple red cheatlines marked the all white fuselage. A red band with white stripes and a small 'SBZ' title was shown on the tail. A further two -30s, F-BTDB and F-GHOI, were temporarily leased in late1993. Whereas F-BTDB had a small 'European Airlift' sticker on the fuselage, F-GHOI had a small 'Taino' title on the forward fuselage. The leases of both aircraft were terminated in December 1993 and no further DC-10 operations by SBZ have taken place since.

Seaboard World Airlines

Seaboard World was a prospective customer for the -30CF, but no new aircraft were acquired from McDD. Operating a fleet of DC-8-63CFs and 747Fs and 'Cs, the cargo carrier bought a single -30CF, N1035F, in October 1978. The aircraft had been delivered to Overseas National Airways on 8th September, the same month the carrier ceased operations. It was immediately leased to the leasing company United Air Carriers Inc and put into service with Icelandair-Loftleidir, Garuda Indonesian Airways and Air Florida before it was sold by Seaboard in September 1980. The aircraft never flew in the airline's livery, a black nose and cheatline with a bold 'Seaboard World' fuselage title and a golden tail fin with the white and black 'SW' logo. Seaboard ceased to exist when it was acquired by The Flying Tiger Line (Flying Tigers) in the early 1980s.

Shabair

This airline operates international and domestic passenger and freight services. A DC-10-10, 9Q-CSS, was leased in August 1993 and returned to the lessor in September 1994.

The white upper fuselage and highly polished bare metal belly were separated by a black cheatline. Another black cheatline ran parallel just above the lower one on the white upper part. The double black striping was repeated on all engines. Winged 'Shabair' title appeared above the windows between door two and three.

The carrier received another DC-10, this time a -30, in September 1994. F-OKBB started Brussels-Kinshasa services the same month but was returned to the leasing company three months later. From December 1994 until February 1995 Shabair leased Skyjet -30 OO-PHN. The aircraft was operated in full Skyjet colours with large additional Shabair titles on the fuselage. At the time of writing the carrier does not operate wide-body equipment.

Singapore Airlines

The airline ordered four -30s as a replacement for 707s in the fleet and had options on another three of the type. The first aircraft was delivered on 23rd October 1978 with the sixth and last aircraft to be accepted on 30th November 1979. The seventh example was never placed into service and was sold to VARIG upon completion at Long Beach. The carrier has always been a strong Boeing customer and with an ever-increasing fleet of 747s replacement of the DC-10s by the latter type was determined. By the end of 1983 all DC-10s were sold.

Singapore Airlines' attractive colour scheme with blue and yellow cheatlines on a white fuselage was very impressive on the DC-10. The superimposed stylised yellow bird fitted well on the blue tail section. This company logo was also placed in a small blue circle on the wing mounted engines. The blue 'Singapore Airlines' title alongside the national flag appeared on the upper fuselage. A large 'California here we come' title with a stylised US flag alongside the 'Singapore Airlines' title.was applied in1979 to commemorate the start of the airline's San Francisco service.

Skyjet SA / Skyjet Antigua / Skyjet Brazil

Both Skyjet Antigua and Skyjet Brazil were established as sister companies of Skyjet SA in Brussels. Passenger holiday charters are operated between Europe, Africa, South America, the Caribbean and the USA. Hadj pilgrimage flights are also undertaken. Skyjet Brazil also operated charter flights to Mexico, Venezuela, the USA and the US Virgin Islands.

The first DC-10 operated by Skyjet SA was Series 30 OO-PHN, formerly V2-LEA, which has been in service since November 1992. Another of the type, V2-LEH, followed in April 1995. In June 1996 Skyjet SA acquired ex-Mexicana -15 V2-LER. The aircraft features the same livery as sistership OO-PHN with a completely white fuselage, engines and a dark blue tail. Placement of logos and title is the same as for the Skyjet Brazil aircraft. V2-LER carried the name *El Coyote* until being renamed *Gerard Mercator*. In September 1996 -30 V2-LEH was returned to its lessor, CIT Leasing. Another former Mexicana -15, V2-LEX, joined the fleet in May 1997. This aircraft, unlike the others, has a yellow company logo.

Skyjet Brazil acquired a -30 from Lufthansa in September 1994. The livery was basically the same as that of the latter carrier with the turquoise Skyjet logo on the dark blue tail fin. A smaller company logo and a blue bold 'Skyjet' title were placed on the upper white fuselage together with a small 'Brazil' title and the nation's flag. Formerly D-ADKO, with Skyjet Brazil it became PP-AJM and returned to the leasing company at the end of 1996. In December 1996 Skyjet Brazil was wound up by parent company, Skyjet SA Belgium.

Sobelair

The charter subsidiary of Sabena operates flights to destinations in the Mediterranean, the Canary Islands and North Africa. Sobelair leased Skyjet -30 V2-LEA, as OO-PHN, during 1994 to augment capacity and back up the only wide-body aircraft in the fleet, a 767-300ER. The aircraft had the Skyjet livery with additional small 'Sobelair' titles applied next to the forward entry doors.

Spantax

With bases at Last Palmas and Palma de Mallorca this carrier operated charter flights to European and to North and South American destinations. The airline operated with a fleet of 737s, Convair CV-990 Coronados, MD-83s, DC-8s and DC-10s. A DC-10-30CF was bought from ONA in December 1978. Formerly registered N1034F, EC-DEG (f/n 238) was destroyed by fire after an aborted take-off at Malaga, Spain on 13th September 1982. A variety of DC-10s were leased from 1982 until 1988. The

airline, plagued by severe financial problems, ceased all operations in March 1988.

The paint scheme used until 1983 differed on the aircraft operated. A blue cheatline with one or two pinstripes on a white upper fuselage were used at the same time. The company's logo was displayed under the cockpit windows and on some aircraft also on the tail fin. The attractive new livery featured a triple light blue, red and dark blue cheatline and a dark blue 'Spantax' title on the white cabin roof. A new stylised 'S' logo was displayed on the fin as well as on the wing mounted engines.

STAF – Servicios de portes Aéreos Fueguinos

Founded in 1985, the Argentine carrier operates charter flights with aircraft leased from other companies when required. Since early 1996 STAF has operated -30CF XA-TDC *Petete* first on cargo flights between Mexico and Miami, Florida, and then on a worldwide basis, in co-operation with TAESA.

Black diagonal 'STAF' and 'Cargo' titles are applied on the forward fuselage. The all-white fuselage features a thin yellow cheatline encompassing the 'Cargo' title at the front. The complete tail section was painted a solid yellow until February 1997 when a black 'STAF' title on the tail engine and a black sun on the tail fin were applied. The Argentine and Mexican flags with a 'Working Together' title are placed below the cockpit windows, while a separate Mexican flag is shown on the upper fuselage.

Sudan Airways

Finnair -30 OH-LHB operated briefly for the Sudanese flag carrier from 29th September until 3rd October 1981.

Sun Country Airlines

The charter carrier conducts scheduled and charter passenger services within the USA and to destinations in the Caribbean, Canada, Mexico and Europe utilising 727s and DC-10s. The first DC-10 to join the airline's fleet in 1986 was a leased Northwest -40 which was returned to that carrier in July 1991.

KLM DC-10-30 PH-DTH, together with sistership PH-DTG, were directly delivered to VIASA upon completion. McDonnell Douglas

VIASA DC-10-30 YV-137C displaying the second paint scheme with the seven stars.
McDonnell Douglas

DC-10-30 YV-134C in the new VIASA livery at Frankfurt/Main Airport in August 1996.
Author's collection

Wardair Canada DC-10-30 C-GXRC *W R Wop May*, was the first of two aircraft delivered new to the airline. Canadian Airlines International

First of 13 DC-10-10s operated, Western Airlines N901WA at the Long Beach factory. McDonnell Douglas

Before the takeover by Delta Air Lines, Western aircraft sported the bare metal livery. Fred Lerch

DC-10-30CF N103WA was the first of many DC-10s in operation with World Airways. McDonnell Douglas

Displaying the second paint scheme, World Airways DC-10-10 N1826U *Employee One* is cheered by company staff. World Airways

DC-10-30CF N112WA the World paint scheme of the early 1990s. Fred Lerch

World Airways Series 30CF N106WA in the carrier's current livery. Fred Lerch

Today, Sun County operates a fleet of ten 727s, two DC-10-10s and four -15s. From September 1995 to November 1996 four Gemini Air Cargo -30Fs were operated on Gemini's behalf by Sun Country.

The striking first livery conveyed a holiday feeling with a large red, orange and yellow sun at the forward fuselage followed by a triple cheatline in the same colours which was interrupted by a large red 'Sun Country' title. In 1995 the airline introduced a revised livery with orange and red diagonal bands and huge dark red 'Sun Country' titles across the fuselage. The new logo, a stylised red and white sun with the letter 'S', is displayed on the fin.

Swissair

Swissair was the first European carrier to put the -30 into service, when HB-IHA went on its inaugural flight, Zurich-Montreal-Chicago on 15th December 1972. By April 1982 the carrier operated 13 -30s of which four were -30ERs, all used on the whole Swissair international network. As a replacement of the DC-10, Swissair currently operates a fleet of 16 MD-11s.

When the DC-10 entered service the paint scheme consisted of a red window cheatline on the white upper fuselage, a highly polished lower fuselage and the Swiss flag on the fin. The company logo appeared alongside the black 'Swissair' title on the forward top. (See page 116.) On the occasion of Swissair's 50th birthday in 1981 a new livery was introduced, constituting a straight twin light and dark brown cheatline separating the upper white fuselage with a bold red 'Swissair' title, from the polished belly. The red of the flag was extended to include the tail engine. (See page 25.)

Swissair operated DC-10s for Air Afrique on many occasions. Small 'Air Afrique' titles were added to the regular Swissair paint scheme below the cheatlines, at the front and back.

In 1991 a special sticker with a 'growing' Swiss cross and '700th Anniversary of the Swiss Confederation' was applied on all aircraft alongside the 'Swissair' title to commemorate the event. A tribute to a great aircraft was paid when HB-IHI returned from the last Swissair DC-10 operation, Toronto–Montreal–Zurich on 30th May 1992, with a special 'Farewell DC-10' title on the forward fuselage.

HB-IHA	*St Gallen*
HB-IHB	*Schaffhausen*
HB-IHC	*Luzern*, renamed *Obwalden*
HB-IHD	*Bern*, renamed *Thurgau*
HB-IHE	*Vaud*
HB-IHF	*Nidwalden*
HB-IHG	*Grisons*, renamed *Graubunden*
HB-IHH	*Basel-Stadt*, renamed *Schaffhausen*
HB-IHI	*Fribourg*
HB-IHL	*Ticino*, renamed *Thurgau*
HB-IHM	*Valais/Wallis*
HB-IHN	*St Gallen*
HB-IHO	*Uri*

TAESA – Transportes Aéreos Ejecutivos SA

The Mexican carrier has an extensive fleet of Gates Learjet, Lockheed JetStar and Gulfstream executive jets as well as DC-9s, 727s, 737s, and one 757. From June 1995 a Series 30 was leased from GE Capital Aviation Services and operated in the first instance on charters between the Dominican Republic and Germany on behalf of Dominicana de Aviacion. Flight operations for Dominicana were stopped in July 1996.

Thereafter the aircraft was employed on the airline's own Mexico City to Tijuana route and on international charter flights, including work for Caledonian Airways and Leisure International for instance. In January 1997 the -30 left the TAESA fleet on a three year lease to Premiair Denmark.

In April 1996 TAESA leased -30CF XA-TDC, last in service with Avcom Aviation. This aircraft is operated on behalf of STAF Argentina on world-wide cargo flights. Former Skyjet Series 30 V2-LEH (N39081 with the CIT Group) was leased from December 1996 through to March 1997 as XA-TFM.

Although XA-SYE first had an all white fuselage with red 'Dominicana' titles only, it later displayed the TAESA colour scheme with added 'Dominicana' title. A large blue 'TAESA' title alongside a stylised eagle logo was displayed on the forward white fuselage and this title-logo combination was repeated on the yellow tail section. The flags of Mexico and Dominica along with a 'Working Together' title were applied below the cockpit windows.

Taino Airlines

Founded in 1974 the carrier operates charter flights using leased equipment. Charter operations included flights from its base in the Dominican Republic to Frankfurt, Germany.

Series 30 F-GHOI, was sub-leased from Scibe Airlift Zaire (SBZ) from June until December 1993. The aircraft was operated in the standard SBZ paint scheme but carried additional small red 'Taino' titles added on the upper forward fuselage.

TAP Air Portugal

The Portuguese flag carrier operated with Lockheed TriStar 500s on its long range network, now replaced with Airbus A340-211s. In July 1997, to supplement the wide-body fleet, Skyjet DC-10-15 V2-LEX was deployed to TAP.

Tarom

With the loss of A310-324 YR-LCC after take-off from Bucharest on 31st March 1995, Tarom required additional equipment to keep up their international flights. ChallengAir -30 OO-JOT was leased by the airline until the end of 1995. The aircraft was operated in a full white colour scheme with large dark blue 'Tarom' titling on the lower forward fuselage and the company's logo, a stylised bird in a circle, on the tail.

Thai Airways International

The DC-10 fleet in 1975 and 1976 consisted of three -30s on lease from KLM, UTA and Air Afrique to replace the airline's DC-8s. In March and May 1977 Thai took delivery of its first two own -30s. These two aircraft were sold to SAS in February 1987 and immediately leased back by the airline until the delivery of two -30ERs in December of the same year. Another of the type joined the fleet in May 1988. As a replacement four MD-11s were ordered and are now in service with the carrier.

Although the three DC-10s were stored and 'up for sale' during 1994, all were reactivated. In October 1997 the carrier announced the sale of its DC-10s to Euro Aircraft Trading who subsequently transferred them to Aviation Investor Services. Through a lease-back arrangement, the aircraft will remain a part of the wide-body fleet until April 1998.

Thai's attractive colour scheme is based on a pure white fuselage. Two dark purple cheatlines are separated by a light purple one and accentuated by gold pinstriping. The cheat lines flow out of a stylised orchid. The same motive is superimposed on the tail section followed by the 'Thai' title.

HS-TGC	*Sriwanna*
HS-TGD	*Phimara*
HS-TMA	*Kwaniyuang*
HS-TMB	*Thepalai*
HS-TMC	*Chaiprakarn*
HS-TMC	*Sri Ubon*
HS-TMD	*Hariphunchai*

The Hawaii Express

Another carrier wanting to take part in the lucrative passenger charter business, The Hawaii Express leased -10s, N904WA and N905WA, from April to December 1983. After their return to the lessor, the carrier stopped operations.

A black 'The Hawaii Express' title alongside the USA flag above the windows and a rainbow coloured cheatline flowing toward the completely yellow tail section with a large white pineapple on the fin, formed the livery.

TransAer International Airlines

The Irish carrier is a member of All Leisure Travel Holdings and operates international and regional scheduled and charter flights. Destinations include Athens, the Canary Islands, Last Palmas, Los Angeles, Malaga, Orlando, Palma and Tenerife. The current fleet consists of six A320s and four A300B4s. In May 1997, Skyjet Belgium DC-10-15 V2-LER was used with TransAer for charters.

Transaero Airlines

Transaero was founded in 1990 and is based at Moscow's Sheremetyevo Airport. It was the first non-Aeroflot company allowed to operate scheduled passenger services in Russia. The route network includes scheduled domestic services to Alma Ata, Baku, Kiev, Minsk, Odessa, Omsk, Riga, St Petersburg, Tashkent amongst others and international destinations such as Berlin, Frankfurt, Orlando, London, Los Angeles, Paris, and Tel-Aviv. Charters are conducted to Faro, Istanbul, Rimini, Malaga and Palma de Mallorca. Services from Moscow to Chicago were intended to commence in the spring of 1997. The carrier was further granted traffic rights by the US Department of Transportation for schedules to Dallas, Seattle and Washington DC. The short and medium haul fleet presently consists of five 737-200s, five 757-200s and one Ilyushin Il-86.

To fulfill the need of long range equipment operations started with three -30s in 1996. The American Airlines aircraft are sub-leased from the FIN 3 leasing organisation. Besides the Los Angeles and Orlando routes, the DC-10s are also used on charter flights from Moscow to Faro and Palma de Mallorca, for example.

The DC-10s sport a natural metal fuselage with the blue, white and red cheatlines of American with exta blue and red pinstripes within the white cheatline. The red, white, and blue striped delta-shaped logo is placed on the fin. The first aircraft delivered, N141AA *Los Angeles*, has a dark blue 'Transaero' title on the forward upper section, the other aircraft carry a larger white-outlined dark blue title, extending from door one to door three.

Trans International Airlines – Transamerica Airlines

TIA operated an extensive fleet of DC-8s on long haul charter operations. The DC-10 was the first wide-body aircraft for the airline. The second -30CF built by McDD, N101TV, was delivered to the airline on 19th April 1973. Two more sisterships were soon to follow, N102TV and N103TV were accepted on 4th June and 2nd July 1973.

After TIA had taken over Saturn Airways, the company changed the name to Transamerica in October 1979. A total of five 747s were ordered of which only three were delivered. The DC-10s were sold to Federal Express between February and April 1984. Bigger is not always better, Transamerica Airlines stopped all operations on 30th September 1986.

It was always easy to recognise a TIA or Transamerica aircraft due to the turquoise on

white livery. The turquoise cheatline ran along the fuselage and extended into the tail, the colour progressively turning darker at the top of the fin. TIA aircraft had large 'Trans International' titles on the forward fuselage, 'TIA' and 'DC-10' titling on the tail section. Small turquoise and white bands with 'DC-10 TIA' were applied on engines Nos.1 and 3. Transamerica aircraft of course differed in the 'Transamerica' titling on the fuselage, but the most remarkable difference was the Transamerica insignia on the tail.

Transmile Air Services

Founded in 1992, this Malaysian company started operations as a scheduled and charter passenger and cargo airline in November 1993 with both domestic and international routes. The fleet consisted of four Cessna Caravans and five Boeing 737s. In December 1997 it was planned to acquire two former Malaysian Air-

lines DC-10-30s for long range charter flights to Australia and New Zealand. The aircraft, registered 9M-TGA and 9M-TGB, were not accepted by Transmile and remain withdrawn and in store at Marana, Arizona.

Transtar Airlines

Transtar planned to start international charter passenger flights in 1993 and leased a -10, N102UA, in May of that year from Orlando, USA. The white upper and dark blue lower colouring of the fuselage continued on the tail section. A double green and single red pinstripe accompanied this. This triple pinstriping was repeated on the cowlings of the dark blue wing-mounted engines. The handwritten-style 'Transtar' title appeared on the forward fuselage. The carrier ceased operations in late 1993 with the intention to restart during 1994, however no activities have taken place since.

DC-10-30 N3016Z *Nkwazi* **was in service with Zambia Airways for over ten years and is now operated by Monarch Airlines.** Author's collection

Lufthansa Series 30 D-ADBO re-registered 9J-AFN, awaiting delivery to Zambia Airways at Frankfurt/Main Airport. Author's collection

The airline took delivery of its first -10 on the same day as American, 29th July 1971, but the first passenger service was undertaken a few days later, on 14th August, from San Francisco to Washington DC. The first three -30s came to the carrier in 1983 through a lease agreement with CP Air; these were used for the Hong Kong services. With the extension of the Far Eastern and European network, further Series 30s were acquired. McDD built only nine -10CFs of which eight were ordered by Continental. United took delivery of the ninth -10CF on 20th September 1982, and this was the last DC-10 for United.

The only DC-10 fatality occurred when -10 N1819U (f/n 118) crashed during an emergency landing at Sioux City Gateway Airport, Iowa on 19th July 1989.

Currently, United operates 28 -10s, one -30, three -30CFs and four -30Fs. Eleven -10s have been stored or withdrawn from use. As far as wide-body aircraft are concerned, the airline also has a large fleet of 747s, 767s and was a launch customer for the 777. In September 1996 United agreed to sell 36 -10s to Federal Express in exchange for the delivery of hushkits for 59 United 727-200s by Federal Express Aviation Services. The first aircraft left the United DC-10 fleet in early 1997.

In March 1997 United Airlines' World Cargo Division started all-cargo services from Chicago and Los Angeles to Anchorage, Osaka, Manila and Taipei with DC-10 freighters. The carrier deploys four -30 freighters; three -30s and one -30CF from the United passenger fleet were converted to full freighters by the Aeronavali division of Alenia, Italy.

The bright early paint scheme, a triple blue, white and red cheatline on a white upper and polished lower fuselage remained until 1974. Four stars alongside the 'United' and 'DC-10 Friend Ship' title, were displayed on the cabin roof. The star motif was repeated on the tail engine and a red and blue vertical band, respectively above and below the 'United' title appeared on the tail fin. It should be noted that early aircraft were delivered without the 'star treatment'. In this case the 'DC-10 Friend Ship' title was located on the tail engine.

The livery introduced in 1974 featured a triple orange, red and blue cheatline running from the nose to the tail. The new company orange and blue logo and 'United' title, were placed above the cheatlines while the motif alone was superimposed on the tail. First a small logo and title positioned between the first and second door was used. This was later changed to a much larger logo and title positioned over the second door.

Tunisair

World Airways -30CF N108WA flew for Tunisair from 26th August to 21st September and from 4th to 24th October 1982 to conduct pilgrim flights to Mecca. Both of the Skyjet Belgium Series 15s, V2-LER and 'LEX, operated numerous flights for the carrier during 1997.

Türk Hava Yollari – THY

THY ordered three -10s from McDD. The first two aircraft, TC-JAU and TC-JAV were delivered in December 1972. The third, TC-JAY, followed in February 1973. The second DC-10 to ever be involved in a crash, TC-JAV, (f/n 29), was lost on 3rd March 1974 near Ermenonville, France after take-off from Paris Orly Airport. Together with three 707s, the DC-10s were the long range equipment of the company to destinations in Europe, the Middle and Far East and North Africa.

The red and white paint scheme represented the colours of the national flag. The cheatline comprised five red pinstripes along the fuselage on a white upper body. The name of the airline in English as well as in Turkish was displayed on the upper fuselage. The carrier's bird logo in a white circle, surrounded by six red stripes, appeared on the tail.

The DC-10s were withdrawn from service during 1987 and leased to Bogaziçi BHT, having been replaced by A310-304s. TC-JAU returned from Bogaziçi BHT to THY in February 1989 and was sold to FedEx in November 1989. The aircraft served as a test-bed for a new name and colour scheme to be introduced in 1990. A red thin cheatline and 'Turkish Air' title in the same colour were applied on the fully white fuselage. A white circle with the red bird logo within a wide red band, together with two red stripes formed the scheme on the tail. This livery was not adopted. In January 1990, sistership TC-JAY was also sold to FedEx. THY once more operated a -30 with OH-LHE, on short term lease from Finnair, for Hadj operations in May and June 1993.

TC-JAU	*Istanbul*
TC-JAV	*Ankara*
TC-JAY	*Izmir*

Turkish Air

See Türk Hava Yollari – THY.

United Airlines

Although American Airlines was the launch customer for the DC-10, the order for 30 -10s from United was a breakthrough for the aircraft.

The current livery was introduced in January 1993 – see page 14. A narrow red cheatline separates the dark blue belly from the grey upper fuselage which carries the large white 'United Airlines' title. Royal and dark blue stripes are applied on the engines and tail section. One DC-10 has been named, N1804U *Curtiss Barkes*.

For the freighters, the beautiful United paint scheme is highlighted by a large white 'World-wide Cargo' title. The letter 'O' in the word 'World' appears in the form of a stylised globe. A small logo and a white 'United Airlines' title is placed in front of the forward entry doors.

UTA – Union de Transports Aériens

Once the largest independent French carrier, UTA merged with Air France in October 1991. UTA bought five -30s from the manufacturer which were later supplemented by two leased units of the same type. The aircraft were in service on the routes to Africa, the USA, Australia and the Pacific area. On 19th September 1989, UTA became a victim of terrorism when one of its DC-10s, N54629 (f/n 93), was blown up in flight by a bomb over Niger on a scheduled flight from Abidjan to Paris. After the merger with Air France, the UTA DC-10s were incorporated into the Air France fleet.

The airline's livery was striking indeed with bright green doors on an overall white fuselage and dark blue tail assembly extending to the belly. Huge dark blue 'UTA' lettering on the forward fuselage made an identification unmistakable. A small white winged UTA symbol was placed on the upper fin.

VARIG – Viação Aérea Rio-Grandense, SA

The Brazilian carrier started DC-10 operations with three -30s in 1974. Further examples were acquired and a total of 12 were in the fleet by 1981. VARIG has a fleet of two -30Fs (CFs) and seven -30s. One -30 is on long term lease to PLUNA, Uruguay. The DC-10s together with nine MD-11s, ten 767-200s and -300s and five 747-300s form the present long range fleet.

The former livery dates back to 1955 and was only changed once, in 1960, when the Icarus motif on the tail was substituted by a mariner's compass. A broad light blue cheatline with twin white pinstripes started at the nose and extended to the rear of the aircraft. A large blue 'VARIG' title was displayed over the wings on the white upper fuselage which also showed the black 'Brazil' title and national flag at the front section. The compass, together with a small black 'VARIG' title were placed on the tail fin. It is note-worthy that some aircraft are operated with a natural metal as well as a white underside. The carrier's two -30Fs, PP-VMT and PP-VMU, displayed an additional bold red 'Cargo' title on the cabin roof.

To commemorate the country winning the football world championship in 1994, PP-VMD received a special paint job. A broad yellow and blue band, separated by the 'VARIG' title, ran diagonally across the fuselage with the 'Campeao Mundial de Futebol USA '94' title prominently displayed. The mascot of the games highlighted the light grey painted wing engines.

In October 1996 VARIG unveiled a new livery, replacing the still-attractive former scheme. First aircraft to carry the livery was Boeing 747-300 PP-VNH, featuring an overall white fuselage with deep blue lower section. The engines and the tail – which displays a redesigned golden and white compass logo – are also deep blue. An elegantly written, golden 'Brazil' title is added to the blue 'VARIG' lettering on the upper fuselage. A golden 'Cargo' title is displayed on the freighters.

VASP – Viação Aérea São Paulo

VASP is Brazil's second largest carrier and operates scheduled passenger and cargo flights on its domestic and international network. Three -30s were leased in 1991 but were returned to the leasing companies. The aircraft involved were Canadian Airlines International DC-10s, two of which are back in service with the Canadian carrier under their former registrations C-FCRD and C-FCRE. During 1995, Skyjet -30 OO-PHN was leased by the Brazilian carrier, this was returned to Skyjet in February 1996. The passenger fleet currently consists of 22 737s, three A300B2s and nine MD-11s.

The DC-10s carried the airline's livery with a low twin blue and black cheatline separating the light grey belly from the white upper fuselage. Large blue 'VASP' titles are displayed between the second entry and the overwing door. The tail section which is also kept in the blue colour displays the stylised white company bird motif.

In March 1997 the airline formed a new cargo division, named VASPEX. Operations started with a 727-200F and two 737-200Fs. A -30CF, leased from World Airways, was added to the cargo fleet in June 1997. The aircraft features a large VASPEX title on the fuselage and a white 'Cargo' title on the tail engine.

VIASA – Venezolana Internacional de Aviacion SA

The Venezuelan airline was 45% owned by Iberia, 30% by the Venezuelan national investment fund and 15% by the country's Banco Provincial. The carrier received its first -30 in April 1974 and a second followed in April 1975. Both aircraft, PH-DTG and PH-DTH, were KLM orders, delivered on lease to VIASA immediately and thereafter bought by the carrier. DC-10s replaced DC-8s on the airline's international route network which included destinations in Europe, the USA and South America. During the Canadian winter season charter flights were flown to Toronto and Vancouver. In 1996 the fleet consisted of seven 727s and the company's own four -30s. The airline operated a further -30, YV-139C, on lease from Iberia from 31st March 1994, though this was returned to the Spanish carrier in January 1997. Facing heavy losses and a lack of cash flow, VIASA was forced to cease flight operations on 23rd January 1997. The company was liquidated in March 1997.

On 26th November 1993 -30 YV-135C sustained major damage while overshooting the runway after landing at Buenos Aires' Ezeiza Airport, Argentina. VIASA determined for economic reasons not to repair the aircraft (f/n 258) and it was put into storage at Ezeiza.

When the DC-10s entered service with the airline, the paint scheme consisted of a white cabin roof, divided by a wide dark blue cheatline from the bare metal lower fuselage. The dark blue 'VIASA' and orange 'Venezuela' titles were applied above the passenger windows. The oval company 'VIASA' logo was shown on the completely orange tail section. The second livery, introduced in 1979, differed only slightly from the first one in that the oval company logo on the tail fin had been replaced by a white 'VIASA' title on the tail engine. Aircraft with the first and second livery were operated with and without the seven stars alongside the 'VIASA' title on the upper fuselage.

A new livery was first applied to -30 YV-134C in August 1996, following the pattern used by Iberia. Wide orange and dark blue bands, which flowed over the cabin roof, were applied on the white fuselage. The orange band displayed a white 'VIASA' title, while an orange 'VIASA' title was applied to all three engines. A 'Venezuela' title alongside the national flag was placed on the forward lower fuselage.

Wardair Canada

Maxwell 'Max' W Ward's charter airline took delivery of three -30s in 1978. Two examples were delivered by McDD, one was a former Singapore Airlines aircraft. At that time, the DC-10s together with three 747s formed the airline's fleet. International charters were flown to Amsterdam, Frankfurt and destinations in the UK.

In 1986 the airline started to operate domestic schedules between Vancouver, Calgary, Edmonton, Winnipeg, Toronto, Ottawa and Montreal. International schedules were offered from Vancouver, Calgary, Edmonton, Toronto and Ottawa to London, Manchester, Birmingham, Leeds, Newcastle, Cardiff and Prestwick. Further international scheduled services linked Montreal with San Juan, Puerto Rico and Puerto Plata, Dominican Republic. On 15th January 1990 the carrier was taken over by Canadian Airlines International. Prior to the merger, the three DC-10s were sold to the GPA Group during 1988 and 1989.

A blue 'Wardair' title appeared above the windows, followed by a red cheatline widening into the tail section. Below the windows a narrow line extended from the front to the rear on the white upper fuselage. To underscore the origin of the carrier the tail engine showed a 'Wardair Canada' title.

C-GFHX   S R Stan MacMillan
C-GXRB   C H Punch Dickens
C-GXRC   W R Wop May

Western Airlines

With the accent on operations in the western states, Western also operated flights to Alaska, Mexico, Honolulu, New York and Washington DC. A total of 13 DC-10-10s were acquired by the airline. Fate struck the airline when N903WA (f/n 107) was lost after landing in dense fog on the wrong runway at Mexico City 31st October 1979. A Honolulu to Anchorage to London-Gatwick service was introduced using a -10, to be replaced in 1981 by a more suitable leased Series 30, N821L. Due to poor financial results this operation was soon stopped and the aircraft returned. The end of one of the oldest US carriers came when Western was taken over by Delta Airlines on 1st April 1987.

Over the years, two basically similar liveries were applied. The original livery featured a wide red cheatline beginning with a large 'W' on a fully white fuselage, small 'Western' title on the upper forward fuselage and a large diagonal 'Western' title on the tail section. The second paint scheme had a natural metal fuselage with a red 'W'-cheatline, accentuated by black and white striping, and the diagonal 'Western' title only on the tail section.

World Airways

World Airways was founded in 1948 and developed into a noted charter airline. The carrier received the first of nine -30CFs on 7th March 1978. Domestic low fare scheduled services were offered in 1979 and scheduled international services to London, Frankfurt and Hawaii commenced in 1980. At that time the fleet consisted of three 727s, three 747Cs, one 747F, four DC-8-63CFs and nine -30CFs. The airline withdrew from scheduled flights during 1988 and continued with passenger and cargo charter operations.

The airline restarted scheduled passenger services in July 1995 from Newark to Tel Aviv and from Newark via Dakar to Johannesburg, Dublin and Shannon in June 1996. Due to poor financial results, all scheduled passenger services, as well as all charters to Europe, were dropped in August and September 1996.

World Airways is a successful lessor of aircraft to other airlines, with strong ties to Garuda Indonesia and Malaysia Airlines, and presently has a fleet of three -30, one -30CF, plus three MD-11s, one MD-11F, two MD-11CFs and two MD-11ERs. One of the three -30s, N117WA, was the last DC-10 built (f/n 446). One -30CF was lost when N113WA (f/n 320) skidded into

the harbour at Boston after landing on an icy runway on 23rd January 1982.

Over the years several different liveries have been applied. The first paint scheme displayed a broad red cheatline splitting up in a double gold and red line at the tail section. A red 'World Airways' and a 'World' title were placed on the fuselage and tail engine respectively, while the tail fin showed the red company 'globe' logo. In 1986 an all-white fuselage formed the background for a huge red and blue 'World' title in the second paint scheme, repeated on the tail engine and the stylised letter 'W' of the title was placed on the fin. Series 10 N1826U, on lease from United Airlines, featuring this livery was named *Employee One*.

In 1990 some DC-10s featured a white fuselage with a dark blue thin line starting at the nose, gradually widening to encompass the whole tail section. The stylised globe appeared in white and blue on the fin and was used in reversed colours to form the letter 'O' in the 'World' title on the fuselage.

Finnair -30 OH-LHA which was leased by World from October 1994 until August 1995 can be called a one-off. It flew in the colours of its former lessee, Express One International with added 'World' titles and logo.

The current livery has a white fuselage with a 'World' title on the cabin roof and the company globe on the fin, while the cargo aircraft carry an extra 'Cargo' title on the tail engine.

World Brazilian Air

World Brazilian Airlines was founded in December 1996 by the Brazilian partners of former Skyjet Brazil. The charter carrier leased a former Mexicana -15, N1003L, registered PP-AJN. Until delivery of this aircraft, charter flights to Miami, St Maarten and Cancun were conducted with equipment wet-leased from other carriers, eg 747s from Tower Air, DC-10s from Sun Country and TAESA and a TriStar from Air Atlanta. The Series 15 was not delivered and remained with the Greyhound Finance Corporation. World Brazilian suspended operations in March 1997.

The livery consisted of a white fuselage with a large dark blue 'World Brazilian Air' title and the company logo, a yellow sun with a stylised white bird, above the passenger windows. This theme was repeated on the dark blue wing engines. The company logo was also shown on the dark blue fin.

Zambia Airways

The airline took delivery of a new -30, initially ordered by Egypt Air, on 20th July 1984. N3016Z *Nkwazi*, leased from Chemco, was put into service on 31st July 1984 on the international routes to Frankfurt, London, Rome, New York and Bombay. A further -30, D-ADBO of Lufthansa, was to be leased through Aircraft Trading & Services. Registered 9J-AFN, the aircraft awaited delivery in Frankfurt for over half a year when financial difficulties led to the cancellation of the arrangement. Thereafter Lufthansa re-purchased the aircraft from the leasing company in July 1991. In December Zambia Airways ceased operations and N3016Z was returned to the leasing company.

Representing the colours of the nation's flag, a green, red, black and orange cheatline along the fuselage marked the airline's livery. The green line continued into the tail section where the company's logo, an orange predatory bird in the form of the letter 'Z' in an orange circle, was placed. The black 'Zambia Airways' title was located on the forward fuselage.

Omni Air International DC-10-10 N450AX at Shannon, Ireland, on a transatlantic route proving flight, 8th November 1997.
Malcolm Nason

IATA Codes of DC-10 Operators, Past and Present

To aid reference, the airline name is followed by its country of origin, plus page references in italic (sloping) characters for the illustration(s) and in roman (upright) characters for the narrative description.

Where IATA codes are not applicable, three-letter ICAO codes are given and two airlines without any designators are included for completeness.

AA	American Airlines, USA; *3, 12, 17,* 40
AF	Air France, France; *30,* 34
AH	Air Algerie, Algeria; 32
AM	Aeromexico, Mexico; *27,* 28
AQ	Aloha Airlines, USA; *34,* 39
AY	Finnair, Finland; *49, 51,* 60
AZ	Alitalia, Italy; *34,* 39
BA	British Airways, UK; *37, 38,* 42
BB	Balair, Switzerland; *36,* 40
BG	Biman Bangladesh AL, Bangladesh; *36, 37,* 41
BR	British Caledonian Airways, UK; *38,* 45
BX	Spantax, Spain; *78,* 90
CAP	Capitol International Airways, USA; *44,* 50
CHG	ChallengAir, Belgium; *44,* 50
CI	China Airlines, Taiwan; 50
CO	Continental Airlines, USA; *17, 45, 46, 51*
CP	CP Air/Canadian Airlines Int'l, Canada; *42, 43, 49,* 50
CU	Cubana, Cuba; *46,* 55
DD	AeroLyon, France; *26,* 27
DE	Condor Flug (as of 1990), Germany; *20, 44, 45,* 50
DF	Condor Flug (until 1990); see above
DK	Scanair, Sweden; *75,* 89
DK	Premiair, Denmark; *73, 74,* 87
DL	Delta Air Lines, USA; *47,* 55
DO	Dominicana de Aviacion, Dominica; *47,* 57
EA	Eastern Airlines, USA; *47,* 59
EG	Japan Asia Airways, Japan; *55, 56,* 65
EN	Cal Air International, UK; *38,* 46
EN	Novair International Airways, UK; *69,* 82
EO	Express One International, USA; *49,* 50
EU	Ecuatoriana, Ecuador; *48,* 59
EXC	Excalibur Airways, UK; 60
FG	Ariana Afghan Airlines, Afghanistan; *35,* 40
FI	Icelandair-Loftleidir, Iceland; *35,* 65
FJ	Air Pacific, Fiji; *32,* 39
FM	Federal Express (until July 1996), USA; see FX
FS	STAF, Argentina; *79,* 90
FX	Fed' Express (July 1996 on), USA; *23, 49,* 60
GA	Garuda Indonesian, Indonesia; *51,* 61
GD	TAESA, Mexico; *80,* 94
GH	Ghana Airways, Ghana; *52,* 64
GK	Laker Airways, UK; *59,* 71
GR	Gemini Air Cargo, USA; *51, 52,* 63

HA	Hawaiian Air, USA; *53,* 65
HM	Air Seychelles, Seychelles; *33,* 39
HP	Air Hawaii, USA; *30,* 35
HT	Air Tchad, Chad; 39
IB	Iberia, Spain; *53,* 65
IJ	Air Liberté, France; *31,* 36
IQ	Caribbean Airways, Barbados; *44,* 50
IW	Minerve, France; *66,* 81
IW	AOM French Airlines, France; *31, 32,* 36
JB	British Caledonian Air Charter, UK; *41,* 45
JD	Japan Air System, Japan; *55,* 65
JL	Japan Air Lines, Japan; *14, 54,* 65
JU	Jugoslovenski AT, Yugoslavia; *56, 57,* 68
JW	Arrow Air, USA; *35,* 40
JZ	Japan Air Charter, Japan; *55,* 65
J6	Avcom Aviation Commercial, Russi; *36,* 40
KE	Korean Air Lines, S Korea; *58,* 71
KG	Caledonian Airways, UK; *41,* 47
KL	KLM Royal Dutch Airlines, Netherlands *57,* 70
KQ	Kenya Airways, Kenya; 68
KT	Birgenair, Turkey; *37,* 41
KU	Kuwait Airways, Kuwait; *59,* 71
LA	LAN Chile, Chile; *61,* 71
LH	Lufthansa, Germany; *1, 2, 62, rear cover,* 74
LO	LOT Polskie Linie Lotnicze, Poland; *62,* 74
L8	Leisure Air, USA; *61,* 72
MH	Malaysian Airline System, Malaysia; *63,* 76
MP	Martinair Holland, Netherlands; *64,* 78
MS	Egypt Air, Egypt; 60
MT	Flying Colours Airlines, UK; 61
MX	Mexicana, Mexico *64, 66,* 80
NA	National Airlines, USA *67,* 81
NG	Lauda Air, Austria; 71
NO	Atlantis, Germany; *35,* 40
NW	Northwest Orient/ Northwest, USA; *68, 69,* 81
NZ	Air New Zealand, New Zealand; *31,* 37
OP	Air Panama, Panama; *32,* 39
OV	Overseas National Airways, USA; *70,* 84
PA	Pan American World Airways, USA; *72,* 84
PE	Air Europe, Italy; *29;* 33
PK	Pakistan Int'l Airlines, Pakistan; *70, 72,* 84
PL	Aero Peru, Peru; *27,* 30
PN	Air Martinique, Martinique; *31,* 36
PQ	Bogaziçi Hava Tasimaciligi, Turkey; *37,* 42
PR	Philippine Airlines, Philippines; *72, 73,* 84
PU	PLUNA, Uruguay; *73,* 84
PZ	Lineas Aéreas Paraguayas, Paraguay; *62,* 73
QC	Air Zaire, Zaire; *33, 34,* 39
QF	Qantas, Australia; 88
QH	Air Florida, USA; *29, 30,* 33
QK	Aéromaritime, France; *26,* 27
QN	Air Outre Mer, France; 37
QSC	African Safari Airways, Switzerland; *28,* 30
QZ	Zambia Airways, Zambia; *96,* 98
RE	Aerocancun, Mexico; *26, 26*
RG	VARIG, Brazil; *87, 88,* 97
RI	Mandala Airlines, Indonesia; 77

RK	Air Afrique, Ivory Coast; *28,* 32
RO	Tarom, Romania; *82,* 94
SB	Seaboard World, USA,; *76,* 89
SD	Sudan Airways, Sudan; 90
SE	DAS Air Cargo, UK; *47,* 55
SK	Scandinavian Airlines System, Sweden; *76,* 89
SKA	Skyjet Brazil – World Brazilian Airlines, Brazil; *78,* 90, *95,* 98
SKJ	Skyjet Antigua, Antigua; 90
SKT	Skyjet Belgium, Belgium; *78,* 90
SL	Transtar Airlines, USA; *83,* 95
SM	Taino Airlines, Dominica; *80,* 94 -
SN	Sabena, Belgium; *74, 75,* 88
SQ	Singapore Airlines, Singapore; *77,* 90
SR	Swissair, Switzerland; *25, 80, 93 -*
SS	Corsair, France; *46,* 54
SS	Shabair, Zaire; *77,* 90
SU	Aeroflot Russian Int'l Airlines, Russia; *26, 26*
SV	Saudi Arabian Airlines, Saudi Arabia; 89
SY	Sun Country Airlines. USA; *79,* 90
S3	Sobelair, Belgium; 90
TG	Thai Airways Int'l, Thailand; *82,* 94
TK	Turk Hava Yollari, Turkey; *85,* 96
TM	Linhas Aéreas de Mocambique, Mozambique; *61,* 73
TP	TAP Air Portugal, Portugal; 94
TU	Tunisair, Tunisia; 96
TV	Trans Int'l Airlines/Transamerica, USA; *83,* 95
TX	Air Guadeloupe, Guadeloupe; *30,* 35
TZ	American Trans Air, USA; *34,* 40
T8	TransAer Int'l Airways, Ireland; 94
UA	United Airlines, USA; *13, 14, 85, 86,* 96
UN	Transaero Airlines, Russia; *82,* 94
UT	Union de Transports Aériens, France; *87,* 97
VA	VIASA, Venezuela; *91,* 97
VP	VASP, Brazil; *88,* 97
WA	Western Airlines, USA; *92,* 98
WD	Wardair Canada, Canada; *92,* 97
WE	Challenge Air Cargo, USA; 50
WO	World Airways, USA; *93, 95,* 98
WT	Nigeria Airways, Nigeria; *67,* 81
X9	Omni Air Express, Omni Air Int'l, USA; 84 , *98*
YV	Air Siam, Thailand; *33,* 39
ZA	USAF – internal McDD code
ZB	Monarch Airlines, UK; *67,* 81
ZM	Scibe Airlift Zaire, Zaire; *76,* 89
ZN	Key Airlines, USA; *57,* 68
ZU	ARCA Colombia, Colombia; 40
2J	Jet 24 Int'l Charter Service, USA; *56,* 66
3F	African West-Air, Senegal; *28,* 31
6F	Laker Airways, USA; *59,* 71
6P	Pacific East Air, USA; *70,* 84
7B	Kras Air - Krasnoyarsk AL, Russia; *58,* 71
9H	Okada Air, Nigeria; *69,* 82
9P	Transmile Air Services, Thailand; 95
–	Air America, USA; *28,* 32
–	The Hawaii Express, USA; *82,* 94

On 3rd November 1997, Munich Airport was the scene of an emergency exercise in which over 1,000 employees of the airport, Federal Border Guard, Federal Armed Forces, police, rescue services and other organisations took part. DC-10 D-ADPO was supplied by Condor for the exercise, which included a simulated emergency landing with an actual evacuation of 350 'passengers' – from the Border Guard and Armed Forces. The airline involved carried the fictitious name 'Trans Bavarian Airlines'. The evacuation took place over the smaller slide at door No.1 and the larger slides at door Nos.2 and 4 on the starboard side. The emergency slides, which can be used as rafts in an emergency ditching, are described in Chapter Two. Transport of the 'casualties' to surrounding hospitals also was a challenge of logistics with the deployment of over 200 emergency and rescue vehicles, as well as eight helicopters. Photo Christofer Witt

Hughes Aircraft Company / Raytheon

Hughes Aircraft Company (HAC) was a subsidiary of the Hughes Electronics Corporation which in turn is owned by General Motors (GM).

On 16th January 1997, GM, Hughes and Raytheon, announced their plan to spin off HAC after which it would merge with Raytheon. This was approved on 2nd October 1997 and completed at the end of the year.

HAC, an acknowledged leader in missile, sensor and information systems, had three primary business segments. Sensors and Communications Systems, including work in space, airborne and surface-based radars; lasers, infra-red and other sensors; and military communications. The Weapons Systems segment was responsible for numerous cruise missile and tactical programmes and shipboard display and control systems. Third was Information Systems, focusing HAC's expertise in building complex software-intensive systems for command and control, air defence, training and simulation and intelligence gathering.

Following the merger, a new company, named Raytheon Systems, headquartered at Washington DC, was formed, combining the operations of Hughes with those of Raytheon Electronic Systems, Raytheon E-Systems and Raytheon TI Systems.

In September 1995 HAC acquired former American Airlines DC-10-10 N124AA, which had been withdrawn from use and stored at Marana, Arizona, since February of that year, from the GATX Capital Corporation. The aircraft was re-registered N910SF and named *Sweet Judy*. After extensive modifications, the DC-10 left Los Angeles for an unknown location in May 1997. Most notable on the flying test-bed is the enormous bulge on the forward port side of the fuselage and a smaller fairing just aft of the nose gear assembly. No further details are available.

The military-like paint scheme consists of a white upper and light grey lower fuselage divided by a thin blue cheatline. A small US flag is displayed on the white tail fin.

NMB Air Operations Corporation

Minebea Technologies Pte, Ltd, is a joint venture of NMB Nippon Miniature Ballbearing Co and NHBB New Hampshire Ball Bearings Inc. The private company conducts non-commercial corporate flights between Singapore and Japan. Formerly 707 N707MB was operated but this aircraft was replaced with former Sabena -30CF OO-SLB in August 1994. It received the appropriate registration N10MB.

A red pinstripe separates the dark blue belly from the first light blue cheatline. Another light blue line starts on the white upper fuselage and widens up into the tail. The name 'Minebea' appears in dark blue on the forward fuselage, while 'NMB' in white is displayed on the fin. The DC-10 is based at Singapore-Changi Airport.

Orbis International

A subject in itself, it is covered in Chapter Four – opposite.

Undoubtedly the world's most mysterious DC-10, Hughes Aircraft Company's (now Raytheon Systems) flying test-bed N910SF at Los Angeles International Airport. Derek Hellmann

Private operator Minebea Technologies acquired DC-10-30CF N10MB from Sabena. Exavia

Flying Eye Hospital

Orbis International replaced its ageing DC-8 flying eye surgery hospital with DC-10-10 N220AU in 1994. The aircraft with its team of doctors and nurses bring back eyesight to the curable blind in countries around the world.
Orbis International

Orbis International started operations in 1982 as Project Orbis, a neutral and voluntary organisation with the aim of sharing the gift of knowledge and the dedication to bringing eyesight to many who have lived in darkness most of their lives. The New York-based organisation is funded by donations and gifts from corporations, foundations and individuals and by a grant from the United States Agency for International Development.

Until 1994, the main vehicle for Orbis' work was the world's only fully-equipped surgical teaching facility inside an aircraft, DC-8-21 N220RB which was donated by United Airlines. Between 1982 and 1994 missions were flown to more than 70 countries. During this period the medical team on board worked side-by-side with 28,000 doctors and nurses and restored sight directly to 18,000 people. In May 1994,

after 12 years of service with Orbis, the 33 year old DC-8 retired to the China Air Museum at Datanshan, near Beijing, China.

Through the donations of Hong Kong businessman Ho Ying-Chie and FlightSafety International President Albert L Ueltschi, a founder and chairman of Orbis, a DC-10-10 was bought from the Rank Organisation. The aircraft began as any other commercial airliner, flying passengers to destinations around the world for business or pleasure. The Orbis aircraft was the second DC-10 to roll off the production line at Long Beach. After having served as a flight test aircraft as N101AA and N10DC, it was sold to Laker on 3rd June 1977 becoming G-BELO *Southern Belle*. The aircraft was also operated by American Trans Air, Air Hawaii and Cal Air (renamed Novair International Airways) until the Rank Organisation closed down the charter operations of the latter carrier.

Numerous reasons led to the purchase of the DC-10. Reliability, availability of spare parts, operating and maintenance costs, an airframe young enough to provide 70 years of service and of course the greatly expanded capacity played a key role.

When the aircraft was bought on 26th

November 1991 it had only 35,491 flight hours and 10,266 landings to its name. Orbis took the unusual step of becoming its own prime contractor for the conversion project which took over two years to be completed. The work was done by Aerospace Engineering at Mobile, Alabama. The Schwartz Engineering Company of San Antonio, Texas, and Avionics Engineering Services of Tucson, Arizona, were selected by Orbis for structural and electrical work as well as Federal Aviation Administration certification services.

McDonnell Douglas actively supported the project. Technical data and maintenance information were provided by the Design & Technology and Product Support staff. Douglas Aircraft Distribution and Spares granted Orbis access to spare parts. Contractual Data provided proprietary data involving stress and load analysis to bring the Orbis design to completion within budget. In a great gesture, several Douglas engineers volunteered hundreds of off-duty hours.

During the conversion, the aircraft was completely gutted from the top of the vertical stabiliser to the bottom of the airframe hull, steam cleaned and repainted where appropriate. New hydraulic, electrical, pneumatic, environmental and air conditioning systems were installed. The airframe was modified and floor panels strengthened to minimise vibrations, an Orbis requirement to secure the safest possible laser eye operations. Special features of the new flying hospital include a water purification system, an auxiliary air conditioning and an oxygen generation system.

Based on the experience of the DC-8 operation, a team of medical doctors, engineers and technicians, constructed a styrofoam mock-up to be placed in the empty DC-10 cabin in order to obtain a perfect layout. Runge Industries of Sulphur Springs, Texas, carried out the installation of the final interior-design.

A 52 seat classroom is located at the front and is equipped with an interactive video system. An adjacent audio-visual studio can transmit surgery being performed to the classroom and conference room. For teaching purposes 12 cameras have been installed throughout the aircraft. A three-station examination and laser room is followed by a conference area which has glass partitions towards the operational theatre. The patient preparation and recovery room is located next to the operating room. Finally, a communications centre finds its place at the rear of the aircraft. An advantage over the DC-8 is the hallway extending along the left side of the fuselage enabling separate entrances to the different areas.

The all-white fuselage shows the blue 'Orbis' title and a small red cross. The stylised Orbis emblem, two white hands protecting an eye within a blue circle, is displayed on the tail fin.

The DC-10, N220AU, now a fully equipped eye surgery hospital and training facility, took to the sky on 23rd July 1994 for a three-week mission to Beijing, China. Further missions were flown to Myanmar, Sudan, Bulgaria, Romania, Latvia. Lithuania, Peru and El Sal-vador. For 1996 the programme included destinations in India, China, Bangladesh, Mongolia, Cameroon, Ethiopia and Sudan.

Orbis continued its fight against blindness in 1997. Besides land-based regional training centres carrying out programmes in, for example Taiyuan, Shanxi Province, China and Hyderabad, India, Orbis staged 'SightFlight' programmes in Bulgaria, China, Myanmar, Syria and Uzbekistan, among others. The first DC-10 mission in 1998 was flown to Dhaka, Bangladesh.

Former chief pilot Captain Jack Race said, 'The spirit of Orbis is to love one's neighbour – the world – through the gift of healing'. Playing a major role in this spirit is the DC-10.

This extraordinary aircraft will carry more than its international medical team. It will carry hope and sight to millions worldwide who are curably blind.

N220AU was the second DC-10 built, originally used as a flight test aircraft and delivered to Laker Airways in 1977. Orbis International

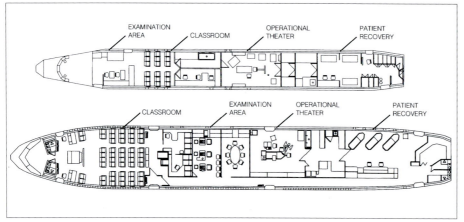

Comparative graphics of the Orbis DC-8 and DC-10 indicate the enormous increase in working area in the latter aircraft. The passage-way alongside the left side of the DC-10 fuselage is a major advantage. Orbis International

Chapter Five

Global Reach
Tanker/Transports

US Air Force KC-10A Extender 79-1711 is shown accompanying the US Navy 'Blue Angels' flight demonstration team on a transcontinental mission. Another Douglas product, the A-4F Skyhawk was the team's demonstrator for 13 years. McDonnell Douglas

Douglas' experience in aerial refuelling goes back a long time. In early 1929, two Douglas C-1s refuelled a Fokker C-2 tri-motor, keeping it aloft for seven days. It was not until 1948 that aerial refuelling as a means of extending the range of fighters and bombers as part of day-to-day operations was introduced with the conversion of Boeing B-29 Superfortresses into KB-29M flying tankers. Following the KB-29 came the more advanced KB-50 and then Boeing modified the C-97 Stratofreighter into the KC-97 tanker which provided the backbone until the military variant of the 707 jetliner – the KC-135 Stratotanker – entered US Air Force (USAF) service in large numbers. (For a detailed examination of US aerial refuelling see the Aerofax title, *Boeing KC-135 Stratotanker – More Than Just a Tanker* by Robert S Hopkins.) The KC-135 was the *original* Boeing Model 717 – see page 125.

Operation 'Nickel Grass', the emergency resupply of Israel during the 1973 Yom Kippur War, sorely tested US airlift capability, both in terms of capacity and aerial refuelling. Unlike the Lockheed C-5A Galaxy, the C-141A Starlifter could not be refuelled in flight. It was then decided to stretch the Lockheed C-141s and at the same time add the refuelling capability, producing the C-141B.

As a longer term measure, the USAF decided to purchase an Advanced Tanker Cargo Aircraft (ATCA). Both McDonnell Douglas and Boeing were in the running for an order. Although Lockheed might have had a contender with a military version of the L-1011, they did not participate in the programme.

The Boeing proposal was based on the 747 and was initially referred to as the 747MF/T (Military Freighter/Tanker), later the 747 ATCA. This offered an aerial refuelling 'flying' boom (the USAF's chosen system of aerial refuelling) and wing-mounted hose drum unit refuelling systems (the system adopted by the US Navy and Marines, the Royal Air Force in the UK and many other air forces). With the additional large capacity for personnel and freight available on the upper deck, Boeing thought they had the ideal aircraft on offer.

This was not the case; on 19th December 1977, the decision in favour of the McDonnell Douglas proposal was announced. Despite the fact that the KC-10A Extender (as it was designated and named) could not match the capacity of the 747 ATCA, the advantage that the aircraft

could lift off with a maximum load from airfields with shorter runways had played a major role in the decision. The company received an initial order for 12 KC-10As, a derivative of the DC-10-30CF. In all 60 Extenders were eventually procured.

KC-10A Serial Blocks

79-0433	to	79-0434	– 2 aircraft
79-1710	to	79-1713	– 4 aircraft
79-1946	to	79-1951	– 6 aircraft
82-0190	to	82-0193	– 4 aircraft
83-0075	to	83-0082	– 8 aircraft
84-0185	to	84-0192	– 8 aircraft
85-0027	to	85-0034	– 8 aircraft
86-0027	to	86-0038	– 12 aircraft
87-0117	to	87-0124	– 8 aircraft
			total 60 aircraft

The KC-10A made its first flight on 12th July 1980 and the first aircraft were delivered to Barksdale Air Force Base (AFB), Louisiana, in March 1981. They featured the original attractive livery with a white roof, a light grey belly, a blue cheatline and a blue nose section used on early aircraft. Later aircraft were delivered in a green-grey camouflage scheme that is now being replaced with an overall mid-grey.

Barksdale AFB was the home of the 2nd Bombardment Wing (BW) comprising the 32nd Air Refueling Squadron (ARS) and associate 78th ARS of the Air Force Reserve (AFRES). The 722nd Air Refueling Wing (ARW) at March AFB, California, was the second wing to receive the KC-10A for its 9th ARS and AFRES associate, the 79th ARS. Of the early bases, the 68th ARW at Seymour-Johnson AFB, North Carolina, was the last recipient of KC-10As, assigned to the 334th, 911th and its AFRES associate, the 77th ARS.

The 60 Extenders were equally divided over the three bases, although one aircraft, 82-0190 (fuselage number 382) was destroyed by fire at Barksdale AFB on 17th September 1987.

On 1st June 1992 Air Mobility Command (AMC) at Scott AFB, Illinois, was formed from the assets of Strategic Air Command and Military Airlift Command. As America's 'Global Reach Team', AMC provides aerial refuelling, airlift, aeromedical evacuation and combat rescue for all of America's armed forces. It further continues a tradition of humanitarian airlift support at home and around the world.

AMC's agency for centralised command and control, the Tanker Airlift Control Center is responsible for scheduling and tracking strategic tanker and airlift resources worldwide. Air Force and Department of Defense support taskings are channelled through this state-of-the-art hub of Mobility Control. AMC assigns its active duty resources to two Air Forces, the 15th at Travis AFB, California, and the 21st at McGuire AFB, New Jersey. The command has ten US bases in addition to its headquarters and has a presence at almost 100 bases worldwide. AMC's strategic mobility aircraft include the McDonnell Douglas C-9 Nightingale, C-17 Globemaster III, Lockheed C-5 Galaxy, C-141 Starlifter, Boeing KC-135 Stratotanker and the KC-10A Extender.

Following the creation of AMC, restructuring included the assignment of the KC-10A fleet to only one west coast and one east coast AFB. The 305th Air Mobility Wing (AMW) at McGuire AFB, New Jersey, became a KC-10 base in October 1994 when the first aircraft were transferred from Barksdale AFB, Louisiana, and Seymour-Johnson AFB, North Carolina. The 2nd and 32nd ARS each operate 16 KC-10As. The aircraft are also flown by crews of the 76th and 78th ARS, AFRES.

Known as the 'Gateway to the Pacific', Travis AFB, California, is the west coast KC-10 base. The 60th AMW is the largest and busiest base in the Air Mobility Command, operating half of the command's C-5 Galaxy fleet and a sixth of

the C-141 Starlifter fleet. During 1994 and 1995, the 60th AMW received 13 and 14 aircraft respectively for its 6th and 9th ARS. The KC-10s of the active squadrons are also flown by crews of the 70th and 79th ARS AFRES units.

The addition of the KC-10A Extenders further solidified the wing's prominence as the largest airlift wing in the USAF and the centrepiece of AMC. Fulfilling AMC's primary mission of rapid, global mobility and sustainment for America's armed forces, the KC-10s are the lifeline of 'Global Reach'.

KC-10A Disposition (as of late 1997)

60th AMW, Travis AFB
– 6th ARS and 9th ARS
79-1946, 79-1947, 79-1948, 79-1950, 79-1951, 82-0191, 82-0192, 82-0193, 83-0076, 83-0077, 83-0078, 83-0080, 84-0185, 84-0187, 84-0189, 84-0191, 85-0029, 86-0029, 86-0031, 86-0032, 86-0033, 86-0036, 86-0037, 86-0038, 87-0117, 87-0118, 87-0119.

305th AMW, McGuire AFB
– 2nd ARS and 32nd ARS
79-0433, 79-0434, 79-1710, 79-1711, 79-1712, 79-1713, 79-1949, 83-0075, 83-0079, 83-0081, 83-0082, 84-0186, 84-0188, 84-0190, 84-0192, 85-0027, 85-0028, 85-0030, 85-0031, 85-0032, 85-0033, 85-0034, 86-0027, 86-0028, 86-0030, 86-0034, 86-0035, 87-0120, 87-0121, 87-0122, 87-0123, 87-0124.

KC-10 Described

With the KC-10A the USAF not only obtained an aircraft fulfilling its task as an aerial refuelling tanker but could also haul 170,000lb (7,711kg) of equipment. Up to 27 pallets can be accommodated inside the cargo compartment. If necessary 75 seats for support personnel can be installed in the forward section. In this case, 146,000lb (66,225kg) of cargo on 17 pallets can be transported.

The pallets can be loaded through the large 140in x 102in (3.56m x 2.59m) port side cargo door. Loading and unloading of heavy equipment is facilitated by powered rollers and winches inside the cargo compartment.

Whereas the Boeing KC-135 can only be fitted on ground with either a refuelling boom or an aerial hose and drogue system, the KC-10A carries both a centreline aerial refuelling boom and an aerial hose and drogue system on the port side of the fuselage. By employing either system the KC-10 can refuel a wide variety of USAF, US Navy, US Marine Corps aircraft as well as aircraft from allied nations on the same mission.

Unlike most KC-135s, the KC-10A has a receptacle allowing it to be refuelled in flight by a KC-135 or another KC-10A, so increasing its delivery range or time-on-station. With a fuel capacity of 356,000lb (16,148kg), the KC-10A carries nearly twice as much fuel as the Stratotanker. In addition to the wing and centre wing area fuel tanks, the KC-10A has two large

fuel tanks under the cargo floor, one in the forward lower cargo compartment and one in the aft lower cargo compartment. The forward and the aft tank consist of three and four bladder cells respectively. Each cell has a separate access for maintenance and inspection via the bottom of the fuselage.

The aerial refuelling operator (ARO) station is located at the rear of the aircraft and provides seating for the operator, an instructor and a student or an observer. Compared to the KC-135, the working area is far more comfortable and includes state-of-the-art control systems. The hand controls for the aerial refuelling boom are located at the operator's armrests with the instructor's controls positioned on a special console. A large window allows the boom operator to monitor the refuelling process.

The advanced refuelling boom can transfer 1,200 US gallons (4,542 litres) per minute to the receiving aircraft and is controlled by the operator by means of a digital fly-by-wire system. The separate hose and drogue unit (HDU) system has a flow rate of over 600 US gallons per minute (2,271 litres), exceeding that of any in-service system and matching the requirement of the most demanding receiver.

With an 88% systems commonality with the commercial DC-10, the KC-10 benefits significantly from the available worldwide commercial support system. Besides material available from subcontracted airlines, Douglas as well as the engine manufacturer maintain spare parts inventories and service personnel at selected locations around the world.

During Operations 'Desert Shield' and 'Desert Storm' the KC-10A proved to be a reliable tanker/cargo aircraft. In the early stages of 'Desert Shield', inflight refuelling was the key to rapid airlift of material and forces. In addition to refuelling airlift aircraft, the KC-10, along with the smaller KC-135, moved thousands of tons of cargo and thousands of troops in support of the massive Persian Gulf build-up.

During 'Desert Storm', inflight refuelling extended the range and capability of all US and Coalition warplanes. Air operations continued without the costly and time-consuming ground refuelling. KC-10A and the KC-135 tankers conducted about 51,700 separate refuelling operations and delivered 125 million gallons of fuel to US and Coalition forces aircraft, without missing a single scheduled rendezvous.

Photographs on the opposite page:

An early flight demonstration with McDonnell Douglas A-4B Skyhawk N905MD (previously US Navy 142905 and used as a 'chase plane') proved smaller aircraft could safely fly in trail of the wide-body trijet, a necessary step before offering the DC-10 to the USAF ATCA competition. Note the calibration markings under the tailplanes and the rear fuselage. McDonnell Douglas

Accompanied by a Boeing KC-135, a Lockheed C-5A Galaxy is refuelled by the KC-10A during compatibility assessment. McDonnell Douglas

Above : **Both KLu KDC-10s, T-235 *Jan Scheffer* and T-264 *Prins Bernhard*, on a joint mission.** Koninklijke Luchtmacht, Eindhoven AFB Public Affairs

Below: **The Royal Netherlands Air Force is the world's first air force to deploy the KDC-10. T-264 *Prins Bernhard* over the North Sea with KLu Lockheed Martin F-16A and F-16B Fighting Falcon fighters.** Koninklijke Luchtmacht, Eindhoven AFB Public Affairs

The 60th and final KC-10 delivered to the USAF (on 29th November 1988) was the first aircraft to be equipped with removable wingtip Flight Refuelling (Cobham) Mk.32B HDUs. In this case, up to three US Navy or NATO aircraft can connect refuelling probes into the funnel-shape devices ('baskets') to receive fuel. Under a recent modification programme, 20 KC-10As have been fitted with these wing-mounted HDUs to further enhance refuelling capabilities. The wing-mounted refuelling pods are in addition to the existing centreline refuelling boom and separate refuelling hose which make the KC-10 the most versatile tanker ever to fly. The maximum delivery flow rate from the wing pods is 600 US gallons (2,271 litres) per minute.

KC-10A Specification

Capacity		
Passengers/Cargo	27 pallets or	
	75 passengers and 17 pallets	
Max cargo payload	170,000lb	77,112kg
Max fuel load	356,000lb	161,481kg
Dimensions		
Wingspan	165ft 4in	50.39m
Length	181ft 7in	55.35m
Height	58ft 1in	17.7m
Cargo door	140in x 102in	3.56m x 2.59m
Engines	Three GE F103-GE-100	
Take-off thrust	52,500lb st	233.5kN each
Weights		
Empty	240,065lb	108,891kg
Maximum take-off	590,000lb	267,624kg
Performance		
Max speed at		
25,000ft (7,620m)	610mph	982km/h
Cruise at		
30,000ft (9,145m)	564mph	908km/h
Range		
Ferry range	11,500 miles	18,507km
Max range with		
max payload	4,370 miles	7,032km
Crew	Pilot, Co-pilot, Flight Engineer and Boom Operator	

KDC-10 – Dutch Global Reach

The Gulf War taught many lessons, and to several of the Coalition forces it showed chronic deficiencies in airlift and tanker capability. (In early 1991 even the UK's Royal Air Force had to lease a Sabena DC-10-30CF to help out with its airlift capacity to and from the Gulf – see Chapter Three.) The first European country to react to this was the Netherlands, whose air force, the Koninklijke Luchtmacht (KLu), acquired two DC-10-30CFs from the Dutch airline Martinair Holland in 1995.

The aircraft were converted to the tanker configuration and are equipped with the centreline boom refuelling system. The conversion was carried out at KLM's Amsterdam Schiphol Airport facilities and the project was supported by McDonnell Douglas. Since the full-passenger/cargo conversion capability is maintained, the aircraft received the appropriate designation KDC-10'. Depending on operational requirements the aircraft can be used in the full cargo or all passenger configuration, or in three different passenger/pallet configurations.

Both are assigned to the 334th Squadron at Eindhoven, greatly enhancing the capabilities of the transport unit who also operate Fokker 50s and 60Us, a Gulfstream IV and Lockheed C-130H-30 Hercules.

The KLu is the world's first (and so far, only) air force to operate the KDC-10. Based upon used DC-10-30s, McDonnell Douglas offered the tanker/transport modification with improvements in tanker technology. The KDC-10 is equipped with an advanced air refuelling boom which has been increased in length and has a larger manoeuvring envelope. The refuelling boom can transfer a maximum of 1,500 US gallons (5,678 litres) per minute to the receiver. As is the case with the KC-10, the KDC-10 can be equipped with two independent wing-mounted HDUs, with a maximum flow rate of 600 US gallons (2,271 litres) per minute each.

Unlike the KC-10A, the KDC-10 has a boom operator station which is located on the main deck, just behind the cockpit. The Remote Aerial Refuelling Operator (RARO) system reduces the complexity of the modification while improving the boom operator's mission effectiveness. By means of the cameras located in a fairing just forward of the boom, the boom operator obtains a three-dimensional view of the refuelling process on video monitors. For HDU refuelling operations from the optional wing pods, the cameras provide the operator with a wing tip to wing tip view.

A sophisticated lighting system has been installed to guide the receiving aircraft to the refuelling boom. A row of red, white and green lights are located at each side of the lower rear fuselage. Whereas the right row of lights indicates the pilot to go up or down, the left row signals the pilot to fly to the left or to the right, or fly steady behind the tanker.

An important feature of the militarised jetliners is the high commonality with Federal Aviation Administration (FAA) certified commercial equivalents. The certification ensures ready availability of a worldwide network of FAA-approved repair stations and a large supply of common, commercial spare parts.

Despite the fact that the livery of the RNLAF KDC-10s has been kept low profile, it nevertheless is quite attractive. The white upper and light grey lower fuselage has a blue cheatline which extends from the front to the rear. The title 'Royal Netherlands Air Force' alongside the Dutch flag appear above the passenger windows. The RNLAF roundel, which is based on the colours of the national flag, is displayed on the tail engine while the aircraft serial number is placed on the tail fin (T-235 and T-264 derived from the fuselage numbers). T-264 is named *Prins Bernhard*, T-235 *Jan Scheffer*.

With the KDC-10, the KLu is able to transport personnel and material to a crisis area within a short period of time. At the same, the accompanying KLu General Dynamics (now Lockheed Martin) F-16 Fighting Falcons can be refuelled.

Besides an increase in transport capacity, the acquisition of the KDC-10s has an environmentally beneficial effect. Aerial refuelling enables the F-16s to extend training missions over the North Sea, significantly reducing the number of take-offs and landings, and thus limiting noise pollution in the surroundings of the air force bases. If necessary, the KDC-10s are used to refuel aircraft of other air forces.

Since the aircraft have been placed in service, they have been subject to a heavy schedule. During 1996 the KDC-10s were deployed in eastern Canada when the KLu, together with Canadian forces, took part in exercise 'Maple Flag', as well as in the Nevada desert, Arizona, for a combined exercise of Dutch, Belgian, Danish and Norwegian forces. Further missions included the transport of troops and equipment to Curacao, Haiti, Italy, Norway and Yugoslavia.

Besides its task as the transport squadron of the KLu, performing flights for the Ministry of Defense and other ministries, the 334th has a high standing of conducting humanitarian aid, disaster relief and medical evacuation flights for the United Nations, the International Red Cross, Médicins sans Frontières (Doctors without Borders) and many other private organisations. From the beginning of the crisis in former Yugoslavia, the squadron played an important role in transporting UN military personnel and relief goods and evacuating sick and wounded persons. The KDC-10s will also play an important role in such operations in the future.

KDC-10 Specification

Capacity		
Passengers	335	
Passengers/Cargo	110 / 170 / 240 passengers / pallet combination	
Cargo	22 pallets total	
Max cargo payload	151,000lb	68,494kg
Dimensions		
Wingspan	165ft 4in	50.39m
Length	181ft 7in	55.35m
Height	58ft 1in	17.70m
Cargo door	140in x 102in	3.56m x 2.59m
Engines	Three GE CF6-50C2s or three GE CF6-50C2B* turbofans	
Take-off thrust:	52,500lb	233.5kN each
or	54,000lb	240kN* each
Weights		
Max take-off	565,000lb	256,284kg
Empty*	257,000lb	116,575kg
Max fuel load	306,000lb	138,801kg
Crew	Pilot, Co-pilot, Flight Engineer and Boom Operator / Loadmaster	

* Tanker configuration with supplemental fuel tanks, centreline boom, wing pods, no cargo handling equipment

Lockheed Martin F-117A Nighthawk 'stealth' fighter refuels from KC-10A 84-0191 during type compatibility trials. March Air Force Base

A Northrop B-2A Spirit 'stealth' bomber ready to make the connection with KC-10A 79-1951. March AFB Public Affairs

A Boeing B-52 is refuelled by the first KC-10A tanker. Note the F-4 Phantom II 'chase plane' in the background. McDonnell Douglas

Photographs on the opposite page:

A March KC-10A with the San Francisco-Oakland Bay Bridge in the background March AFB

Ramp scene at the 68th Air Refueling Wing at Seymour-Johnson AFB. Seymour-Johnson AFB

McDonnell Douglas KC-10A Extender

1. Radome
2. Weather scanner radar
3. Radar mounting
4. Front pressure bulkhead
5. Radome hinge panel
6. Windscreen wipers
7. Windscreen panels
8. Instrument panel shroud
9. Control column
10. Rudder pedals
11. Underfloor radio and electronics racks
12. Flight deck floor level
13. Pilot's seat
14. Overhead systems control
15. Flight engineer's control panel
16. Observer's seat
17. Cockpit doorway
18. Refuelling floodlighting
19. Universal air refuelling receptacle
20. Toilet compartment
21. Crew baggage locker
22. Galley
23. Air condition ram air intake duct
24. Entry doorway
25. Air conditioning system access panels
26. Nose undercarriage leg strut
27. Twin nosewheels
28. Nosewheel leg doors
29. Air conditioning plant
30. Passenger seating, six crew and 14 support personnel
31. Forward cabin roof trim panels
32. Upper formation light
33. IFF aerial
34. Overhead air conditioning ducting
35. Environmental curtain
36. Cargo winch
38. Cargo safety net
39. Powered cargo handling system control box
40. Low voltage formation lighting strip
41. Underfloor oxygen bottle stowage
42. Powered roller cargo handling floor
43. Underfloor water tank
44. Door hydraulic jack
45. Cargo door
46. TACAN aerial
47. VHF aerial
48. Starboard engine nacelle
49. UHF SATCOM aerial, structural provision
50. USAF 463L cargo pallet, 25 pallets in configuration illustration
51. Main cabin doorway
52. Forward underfloor fuel cell group
53. Fuselage frame and stringer construction
54. Director lights, port and starboard
55. Wing root fillet
56. Runway light

57. Electrical system distribution equipment centre
58. Access ladder to equipment bay
59. Central slat drive unit
60. Wing centre section carry-through
61. Single cabin window, port and starboard
62. Centre section fuel tank, aircraft basic fuel system
63. Floor beam construction
64. Wing spar / fuselage main frame
65. Overwing integral fuel tank
66. De-activated centre section doors
67. Anti-collision light
68. Starboard wing integral fuel tank
69. Inboard leading edge slat
70. Engine thrust reverser cascades, open
71. Starboard nacelle pylon
72. Outboard slat drive mechanism
73. Pressure refuelling connections
74. Fuel system piping
75. Slat guide rails
76. Outboard leading edge slat segments
77. Starboard navigation lights
78. Wing tip formation lights
79. Starboard wing tip strobe light
80. Static dischargers
81. Aileron balance weights
82. Aileron hydraulic jack
83. Outboard low speed aileron
84. Fuel jettison pipe
85. Outboard spoiler segments (four), open
86. Spoiler hydraulic jacks
87. Flap hydraulic jacks
88. Flap hinge fairings
89. Outboard double slotted flap, down position
90. High speed aileron
91. Inboard spoiler
92. Inboard double slotted flap, down position
93. Fuselage skin plating
94. UHF aerial
95. Centre fuselage construction
96. Pressure floor above wheel bay
97. Centre undercarriage wheel bay
98. Cargo loading floor
99. Roller conveyors
100. Cabin wall trim panels
101. Access ladder to lower deck refuelling station
102. Drogue refuelling hose reel unit
103. Drogue housing
104. Ground emergency exit doorway
105. Rear cabin air condition duct

106. HF aerial
107. Centre engine pylon construction
108. Centre engine intake
109. Intake duct construction
110. Intake duct ring frames
111. Tailfin attachment point
112. Starboard tailplane
113. Starboard elevator
114. Tailfin construction
115. J-band and I-band beacon antennae
116. VOC localiser No.1 aerial
117. Fin tip fairing
118. VOR localiser No.2 aerial
119. Rudder mass balance
120. Two segment rudder
121. Rudder hydraulic jacks
122. Fin low voltage formation lighting strip
123. Centre engine installation

124. Detachable engine cowlings
125. Bleed air system pre-cooler
126. Engine mounting pylon
127. Hot stream exhaust nozzle
128. Fan air exhaust duct
129. Detachable tailcone fairing
130. Centre engine access ladder

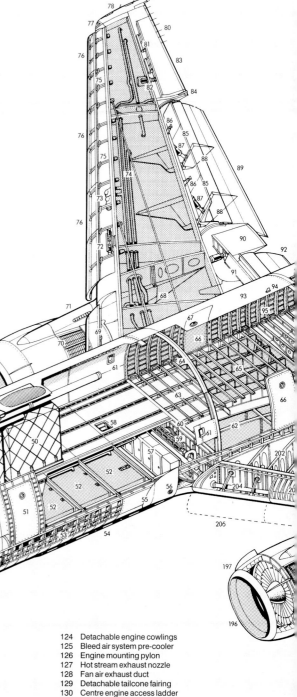

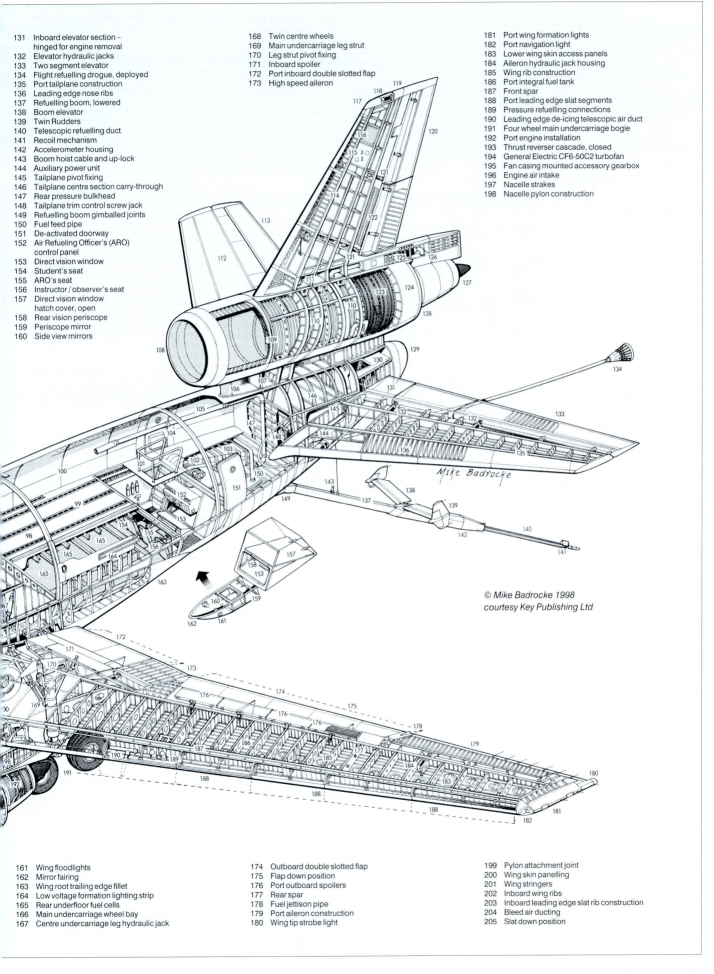

131 Inboard elevator section –
 hinged for engine removal
132 Elevator hydraulic jacks
133 Two segment elevator
134 Flight refuelling drogue, deployed
135 Port tailplane construction
136 Leading edge nose ribs
137 Refuelling boom, lowered
138 Boom elevator
139 Twin Rudders
140 Telescopic refuelling duct
141 Recoil mechanism
142 Accelerometer housing
143 Boom hoist cable and up-lock
144 Auxiliary power unit
145 Tailplane pivot fixing
146 Tailplane centre section carry-through
147 Rear pressure bulkhead
148 Tailplane trim control screw jack
149 Refuelling boom gimballed joints
150 Fuel feed pipe
151 De-activated doorway
152 Air Refueling Officer's (ARO)
 control panel
153 Direct vision window
154 Student's seat
155 ARO's seat
156 Instructor / observer's seat
157 Direct vision window
 hatch cover, open
158 Rear vision periscope
159 Periscope mirror
160 Side view mirrors

168 Twin centre wheels
169 Main undercarriage leg strut
170 Leg strut pivot fixing
171 Inboard spoiler
172 Port inboard double slotted flap
173 High speed aileron

181 Port wing formation lights
182 Port navigation light
183 Lower wing skin access panels
184 Aileron hydraulic jack housing
185 Wing rib construction
186 Port integral fuel tank
187 Front spar
188 Port leading edge slat segments
189 Pressure refuelling connections
190 Leading edge de-icing telescopic air duct
191 Four wheel main undercarriage bogie
192 Port engine installation
193 Thrust reverser cascade, closed
194 General Electric CF6-50C2 turbofan
195 Fan casing mounted accessory gearbox
196 Engine air intake
197 Nacelle strakes
198 Nacelle pylon construction

© Mike Badrocke 1998
courtesy Key Publishing Ltd

Mike Badrocke

161 Wing floodlights
162 Mirror fairing
163 Wing root trailing edge fillet
164 Low voltage formation lighting strip
165 Rear underfloor fuel cells
166 Main undercarriage wheel bay
167 Centre undercarriage leg hydraulic jack

174 Outboard double slotted flap
175 Flap down position
176 Port outboard spoilers
177 Rear spar
178 Fuel jettison pipe
179 Port aileron construction
180 Wing tip strobe light

199 Pylon attachment joint
200 Wing skin panelling
201 Wing stringers
202 Inboard wing ribs
203 Inboard leading edge slat rib construction
204 Bleed air ducting
205 Slat down position

Unlike most Boeing KC-135s, the KC-10A is equipped with a refuelling receptacle. A KC-10A boom operator guides the refuelling boom towards an approaching sister ship.
March AFB Public Affairs

KC-10A layouts show flexibility between a 75 passengers-plus-pallets and an all-pallet configuration. McDonnell Douglas

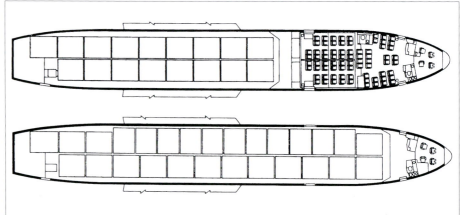

The 60th and last aircraft delivered to the USAF was the first to be equipped with removable wing-tip pods. Note the use of a temporary civil registration – N6204N – in place of the USAF serial number (87-0124) during the trials.
McDonnell Douglas

Production

The following table covers the complete McDonnell Douglas DC-10 production run. As the individual histories of DC-10s are constantly changing, and widely available in other publications, it has been the Author's goal in this chapter to accurately describe the present status of each aircraft at 1st December 1997.

The manufacturer's configuration (config) and cumulative (cum) order, customer abbreviation and its cumulative deserve further explanation. KLM ordered fuselage number 146 (factory serial number – FSN, or constructor's number – 46556), its seventh DC-10 and the 39th Series 30. However, the aircraft was the first of the type for VARIG (VA), to whom it was

directly delivered. (See Chapter Three, page 99 for a full listing of customer codes.) Lufthansa, as the parent company of Condor Flugdienst, ordered DC-10s for its charter division. Aircraft 301 was Condor's second, Lufthansa's 13th and the 130th Series 30.

The status column should take little explanation. Aircraft which do not have an airline or operator are marked with an asterisk (*) and the name of the owner/leasing company. An aircraft is considered withdrawn from use (WFU) when it is temporarily or permanently withdrawn from airline service. The abbreviation (STD) is used when an aircraft has been placed into short or long term storage. In both

cases the aircraft's data plate remains on the aircraft. When an aircraft is retired (RET) the data plate is removed from the aircraft. A retired aircraft can be returned to service, but this will generally involve considerable work to achieve. This being the case, the original data plate will be remounted. An aircraft that is broken up is shown: (BU) while aircraft that are lost in an accident are marked (L).

Three DC-10-30s, nose-to-nose at Long Beach for a presentation ceremony in October 1972 for launch customers KLM, Swissair and UTA – all members of the KSSU Group. American, National and THY examples are in the background.
McDonnell Douglas

Fuse number	FSN	McDD config	McDD cum	Original Registration	Cust-omer	Cust cum	Model/Series	Model cum	Engine	Assembly complete	Customer Accept	Status Config/Cust/WFU/STD/BU/L	Current Regn
1	46500	AA	1	N101AA	AA	1	10	1	CF6-6D	29.07.1970	08.12.1972	FX	N101AA
2	46501	GK	1	G-BELO	GK	4	10	2	CF6-6D1	17.12.1970	03.06.1977	ORBIS	N220AU
3	46502	AA	2	N102AA	AA	2	10	3	CF6-6D	16.10.1970	27.06.1972	FX	N102AA
4	46600	UA	1	N1801U	UA	1	10	4	CF6-6D	18.01.1971	25.05.1972	WFU/STD	N1801U
5	46503	AA	3	N103AA	AA	3	10	5	CF6-6D	11.02.1971	29.07.1971	FX	N103AA
6	46601	UA	2	N1802U	UA	2	10	6	CF6-6D	08.03.1971	29.07.1971	FX	N1802U
7	46504	AA	4	N104AA	AA	4	10	7	CF6-6D	30.03.1971	17.09.1971	BU	
8	46602	UA	3	N1803U	UA	3	10	8	CF6-6D	21.04.1971	03.06.1972	FX	N1803U
9	46505	AA	5	N105AA	AA	5	10	9	CF6-6D	11.05.1971	09.11.1971	FX	N105AA
10	46603	UA	4	N1804U	UA	4	10	10	CF6-6D	28.05.1971	27.09.1971	BU	
11	46604	UA	5	N1805U	UA	5	10	11	CF6-6D	16.06.1971	29.10.1971	BU	
12	46506	AA	6	N106AA	AA	6	10	12	CF6-6D	30.06.1971	10.12.1971	WFU/STD	N106AA
13	46507	AA	7	N107AA	AA	7	10	13	CF6-6D	15.07.1971	15.12.1971	FX	N107AA
14	46700	NA	1	N60NA	NA	1	10	14	CF6-6D	28.07.1971	01.11.1971	AAR Engine Group Inc*	N145AA
15	46605	UA	6	N1806U	UA	6	10	15	CF6-6D	10.08.1971	23.12.1971	FX	N1806U
16	46701	NA	2	N61NA	NA	2	10	16	CF6-6D	23.08.1971	19.11.1971	FX	N146AA
17	46606	UA	7	N1807U	UA	7	10	17	CF6-6D	03.09.1971	20.12.1971	FX	N1807U
18	46702	NA	3	N62NA	NA	3	10	18	CF6-6D	16.09.1971	21.12.1971	X9/RET	N147AA
19	46703	NA	4	N63NA	NA	4	10	19	CF6-6D	28.09.1971	12.01.1972	HA	N148AA
20	46508	AA	8	N108AA	AA	8	10	20	CF6-6D	08.10.1971	31.01.1972	FX	N108AA
21	46509	AA	9	N109AA	AA	9	10	21	CF6-6D	19.10.1971	21.01.1972	BU	
22	46510	AA	10	N110AA	AA	10	10	22	CF6-6D	29.10.1971	28.02.1972	L	
23	46511	AA	11	N111AA	AA	11	10	23	CF6-6D	10.01.1972	15.03.1972	BU	
24	46512	AA	12	N112AA	AA	12	10	24	CF6-6D	14.01.1972	30.03.1972	FX	N112AA
25	46607	UA	8	N1808U	UA	8	10	25	CF6-6D	20.01.1972	27.02.1972	FX	N1808U
26	46608	UA	9	N1809U	UA	9	10	26	CF6-6D	02.02.1972	29.02.1972	FX	N1809U
27	46609	UA	10	N1810U	UA	10	10	27	CF6-6D	09.02.1972	20.04.1972	WFU/STD	N1810U
28	46750	NW	1	N141US	NW	1	40	1	JT9D-20	25.01.1972	13.06.1973	NW	N141US
29	46704	TK	1	TC-JAV	TK	1	10	28	CF6-6D	15.02.1972	10.12.1972	L	
30	46513	AA	13	N113AA	AA	13	10	29	CF6-6D	21.02.1972	20.04.1972	BU	
31	46514	AA	14	N114AA	AA	14	10	30	CF6-6D	28.02.1972	17.05.1972	BU	
32	46610	UA	11	N1811U	UA	11	10	31	CF6-6D	03.03.1972	24.04.1972	WFU/STD	N1811U
33	46705	TK	2	TC-JAU	TK	2	10	32	CF6-6D	09.03.1972	02.12.1972	10F/FX	N68058
34	46900	CO	1	N68041	CO	1	10	33	CF6-6D	15.03.1972	14.04.1972	CO	N68041
35	46611	UA	12	N1812U	UA	12	10	34	CF6-6D	20.03.1972	27.04.1972	FX	N1812U
36	46751	NW	2	N142US	NW	2	40	2	JT9D-20	24.03.1972	16.02.1973	TZ/L	N184AT
37	46515	AA	15	N115AA	AA	15	10	35	CF6-6D	03.04.1972	26.05.1972	FX	N115AA
38	46706	NA	5	N64NA	NA	5	10	36	CF6-6D	08.04.1972	10.05.1972	X9	N360AX
39	46612	UA	13	N1813U	UA	13	10	37	CF6-6D	18.04.1972	27.05.1972	WFU/STD	N1813U
40	46901	CO	2	N68042	CO	2	10	38	CF6-6D	22.04.1972	22.05.1972	CO	N68042
41	46902	CO	3	N68043	CO	3	10	39	CF6-6D	29.04.1972	19.05.1972	CO	N68043
42	46613	UA	14	N1814U	UA	14	10	40	CF6-6D	06.05.1972	23.06.1972	WFU/STD	N1814U
43	46903	CO	4	N68044	CO	4	10	41	CF6-6D	15.05.1972	09.06.1972	CO	N68044
44	46904	CO	5	N68045	CO	5	10	42	CF6-6D	20.05.1972	23.06.1972	L	
45	46614	UA	15	N1815U	UA	15	10	43	CF6-6D	07.06.1972	07.07.1972	UA	N1815U
46	46550	KL	1	PH-DTA	KL	1	30	1	CF6-50A	27.05.1972	15.03.1974	CO	N12089
47	46905	GK	2	G-AZZC	GK	1	10	44	CF6-6D1	14.06.1972	26.10.1972	SY/BU	N573SC
48	46516	AA	16	N116AA	AA	16	10	45	CF6-6D	21.06.1972	14.07.1972	HA	N116AA
49	46517	AA	17	N117AA	AA	17	10	46	CF6-6D	28.06.1972	21.07.1972	FX	N117AA
50	46906	GK	3	G-AZZD	GK	2	10	47	CF6-6D1	06.07.1972	16.11.1972	HA	N171AA
51	46518	AA	18	N118AA	AA	18	10	48	CF6-6D	11.07.1972	29.07.1972	FX	N118AA
52	46519	AA	19	N119AA	AA	19	10	49	CF6-6D	18.07.1972	11.08.1972	HA	N119AA
53	46752	NW	3	N143US	NW	3	40	3	JT9D-20	24.07.1972	10.11.1972	NW	N133JC
54	46520	AA	20	N120AA	AA	20	10	50	CF6-6D	28.07.1972	24.08.1972	FX	N120AA
55	46521	AA	21	N121AA	AA	21	10	51	CF6-6D	03.08.1972	01.09.1972	FX	N121AA
56	46522	AA	22	N122AA	AA	22	10	52	CF6-6D	10.08.1972	18.09.1972	HA	N122AA
57	46575	SR	1	HB-IHA	SR	1	30	2	CF6-50A	16.08.1972	30.11.1972	EU	PP-SFB
58	46523	AA	23	N123AA	AA	23	10	53	CF6-6D	22.08.1972	20.10.1972	WFU/STD	N123AA
59	47965	DL	1	N601DA	DL	1	10	54	CF6-6D	28.08.1972	10.10.1972	FX	N1833U
60	46551	KL	2	PH-DTB	KL	2	30	3	CF6-50A	01.09.1972	03.12.1972	NW	N229NW
61	46707	NA	6	N65NA	NA	6	10	55	CF6-6D	08.09.1972	13.10.1972	HA	N152AA
62	46708	NA	7	N66NA	NA	7	10	56	CF6-6D	15.09.1972	19.10.1972	HA	N153AA
63	46850	UT	1	F-BTDB	UT	1	30	4	CF6-50A	21.09.1972	18.02.1973	CO	N13088
64	47966	DL	2	N602DA	DL	2	10	57	CF6-6D	26.09.1972	10.11.1972	UA	N1834U
65	46524	AA	24	N124AA	AA	24	10	58	CF6-6D	30.09.1972	17.11.1972	Raytheon Systems/HAC	N910SF
66	46753	NW	4	N144US	NW	4	40	4	JT9D-20	05.10.1972	12.12.1972	NW	N144JC
67	47967	DL	3	N603DA	DL	3	10	59	CF6-6D	07.10.1972	28.11.1972	UA/WFU/STD	N1835U
68	46709	NA	8	N67NA	NA	8	10	60	CF6-6D	14.10.1972	30.11.1972	AAR Engine Group Inc*	N154AA
69	47846	NZ	1	ZK-NZL	NZ	1	30	5	CF6-50A	26.10.1972	11.01.1973	AA/L	N136AA
70	46710	NA	9	N68NA	NA	9	10	61	CF6-6D	31.10.1972	12.12.1972	HA	N160AA
71	46552	KL	3	PH-DTC	KL	3	30	6	CF6-50A	03.11.1972	06.02.1973	NW	N230NW
72	46525	AA	25	N125AA	AA	25	10	62	CF6-6D	09.11.1972	19.12.1972	HA	N125AA
73	46576	SR	2	HB-IHB	SR	2	30	7	CF6-50A	14.11.1972	05.02.1973	CO	N19072
74	47968	DL	4	N604DA	DL	4	10	63	CF6-6D	20.11.1972	05.01.1973	UA	N1836U
75	47861	AZ	1	I-DYNA	AZ	1	30	8	CF6-50A	27.11.1972	06.02.1973	CO	N39081
76	46615	UA	16	N1816U	UA	16	10	64	CF6-6D	01.12.1972	30.01.1973	UA	N1816U
77	46890	RK	1	TU-TAL	RK	1	30	9	CF6-50A	06.12.1972	28.02.1973	IW	F-GTDI
78	46907	TK	3	TC-JAY	TK	3	10	65	CF6-6D	11.12.1972	27.02.1973	10F/FX	N68059
79	46754	NW	5	N145US	NW	5	40	5	JT9D-20	15.12.1972	31.01.1973	NW	N145US
80	47969	DL	5	N605DA	DL	5	10	66	CF6-6D	03.01.1973	16.02.1973	UA	N1837U
81	46825	OV	1	N1031F	OV	1	30CF	1	CF6-50A	09.01.1973	21.04.1973	L	
82	46553	KL	4	PH-DTD	KL	4	30	10	CF6-50A	13.01.1973	28.02.1973	CO	N14090
83	46727	GK	4	G-BBSZ	GK	3	10	67	CF6-6D1	18.01.1973	20.05.1974	10F/ZU/STD	N104WA
84	46554	KL	5	PH-DTE	KL	5	30	11	CF6-50A	24.01.1973	09.03.1973	GH	9G-PHN
85	46851	UT	2	F-BTDC	UT	2	30	12	CF6-50A	30.01.1973	19.03.1973	IW	F-GTDH
86	46616	UA	17	N1817U	UA	17	10	68	CF6-6D	03.02.1973	22.03.1973	UA	N1817U
87	46925	IB	1	EC-CBN	IB	1	30	13	CF6-50A	08.02.1973	20.03.1973	L	
88	47862	AZ	2	I-DYNE	AZ	2	30	14	CF6-50A	14.02.1973	21.03.1973	CO	N12064
89	46617	UA	18	N1818U	UA	18	10	69	CF6-6D	20.02.1973	06.04.1973	WFU/STD	N1818U
90	47886	QC	1	9Q-CLI	QC	1	30	15	CF6-50A	24.02.1973	08.06.1973	QC/WFU/STD	9Q-CLI
91	46555	KL	6	PH-DTF	KL	6	30	16	CF6-50A	01.03.1973	13.04.1973	AA	N143AA
92	47800	CO	6	N68046	CO	6	10	70	CF6-6D	07.03.1973	12.04.1973	CO	N68046

Fuse number	FSN	McDD config	McDD cum	Original Registration	Cust-omer	Cust cum	Model/Series	Model cum	Engine	Assembly complete	Customer Accept	Status Config/Cust/WFU/STD/BU/L	Current Regn
93	46852	UT	3	N54629	UT	3	30	17	CF6-50A	13.03.1973	01.05.1973	L	
94	47863	AZ	3	I-DYNI	AZ	3	30	18	CF6-50A	17.03.1973	20.04.1973	CO	N14062
95	46908	WA	1	N901WA	WA	1	10	71	CF6-6D	22.03.1973	19.04.1973	AA	N166AA
96	46800	TV	1	N101TV	TV	1	30CF	2	CF6-50A	27.03.1973	19.04.1973	30F/FX	N301FE
97	46755	NW	6	N146US	NW	6	40	6	JT9D-20	31.03.1973	09.05.1973	NW	N146US
98	47801	CO	7	N68047	CO	7	10	72	CF6-6D	05.04.1973	10.05.1973	CO	N68047
99	46926	IB	2	EC-CBO	IB	2	30	19	CF6-50A	10.04.1973	19.05.1973	CO	N37078
100	46927	IB	3	EC-CBP	IB	3	30	20	CF6-50A	14.04.1973	29.05.1973	CO	N14079
101	47802	CO	8	N68048	CO	8	10	73	CF6-6D	24.04.1973	23.05.1973	FX	N68048
102	46756	NW	7	N147US	NW	7	40	7	JT9D-20	28.04.1973	02.06.1973	NW	N147US
103	46801	TV	2	N102TV	TV	2	30CF	3	CF6-50A	03.05.1973	04.06.1973	30F/FX	N302FE
104	46928	WA	2	N902WA	WA	2	10	74	CF6-6D	09.05.1973	12.06.1973	Chon Dal Inc*	N902WA
105	46711	NA	1	N80NA	NA	10	30	21	CF6-50A	15.05.1973	11.06.1973	AA/L	N139AA
106	46712	NA	2	N81NA	NA	11	30	22	CF6-50A	19.05.1973	18.06.1973	UN	N140AA
107	46929	WA	3	N903WA	WA	3	10	75	CF6-6D	24.05.1973	21.06.1973	L	
108	46757	NW	8	N148US	NW	8	40	8	JT9D-20	31.05.1973	06.07.1973	NW	N148US
109	46826	OV	2	N1032F	OV	2	30CF	4	CF6-50A	06.06.1973	29.06.1973	L	
110	46802	TV	3	N103TV	TV	3	30CF	5	JT9D-20	11.06.1973	02.07.1973	30F/FX	N303FE
111	46758	NW	9	N149US	NW	9	40	9	JT9D-20	15.06.1973	25.07.1973	NW	N149US
112	46930	WA	4	N904WA	WA	4	10	76	CF6-6D	21.06.1973	20.07.1973	AA	N167AA
113	46759	NW	10	N150US	NW	10	40	10	JT9D-20	27.06.1973	31.07.1973	NW	N220NW
114	46577	SR	3	HB-IHC	SR	3	30	23	CF6-50A	02.07.1973	10.09.1973	NW	N220NW
115	47906	SN	1	OO-SLA	SN	1	30CF	6	CF6-50A	09.07.1973	18.09.1973	30F/SE	5X-JOE
116	47847	NZ	2	ZK-NZM	NZ	2	30	24	CF6-50A	13.07.1973	14.09.1973	AA	N137AA
117	47921	LH	1	D-ADAO	LH	1	30	25	CF6-50A	20.07.1973	12.11.1973	30F/GR	N601GC
118	46618	UA	19	N1819U	UA	19	10	77	CF6-6D	27.07.1973	12.04.1974	L	
119	46619	UA	20	N1820U	UA	20	10	78	CF6-6D	03.08.1973	22.02.1974	FX	N1820U
120	46760	NW	11	N151US	NW	11	40	11	JT9D-20	10.08.1973	30.10.1973	NW	N151US
121	47864	AZ	4	I-DYNO	AZ	4	30	26	CF6-50A	17.08.1973	13.11.1973	CO	N14063
122	47922	LH	2	D-ADBO	LH	2	30	27	CF6-50A	24.08.1973	15.01.1974	30F/GR	N603GC
123	47923	LH	3	D-ADCO	LH	3	30	28	CF6-50A	31.08.1973	11.02.1974	30F/GR	N602GC
124	46761	NW	12	N152US	NW	12	40	12	JT9D-20	10.09.1973	07.11.1973	NW	N152US
125	47887	YV	1	HS-VGE	YV	1	30	29	CF6-50C	17.09.1973	25.11.1974	KE/L	HL7328
126	46762	NW	13	N153US	NW	13	40	13	JT9D-20	21.09.1973	14.11.1973	NW	N153US
127	46891	MP	1	PH-MBG	MP	1	30CF	7	CF6-50A	25.09.1973	13.11.1973	GD	XA-TDC
128	46763	NW	14	N154US	NW	14	40	14	JT9D-20	08.10.1973	28.11.1973	NW	N154US
129	47924	LH	4	D-ADDO	LH	4	30	30	CF6-50A	15.10.1973	15.02.1974	30F/GR	N604GC
130	46764	NW	15	N155US	NW	15	40	15	JT9D-20	23.10.1973	12.12.1973	NW	N155US
131	46578	SR	4	HB-IHD	SR	4	30	31	CF6-50A	30.10.1973	06.12.1973	NW	N228NW
132	46579	SR	5	HB-IHE	SR	5	30	32	CF6-50A	06.11.1973	06.02.1974	NW	N221NW
133	46944	RG	1	PP-VMA	RG	1	30	33	CF6-50C	13.11.1973	29.05.1974	RG	PP-VMA
134	46853	UT	4	N54639	UT	4	30	34	CF6-50A	20.11.1973	18.01.1974	IW	F-BTDE
135	47865	AZ	5	I-DYNU	AZ	5	30	35	CF6-50A	29.11.1973	22.01.1974	IJ	F-GPVD
136	47848	NZ	3	ZK-NZN	NZ	3	30	36	CF6-50A	06.12.1973	18.01.1974	AA	N144AA
137	46931	PK	1	AP-AXC	PK	1	30	37	CF6-50C	12.12.1973	01.03.1974	6F	N832LA
138	46620	UA	21	N1821U	UA	21	10	79	CF6-6D	20.12.1973	13.02.1974	FX	N1821U
139	47803	CO	9	N68049	CO	9	10CF	1	CF6-6D	07.01.1974	04.02.1974	FX	N68049
140	46621	UA	22	N1822U	UA	22	10	80	CF6-6D	14.01.1974	25.04.1974	FX	N1822U
141	46940	PK	2	AP-AXD	PK	2	30	38	CF6-50C	21.01.1974	02.04.1974	CO	N76073
142	47804	CO	10	N68050	CO	10	10CF	2	CF6-6D	28.01.1974	04.03.1974	FX	N68050
143	46765	NW	16	N156US	NW	16	40	16	JT9D-20	01.02.1974	08.03.1974	NW	N156US
144	46622	UA	23	N1823U	UA	23	10	81	CF6-6D	11.02.1974	02.05.1974	FX	N388FE
145	47805	CO	11	N68051	CO	11	10CF	3	CF6-6D	18.02.1974	08.04.1974	FX	N68051
146	46556	VA	1	PH-DTG	KL	7	30	39	CF6-50A	25.02.1974	03.04.1974	VA	YV-134C
147	46936	AM	1	XA-DUG	AM	1	30	40	CF6-50C	04.03.1974	17.04.1974	6F	N831LA
148	47806	CO	12	N68052	CO	12	10CF	4	CF6-6D	11.03.1974	11.04.1974	FX	N68052
149	47866	AZ	6	I-DYNB	AZ	6	30	41	CF6-50A	18.03.1974	19.04.1974	CO	N13067
150	47980	IB	4	EC-CEZ	IB	4	30	42	CF6-50A	25.03.1974	19.05.1974	IB	EC-CEZ
151	46766	NW	17	N157US	NW	17	40	17	JT9D-20	01.04.1974	17.05.1974	NW	N157US
152	46937	AM	2	XA-DUH	AM	2	30	43	CF6-50C	08.04.1974	16.05.1974	6F	N833LA
153	46938	WA	5	N905WA	WA	5	10	82	CF6-6D	15.04.1974	14.05.1974	AA	N168AA
154	46623	UA	24	N1824U	UA	24	10	83	CF6-6D	22.04.1974	19.06.1974	WFU/STD	N1824U
155	46624	UA	25	N1825U	UA	25	10	84	CF6-6D	29.04.1974	26.06.1974	FX	N1825U
156	46945	RG	2	PP-VMB	RG	2	30	44	CF6-50C	06.05.1974	18.06.1974	RG	PP-VMB
157	47907	SN	2	OO-SLB	SN	2	30CF	8	CF6-50A	13.05.1974	10.06.1974	NMB Air Operations	N10MB
158	46932	QC	2	9Q-CLT	QC	2	30	45	CF6-50A	20.05.1974	26.06.1974	MT	G-NIUK
159	46933	PR	1	PH-DTI	KL	8	30	46	CF6-50C	28.05.1974	27.06.1974	WO	9M-MAZ
160	46934	KE	1	HL7315	KE	1	30	47	CF6-50C	04.06.1974	20.06.1974	NW	N236NW
161	46767	NW	18	N158US	NW	18	40	18	JT9D-20	11.06.1974	19.07.1974	NW	N158US
162	46942	NA	10	N69NA	NA	12	10	85	CF6-6D	18.06.1974	25.06.1975	X9	N450AX
163	46943	NA	11	N70NA	NA	13	10	86	CF6-6D	25.06.1974	23.06.1975	HA	N162AA
164	46768	NW	19	N159US	NW	19	40	19	JT9D-20	02.07.1974	09.08.1974	NW	N159US
165	46713	NA	3	N82NA	NA	14	30	48	CF6-50A	10.07.1974	20.06.1975	UN	N141AA
166	47925	LH	5	D-ADFO	LH	5	30	49	CF6-50A	17.07.1974	14.11.1974	30F/GR	N605GC
167	46714	NA	4	N83NA	NA	15	30	50	CF6-50A	24.07.1974	16.06.1975	UN	N142AA
168	46769	NW	20	N160US	NW	20	40	20	JT9D-20	31.07.1974	10.09.1974	NW	N160US
169	46625	UA	26	N1826U	UA	26	10	87	CF6-6D	07.08.1974	27.02.1975	FX	N390FE
170	47926	LH	6	D-ADGO	LH	6	30	51	CF6-50A	14.08.1974	03.01.1975	CO	N59083
171	46868	SK	1	LN-RKA	SK	1	30	52	CF6-50A	21.08.1974	01.10.1974	NW	N211NW
172	46935	PK	3	AP-AXE	PK	3	30	53	CF6-50C	28.08.1974	19.10.1974	L	
173	47807	CO	13	N68053	CO	13	10CF	5	CF6-6D	05.09.1974	18.02.1975	FX	N68053
174	46869	SK	2	SE-DFD	SK	2	30	54	CF6-50A	12.09.1974	04.11.1974	IW	F-ODLZ
175	46770	NW	21	N161US	NW	21	40	21	JT9D-20	19.09.1974	05.11.1974	NW	N161US
176	46941	RG	3	PP-VMQ	RG	3	30	55	CF6-50C	26.09.1974	07.11.1974	RG	PP-VMQ
177	47808	CO	14	N68054	CO	14	10CF	6	CF6-6D	03.10.1974	10.03.1975	FX	N68054
178	47867	AZ	7	I-DYNC	AZ	7	30	56	CF6-50A	10.10.1974	18.02.1975	CO	N41068
179	46949	BR	1	G-BEBL	BR	1	30	57	CF6-50C	17.10.1974	31.03.1977	BA	G-BEBL
180	46771	NW	22	N162US	NW	22	40	22	JT9D-20	25.10.1974	06.12.1974	NW	N162US
181	47956	AY	1	OH-LHA	AY	1	30	58	CF6-50C	01.11.1974	27.01.1975	IJ	F-GPVA
182	46910	NZ	4	ZK-NZP	NZ	4	30	59	CF6-50C	08.11.1974	13.12.1974	L	
183	46580	SR	6	HB-IHF	SR	6	30	60	CF6-50A	15.11.1974	11.01.1975	NW	N223NW
184	46581	SR	7	HB-IHG	SR	7	30	61	CF6-50A	22.11.1974	14.02.1975	NW	N224NW

Fuse number	FSN	McDD config	McDD cum	Original Registration	Cust-omer	Cust cum	Model/ Series	Model cum	Engine	Assembly complete	Customer Accept	Status Config/Cust/WFU/STD/BU/L	Current Regn
185	46952	PR	2	PH-DTL	KL	9	30	62	CF6-50A	03.12.1974	26.02.1975	QSC	PH-DTL
186	47981	IB	5	EC-CLB	IB	5	30	63	CF6-50A	10.12.1974	24.01.1975	CO	N12080
187	46582	SR	8	HB-IHH	SR	8	30	64	CF6-50A	17.12.1974	21.02.1975	NW	N225NW
188	46912	KE	2	HL7316	KE	2	30	65	CF6-50C	24.12.1974	07.02.1975	NW	N234NW
189	46911	NZ	5	ZK-NZQ	NZ	5	30	66	CF6-50C	08.01.1975	20.02.1975	CO	N14074
190	47927	LH	7	D-ADHO	LH	7	30	67	CF6-50A	15.01.1975	28.02.1975	CO	N49082
191	47809	CO	15	N68055	CO	15	10CF	7	CF6-6D	22.01.1975	17.03.1975	FX/L	
192	47928	LH	8	D-ADJO	LH	8	30	68	CF6-50A	29.01.1975	10.03.1975	CO	N17087
193	46854	UT	5	N54649	UT	5	30	69	CF6-50A	05.02.1975	19.03.1975	IW	F-GTDF
194	47810	CO	16	N68056	CO	16	10CF	8	CF6-6D	12.02.1975	24.03.1975	FX	N68056
195	46914	PR	3	PH-DTK	KL	10	30	70	CF6-50C	19.02.1975	27.03.1975	AA	N163AA
196	47929	LH	9	D-ADKO	LH	9	30	71	CF6-50A	26.02.1975	31.03.1975	30F/GR	N606GC
197	46557	VA	2	PH-DTH	KL	11	30	72	CF6-50A	05.03.1975	15.04.1975	VA	YV-138C
198	46626	UA	27	N1827U	UA	27	10	88	CF6-6D	12.03.1975	25.04.1975	10F/FX	N392FE
199	46915	KE	3	HL7317	KE	3	30	73	CF6-50C	19.03.1975	25.04.1975	NW	N235NW
200	47868	AZ	8	I-DYND	AZ	8	30	74	CF6-50A	26.03.1975	05.05.1975	CP	C-FCRE
201	47957	AY	2	OH-LHB	AY	2	30	75	CF6-50C	03.04.1975	06.05.1975	CO	N17085
202	46916	RG	4	PP-VMD	RG	4	30	76	CF6-50C	17.04.1975	12.06.1975	CP	C-GBQQ
203	46939	WA	6	N906WA	WA	6	10	89	CF6-6D	29.04.1975	03.06.1975	UA	N1849U
204	46892	RK	2	TU-TAM	RK	2	30	77	CF6-50A	09.05.1975	19.06.1975	IW	F-GNEM
205	46627	UA	28	N1828U	UA	28	10	90	CF6-6D	16.05.1975	23.06.1975	WFU/STD	N1828U
206	46913	JL	1	JA8534	JL	1	40-I	23	JT9D-59A	16.06.1975	23.11.1976	EG	JA8534
207	46628	UA	29	N1829U	UA	29	10	91	CF6-6D	20.06.1975	24.07.1975	UA	N1829U
208	46629	UA	30	N1830U	UA	30	10	92	CF6-6D	30.06.1975	04.08.1975	UA	N1830U
209	46630	UA	31	N1831U	UA	31	10	93	CF6-6D	11.07.1975	20.08.1975	UA	N1831U
210	46631	UA	32	N1832U	UA	32	10	94	CF6-6D	18.07.1975	23.09.1975	FX	N397FE
211	46917	LH	10	D-ADLO	LH	10	30	78	CF6-50C	28.07.1975	01.12.1975	CO	N13086
212	46920	JL	2	JA8530	JL	2	40-D	24	JT9D-59A	06.08.1975	09.04.1976	Ten Forty Corporation*	N157DM
213	47849	NZ	6	ZK-NZR	NZ	6	30	79	CF6-50C	22.08.1975	02.10.1975	IW	F-GNDC
214	46921	BR	2	G-BEBM	BR	2	30	80	CF6-50C	10.09.1975	23.02.1977	BA	G-BEBM
215	47908	SN	3	OO-SLC	SN	3	30CF	9	CF6-50C	26.09.1975	27.10.1975	FX	N322FE
216	46923	JL	3	JA8531	JL	3	40-D	25	JT9D-59A	14.10.1975	12.04.1976	EG	JA8531
217	46870	SK	3	OY-KDA	SK	3	30	81	CF6-50C	18.11.1975	18.12.1975	IW	F-GHOI
218	46924	MP	2	PH-MBN	MP	2	30CF	10	CF6-50C	29.10.1975	26.11.1975	L	
219	46871	SK	4	LN-RKB	SK	4	30	82	CF6-50C	08.12.1975	23.01.1976	30F/FX	N311FE
220	46660	JL	4	JA8532	JL	4	40-I	26	JT9D-59A	31.12.1975	16.04.1976	40-I/EG	JA8532
221	46922	IB	6	EC-CSJ	IB	6	30	83	CF6-50C	19.01.1976	23.02.1976	CO	N14075
222	46946	WA	7	N907WA	WA	7	10	95	CF6-6D	04.02.1976	22.06.1976	6F	N946LL
223	46918	GA	1	PK-GIA	GA	1	30	84	CF6-50C	20.02.1976	22.03.1976	GA	PK-GIA
224	46661	JL	5	JA8533	JL	5	40-D	27	JT9D-59A	09.03.1976	25.05.1976	JL	JA8533
225	46953	IB	7	EC-CSK	IB	7	30	85	CF6-50C	24.03.1976	14.05.1976	IB	EC-GNG
226	46919	GA	2	PK-GIB	GA	2	30	86	CF6-50C	13.04.1976	29.05.1976	GA	PK-GIB
227	46954	NZ	7	ZK-NZS	NZ	7	30	87	CF6-50C	29.04.1976	07.06.1976	IW	F-ODLY

Swissair replaced its DC-8 fleet with DC-10-30s and was the first carrier worldwide to place the type into service.
Series 30 *Schaffhausen*, **HB-IHB, is seen here over an impressive alpine mountain range.** Swissair

Fuse number	FSN	McDD config	McDD cum	Original Registration	Cust-omer	Cust cum	Model/Series	Model cum	Engine	Assembly complete	Customer Accept	Status Config/Cust/WFU/STD/BU/L	Current Regn
228	46955	MH	1	9M-MAS	MH	1	30	88	CF6-50C	17.05.1976	02.08.1976	WFU/STD	9M-MAS
229	47889	PK	4	AP-AYM	PK	4	40-I	28	CF6-50C	03.06.1976	25.08.1976	CP	C-FCRD
230	46662	JL	6	JA8535	JL	6	40-I	28	JT9D-59A	21.06.1976	13.08.1976	JL	JA8535
231	46957	WT	1	5N-ANN	WT	1	30	90	CF6-50C	27.07.1976	14.10.1976	WT	5N-ANN
232	46958	PR	4	RP-C2003	PR	1	30	91	CF6-50C	31.08.1976	22.10.1976	CO	EI-DLA
233	46872	SK	5	SE-DFE	SK	5	30	92	CF6-50C	06.10.1976	02.12.1976	IW	F-ODLX
234	46959	TG	1	HS-TGD	TG	1	30	93	CF6-50C	20.12.1976	03.03.1977	WO	9M-MAW
235	46956	MP	3	PH-MBP	MP	3	30CF	11	CF6-50C	11.11.1976	23.12.1976	KDC-10/RNLAF	T-235
236	46961	TG	2	HS-TGE	TG	2	30	94	CF6-50C	01.02.1977	05.05.1977	NW	N232NW
237	46960	OV	3	N1033F	OV	3	30CF	12	CF6-50C1	08.03.1977	09.05.1977	KE/L	HL7339
238	46962	OV	4	N1034F	OV	4	30CF	13	CF6-50C1	13.04.1977	06.06.1977	BX/L	EC-DEG
239	46964	GA	3	PK-GIC	GA	3	30	95	CF6-50C	16.05.1977	03.10.1977	GA	PK-GIC
240	46640	MH	2	9M-MAT	MH	2	30	96	CF6-50C	27.05.1977	21.09.1977	NW	N233NW
241	46969	SR	9	HB-IHI	SR	9	30	97	CF6-50C	28.06.1977	21.10.1977	NW	N227NW
242	46950	NZ	8	ZK-NZT	NZ	8	30	98	CF6-50C	22.07.1977	10.11.1977	AA	N164AA
243	46968	WT	2	5N-ANR	WT	2	30	99	CF6-50C	12.08.1977	18.10.1977	L	
244	46963	UT	6	F-BTDD	UT	6	30	100	CF6-50C	02.09.1977	02.11.1977	DD	F-BTDD
245	46965	LH	11	D-ADMO	LH	11	30	101	CF6-50C	26.09.1977	09.12.1977	30F/GR	N600GC
246	46951	GA	4	PK-GID	GA	4	30	102	CF6-50C	17.10.1977	13.01.1978	GA	PK-GID
247	46947	AA	26	N126AA	AA	26	10	96	CF6-6D	07.11.1977	10.02.1978	AA	N126AA
248	46975	WO	1	N103WA	WO	1	30CF	14	CF6-50C1	23.11.1977	07.03.1978	UA	N1856U
249	46948	AA	27	N127AA	AA	27	10	97	CF6-6D	09.12.1977	20.03.1978	AA	N127AA
250	46984	AA	28	N128AA	AA	28	10	98	CF6-6D	23.12.1977	01.05.1978	AA	N128AA
251	46977	WA	8	N908WA	WA	8	10	99	CF6-6D	16.01.1978	13.03.1978	SY	N572SC
252	46983	WA	9	N909WA	WA	9	10	100	CF6-6D	30.01.1978	18.05.1978	DK	OY-CNY
253	46986	WO	2	N104WA	WO	2	30CF	15	CF6-50C1	02.05.1978	15.06.1978	UA	N1857U
254	46976	WD	1	C-GXRB	WD	1	30	103	CF6-50C1	23.05.1978	14.12.1978	30F/SE	N400JR
255	46987	WO	3	N105WA	WO	3	30CF	16	CF6-50C1	13.06.1978	04.08.1978	UA	N1858U
256	46978	WD	2	C-GXRC	WD	2	30	104	CF6-50C1	27.06.1978	03.11.1978	30F/GR	N607GC
257	46992	OV	5	N1035F	OV	5	30CF	17	CF6-50C	12.07.1978	08.09.1978	30F/FX	N304FE
258	46971	VA	3	YV-135C	VA	1	30	105	CF6-50C	26.07.1978	21.09.1978	RET	YV-135C
259	46981	JU	1	YU-AMA	JU	1	30	106	CF6-50C1	09.08.1978	08.12.1978	CO	N37077
260	46990	SQ	1	9V-SDA	SQ	1	30	107	CF6-50C1	23.08.1978	23.10.1978	DK	OY-CNO
261	46991	SQ	2	9V-SDC	SQ	2	30	108	CF6-50C1	07.09.1978	31.01.1979	CO	N35084
262	46966	JL	7	JA8536	JL	7	40-D	29	JT9D-59A	21.09.1978	20.11.1978	JL	JA8536
263	46993	SQ	3	9V-SDB	SQ	3	30	109	CF6-50C1	03.10.1978	29.11.1978	BG	S2-ACO
264	46985	MP	4	PH-MBT	MP	4	30CF	18	CF6-50C	13.10.1978	20.12.1978	KDC-10/RNLAF	T-264
265	46967	JL	8	JA8537	JL	8	40-D	30	JT9D-59A	26.10.1978	18.01.1979	40-I/EG	JA8537
266	46590	BR	3	G-BFGI	BR	3	30	110	CF6-50C	06.11.1978	22.01.1979	CO	N68065
267	46998	BB	1	HB-IHK	BB	1	30	111	CF6-50C	15.11.1978	31.01.1979	CHG	OO-LRM
268	46540	CP	1	C-GCPC	CP	1	30	112	CF6-50C1	29.11.1978	27.03.1979	CP	C-GCPC
269	46970	GK	5	G-GFAL	GK	5	10	101	CF6-6D1	07.12.1978	27.02.1979	10F/FX	N10060
270	46996	AA	29	N129AA	AA	29	10	102	CF6-6D	16.12.1978	27.02.1979	AA	N129AA
271	46989	AA	30	N130AA	AA	30	10	103	CF6-6D	03.01.1979	15.03.1979	AA	N130AA
272	46973	GK	6	G-GSKY	GK	6	10	104	CF6-6D1	12.01.1979	21.03.1979	10F/FX	N40061
273	46994	AA	31	N131AA	AA	31	10	105	CF6-6D	22.01.1979	03.04.1979	AA	N131AA
274	46974	JL	9	JA8538	JL	9	40-I	31	JT9D-59A	30.01.1979	04.04.1979	JL	JA8538
275	46995	SQ	4	9V-SDD	SQ	4	30	113	CF6-50C1	08.02.1979	30.03.1979	BG	S2-ACP
276	46972	VA	4	YV-136C	VA	2	30	114	CF6-50C	16.02.1979	20.04.1979	VA	YV-136C
277	46835	WO	4	N106WA	WO	4	30CF	19	CF6-50C2	24.02.1979	27.04.1979	FX	N317FE
278	46988	JU	2	YU-AMB	JU	2	30	115	CF6-50C1	05.03.1979	14.05.1979	JU	YU-AMB
279	47982	IB	8	EC-DEA	IB	8	30	116	CF6-50C	12.03.1979	14.05.1979	IB	EC-DEA
280	46836	WO	5	N107WA	WO	5	30CF	20	CF6-50C2	20.03.1979	21.05.1979	VP	N107WA
281	46541	CP	2	C-GCPD	CP	2	30	117	CF6-50C1	28.03.1979	19.07.1979	CP	C-GCPD
282	46837	WO	6	N108WA	WO	6	30CF	21	CF6-50C2	06.04.1979	29.05.1979	FX	N318FE
283	46645	WA	10	N912WA	WA	10	10	106	CF6-6D	16.04.1979	19.07.1979	SY	N571SC
284	46685	GA	5	PK-GIE	GA	5	30	118	CF6-50C	24.04.1979	27.07.1979	L	
285	46646	WA	11	N913WA	WA	11	10	107	CF6-6D	02.05.1979	26.07.1979	DK	OY-CNS
286	46686	GA	6	PK-GIF	GA	6	30	119	CF6-50C	10.05.1979	22.08.1979	GA	PK-GIF
287	46591	BR	4	G-BGAT	BR	4	30	120	CF6-50C	18.05.1979	08.08.1979	CO	N13066
288	46997	RK	3	TU-TAN	RK	3	30	121	CF6-50C	29.05.1979	10.08.1979	IW	F-GTDG
289	46999	SQ	5	9V-SDE	SQ	5	30	122	CF6-50C	06.06.1979	29.08.1979	30F/SU	M524MD
290	46982	VA	5	YV-137C	VA	3	30	123	CF6-50C	14.06.1979	05.10.1979	VA	YC-137C
291	47888	FG	1	YA-LAST	FG	1	30	124	CF6-50C2	22.06.1979	21.09.1979	BA	G-MULL
292	46583	SR	10	HB-IHL	SR	10	30	125	CF6-50C	02.07.1979	03.03.1980	NW	N226NW
293	46584	SR	11	HB-IHM	SR	11	30	126	CF6-50C	11.07.1979	01.02.1980	CO	N15069
294	47827	AA	32	N132AA	AA	32	10	108	CF6-6D	19.07.1979	13.11.1979	AA	N132AA
295	46542	CP	3	C-GCPE	CP	3	30	127	CF6-50C2	27.07.1979	02.11.1979	CP	C-GCPE
296	46632	UA	33	N1838U	UA	33	10	109	CF6-6D	06.08.1979	30.11.1979	UA	N1838U
297	46633	UA	34	N1839U	UA	34	10	110	CF6-6D	14.08.1979	15.02.1980	WFU/STD	N1839U
298	46634	UA	35	N1841U	UA	35	10	111	CF6-6D	22.08.1979	31.01.1980	WFU/STD	N1841U
299	46595	DF	1	D-ADPO	LH	12	30	128	CF6-50C2	30.08.1979	21.11.1979	DE	D-ADPO
300	47817	SQ	6	PP-VMR	LH	6	30	129	CF6-50C2	10.09.1979	30.11.1979	BG	S2-ACQ
301	46596	DF	2	D-ADQO	LH	13	30	130	CF6-50C2	18.09.1979	15.12.1979	DE	D-ADQO
302	47811	GK	1	G-BGXE	GK	7	30	131	CF6-50C2	26.09.1979	15.12.1979	30F/UA	N1852U
303	47812	GK	2	G-BGXF	GK	8	30	132	CF6-50C2	04.10.1979	05.01.1980	30F/UA	N1853U
304	47822	JL	10	JA8539	JL	10	40-I	32	JT9D-59A	12.10.1979	07.01.1980	JZ	JA8539
305	47818	SQ	7	PP-VMS	SQ	7	30	133	CF6-50C2	23.10.1979	25.01.1980	KG	G-LYON
306	47823	JL	11	JA8540	JL	11	40-D	33	JT9D-59A	31.10.1979	24.12.1979	JL	JA8540
307	46635	UA	36	N1842U	UA	36	10	112	CF6-6D	08.11.1979	28.02.1980	UA	N1842U
308	47824	JL	12	JA8541	JL	12	40-I	34	JT9D-59A	16.11.1979	20.03.1980	JZ	JA8541
309	46636	UA	37	N1843U	UA	37	10	113	CF6-6D	28.11.1979	14.03.1980	UA	N1843U
310	47825	JL	13	JA8542	JL	13	40-I	35	JT9D-59A	06.12.1979	17.04.1980	JL	JA8542
311	48200	ZA	1	79-0433	ZA	1	30CF	22	CF6-50C	14.12.1979	01.10.1981	KC-10A/USAF	79-0433
312	47813	GK	3	G-BGXG	GK	9	30	134	CF6-50C2	24.12.1979	24.03.1980	30F/UA	N1854U
313	47826	JL	14	JA8543	JL	14	40-I	36	JT9D-59A	09.01.1980	22.05.1980	JL	JA8543
314	47819	WO	7	N109WA	WO	7	30CF	23	CF6-50C2	17.01.1980	09.04.1980	30F/UA	N1859U
315	47814	GK	4	G-BGXH	GK	10	30	135	CF6-50C2	25.01.1980	30.04.1980	IW	F-GLMX
316	47816	BR	5	G-BHDH	BR	5	30	136	CF6-50C	04.02.1980	30.04.1980	BA	G-BHDH
317	47820	WO	8	N112WA	WO	8	30CF	24	CF6-50C2	12.02.1980	14.05.1980	FX	N319FE
318	47832	WA	12	N914WA	WA	12	10	114	CF6-6D	20.02.1980	12.05.1980	DK	OY-CNU
319	47828	AA	33	N133AA	AA	33	10	115	CF6-6D	28.02.1980	15.05.1980	AA	N133AA

Fuse number	FSN	McDD config	McDD cum	Original Registration	Cust-omer	Cust cum	Model/Series	Model cum	Engine	Assembly complete	Customer Accept	Status Config/Cust/WFU/STD/BU/L	Current Regn
320	47821	WO	9	N113WA	WO	9	30CF	25	CF6-50C2	07.03.1980	27.05.1980	L	
321	47829	AA	34	N134AA	AA	34	10	116	CF6-6D	17.03.1980	23.05.1980	AA	N134AA
322	47833	WA	13	N915WA	WA	13	10	117	CF6-6D	25.03.1980	05.06.1980	DK	OY-CNT
323	47830	AA	35	N135AA	AA	35	10	118	CF6-6D	03.04.1980	09.06.1980	AA	N135AA
324	47834	IB	9	EC-DHZ	IB	9	30	137	CF6-50C	11.04.1980	23.06.1980	IB	EC-DHZ
325	47815	GK	5	G-BGXI	GK	11	30	138	CF6-50C2	21.04.1980	24.06.1980	IW	F-GKMY
326	47835	SN	4	OO-SLD	SN	4	30CF	26	CF6-50C2	29.04.1980	09.07.1980	FX	N320FE
327	47831	BR	6	G-BHDI	BR	6	30	139	CF6-50C	07.05.1980	21.07.1980	BA	G-BHDI
328	47837	NA	5	N84NA	NA	16	30	140	CF6-50C	15.05.1980	06.08.1980	UA	N1855U
329	47841	RG	5	PP-VMT	RG	5	30	141	CF6-50C2	23.05.1980	31.07.1980	30F/RG	PP-VMT
330	47836	SN	5	OO-SLE	SN	5	30CF	27	CF6-50C2	03.06.1980	14.08.1980	FX	N321FE
331	47850	CO	1	N68060	CO	17	30	142	CF6-50C2	11.06.1980	28.08.1980	CO	N68060
332	47842	RG	6	PP-VMU	RG	6	30	143	CF6-50C2	19.06.1980	05.09.1980	30F/RG	PP-VMU
333	48201	ZA	2	79-0434	ZA	2	30CF	28	CF6-50C2	27.06.1980	17.03.1981	KC-10A/USAF	79-0434
334	47851	CO	2	N12061	CO	18	30	144	CF6-50C2	08.07.1980	25.09.1980	CO	N12061
335	47843	RG	7	PP-VMV	RG	7	30	145	CF6-50C2	16.07.1980	09.10.1980	RG	PP-VMV
336	47844	RG	8	PP-VMW	RG	8	30	146	CF6-50C2	24.07.1980	10.11.1980	RG	PP-VMW
337	47840	BR	7	G-BHDJ	BR	7	30	147	CF6-50C	01.08.1980	16.10.1980	BA	G-BHDJ
338	47838	PR	5	RP-C2114	PR	2	30	148	CF6-50C2	11.08.1980	25.11.1980	KG	G-GOKT
339	47870	NG	1	N305FE	FM	1	30CF	29	CF6-50C2	19.08.1980	07.09.1984	30F/FX	N305FE
340	47852	JL	15	JA8544	JL	15	40-I	37	JT9D-59A	27.08.1980	09.12.1980	JZ	JA8544
341	46543	CP	4	C-GCPF	CP	4	30	149	CF6-50C2	05.09.1980	26.11.1980	CP	C-GCPF
342	48252	DF	3	D-ADSO	LH	14	30	150	CF6-50C2	17.09.1980	22.01.1981	DE	D-ADSO
343	47853	JL	16	JA8545	JL	16	40-I	38	JT9D-59A	29.09.1980	19.12.1980	JL	JA8545
344	48260	UA	38	N1844U	UA	38	10	119	CF6-6D	09.10.1980	09.04.1981	UA	N1844U
345	48265	AY	3	N345HC	AY	3	30	151	CF6-50C2	22.10.1980	11.08.1981	IJ	N345HC
346	48258	MX	1	N1003L	MX	1	15	1	CF6-50C2F	03.11.1980	15.06.1981	SKT	V2-LEX
347	48261	UA	39	N1845U	UA	39	10	120	CF6-6D	13.11.1980	24.04.1981	UA	N1845U
348	48266	MS	1	N3016Z	QZ	1	30	152	CF6-50C2	25.11.1980	20.07.1984	ZB	G-DMCA
349	47855	JL	17	JA8546	JL	17	40-D	39	JT9D-59A	09.12.1980	25.03.1981	JL	JA8546
350	48283	MH	3	9M-MAV	MH	3	30	153	CF6-50C2	19.12.1980	20.02.1981	WFU/STD	9M-MAV
351	48262	UA	40	N1846U	UA	40	10	121	CF6-6D	20.01.1981	08.05.1981	UA	N1846U
352	48285	CP	5	C-GCPG	CP	5	30	154	CF6-50C2	08.01.1981	27.02.1981	CP	C-GCPG
353	48263	UA	41	N1847U	UA	41	10	122	CF6-6D	30.01.1981	22.05.1981	UA	N1847U
354	48277	BR	8	G-DCIO	BR	8	30	155	CF6-50C2	11.02.1981	15.04.1981	BA	G-DCIO
355	48282	RG	9	PP-VMY	RG	9	30	156	CF6-50C2	27.02.1981	30.04.1981	RG	PP-VMY
356	47845	RG	10	PP-VMX	RG	10	30	157	CF6-50C2	17.03.1981	03.06.1981	RG	PP-VMX
357	48259	MX	2	N10045	MX	2	15	2	CF6-50C2F	03.04.1981	29.06.1981	SY	N154SY
358	48275	AM	1	N10038	AM	3	15	3	CF6-50C2F	21.04.1981	30.06.1981	WFU/STD	N10038
359	48202	ZA	3	79-1710	ZA	3	30CF	30	CF6-50C2	07.05.1981	30.07.1981	KC-10A/USAF	79-1710
360	48203	ZA	4	79-1711	ZA	4	30CF	31	CF6-50C2	26.05.1981	28.08.1981	KC-10A/USAF	79-1711
361	48204	ZA	5	79-1712	ZA	5	30CF	32	CF6-50C2	11.06.1981	22.09.1981	KC-10A/USAF	79-1712
362	48276	AM	2	N1003N	AM	4	15	4	CF6-50C2F	29.06.1981	12.11.1981	SY	N153SY
363	48205	ZA	6	79-1713	ZA	6	30CF	33	CF6-50C2	16.07.1981	23.10.1981	KC-10A/USAF	79-1713
364	48288	CP	6	C-GCPH	CP	6	30	158	CF6-50C2	03.08.1981	02.11.1981	CP	C-GCPH
365	48289	MX	3	N1003W	MX	3	15	5	CF6-50C2F	19.08.1981	03.12.1981	SY	N152SY
366	47856	JL	18	JA8547	JL	18	40-I	40	JT9D-59A	04.09.1981	08.12.1981	JZ	JA8547
367	47857	JL	19	JA8548	JL	19	40-D	41	JT9D-59A	23.09.1981	25.01.1982	JL	JA8548
368	48292	SR	12	HB-IHN	SR	12	30	159	CF6-50C2	09.10.1981	27.02.1982	CO	N87070
369	48286	GH	1	9G-ANA	GH	1	30	160	CF6-50C2	02.11.1981	25.02.1983	GH	9G-ANA
370	48296	CP	7	C-GCPI	CP	7	30	161	CF6-50C2	23.11.1981	19.02.1982	CP	C-GCPI
371	48293	SR	13	HB-IHO	SR	13	30	162	CF6-50C2	16.12.1981	01.04.1982	CO	N83071
372	48294	MX	4	XA-MEW	MX	4	15	6	CF6-50C2F	18.01.1982	13.01.1983	SKT	V2-LER
373	48206	ZA	7	79-1946	ZA	7	30CF	34	CF6-50C2	10.02.1982	25.05.1982	KC-10A/USAF	79-1946
374	48295	MX	5	XA-MEX	MX	5	15	7	CF6-50C2F	05.03.1982	13.01.1983	SY	N151SY
375	48207	ZA	8	79-1947	ZA	8	30CF	35	CF6-50C2	30.03.1982	21.06.1982	KC-10A/USAF	79-1947
376	48208	ZA	9	79-1948	ZA	9	30CF	36	CF6-50C2	23.04.1982	23.07.1982	KC-10A/USAF	79-1948
377	48209	ZA	10	79-1949	ZA	10	30CF	37	CF6-50C2	18.05.1982	09.08.1982	KC-10A/USAF	79-1949
378	48210	ZA	11	79-1950	ZA	11	30CF	38	CF6-50C2	11.06.1982	08.09.1982	KC-10A/USAF	79-1950
379	48264	UA	42	N1848U	UA	42	10CF	9	CF6-6D	06.08.1982	20.09.1982	FX	N68057
380	48211	ZA	12	79-1951	ZA	12	30CF	39	CF6-50C2	31.08.1982	18.11.1982	KC-10A/USAF	79-1951
381	48301	JL	20	JA8549	JL	20	40-D	42	JT9D-59A	19.10.1982	15.03.1983	JL	JA8549
382	48212	ZA	13	82-0190	ZA	13	30CF	40	CF6-50C2	20.12.1982	06.04.1983	KC-10A/USAF/L	
383	48213	ZA	14	82-0191	ZA	14	30CF	41	CF6-50C2	08.02.1983	19.04.1983	KC-10A/USAF	82-0191
384	48214	ZA	15	82-0192	ZA	15	30CF	42	CF6-50C2	22.03.1983	20.05.1983	KC-10A/USAF	82-0192
385	48215	ZA	16	82-0193	ZA	16	30CF	43	CF6-50C2	04.05.1983	28.07.1983	KC-10A/USAF	82-0193
386	48216	ZA	17	83-0075	ZA	17	30CF	44	CF6-50C2	16.06.1983	23.08.1983	KC-10A/USAF	83-0075
387	48217	ZA	18	83-0076	ZA	18	30CF	45	CF6-50C2	29.07.1983	16.09.1983	KC-10A/USAF	83-0076
388	48218	ZA	19	83-0077	ZA	19	30CF	46	CF6-50C2	12.09.1983	02.11.1983	KC-10A/USAF	83-0077
389	48219	ZA	20	83-0078	ZA	20	30CF	47	CF6-50C2	25.10.1983	13.12.1983	KC-10A/USAF	83-0078
390	48220	ZA	21	83-0079	ZA	21	30CF	48	CF6-50C2	08.12.1983	27.02.1984	KC-10A/USAF	83-0079
391	48221	ZA	22	83-0080	ZA	22	30CF	49	CF6-50C2	17.02.1984	28.03.1984	KC-10A/USAF	83-0080
392	48222	ZA	23	83-0081	ZA	23	30CF	50	CF6-50C2	27.04.1984	07.06.1984	KC-10A/USAF	83-0081
393	48223	ZA	24	83-0082	ZA	24	30CF	51	CF6-50C2	12.06.1984	19.07.1984	KC-10A/USAF	83-0082
394	48224	ZA	25	84-0185	ZA	25	30CF	52	CF6-50C2	26.07.1984	04.09.1984	KC-10A/USAF	84-0185
395	48225	ZA	26	84-0186	ZA	26	30CF	53	CF6-50C2	30.08.1984	15.10.1984	KC-10A/USAF	84-0186
396	48226	ZA	27	84-0187	ZA	27	30CF	54	CF6-50C2	05.10.1984	27.11.1984	KC-10A/USAF	84-0187
397	48227	ZA	28	84-0188	ZA	28	30CF	55	CF6-50C2	12.11.1984	19.12.1984	KC-10A/USAF	84-0188
398	48228	ZA	29	84-0189	ZA	29	30CF	56	CF6-50C2	19.12.1984	05.02.1985	KC-10A/USAF	84-0189
399	48229	ZA	30	84-0190	ZA	30	30CF	57	CF6-50C2	01.02.1985	16.03.1985	KC-10A/USAF	84-0190
400	48230	ZA	31	84-0191	ZA	31	30CF	58	CF6-50C2	08.03.1985	18.04.1985	KC-10A/USAF	84-0191
401	48231	ZA	32	84-0192	ZA	32	30CF	59	CF6-50C2	12.04.1985	04.06.1985	KC-10A/USAF	84-0192
402	48232	ZA	33	85-0027	ZA	33	30CF	60	CF6-50C2	10.05.1985	21.08.1985	KC-10A/USAF	85-0027
403	48233	ZA	34	85-0028	ZA	34	30CF	61	CF6-50C2	10.06.1985	01.08.1985	KC-10A/USAF	85-0028
404	48234	ZA	35	85-0029	ZA	35	30CF	62	CF6-50C2	09.07.1985	04.09.1985	KC-10A/USAF	85-0029
405	48235	ZA	36	85-0030	ZA	36	30CF	63	CF6-50C2	06.08.1985	19.09.1985	KC-10A/USAF	85-0030
406	48236	ZA	37	85-0031	ZA	37	30CF	64	CF6-50C2	04.09.1985	10.10.1985	KC-10A/USAF	85-0031
407	48237	ZA	38	85-0032	ZA	38	30CF	65	CF6-50C2	25.09.1985	04.11.1985	KC-10A/USAF	85-0032
408	48238	ZA	39	85-0033	ZA	39	30CF	66	CF6-50C2	16.10.1985	03.12.1985	KC-10A/USAF	85-0033
409	48287	FM	1	N306FE	FM	2	30F	1	CF6-50C2	07.11.1985	24.01.1986	FX	N306FE
410	48239	ZA	40	85-0034	ZA	40	30CF	67	CF6-50C2	02.12.1985	04.02.1986	KC-10A/USAF	85-0034
411	48240	ZA	41	86-0027	ZA	41	30CF	68	CF6-50C2	30.12.1985	27.02.1986	KC-10A/USAF	86-0027

Fuse number	FSN	McDD config	McDD cum	Original Registration	Cust-omer	Cust cum	Model/ Series	Model cum	Engine	Assembly complete	Customer Accept	Status Config/Cust/WFU/STD/BU/L	Current Regn
412	48291	FM	2	N307FE	FM	3	30F	2	CF6-50C2	21.01.1986	07.03.1986	FX	N307FE
413	48241	ZA	42	86-0028	ZA	42	30CF	69	CF6-50C2	11.02.1986	29.03.1986	KC-10A/USAF	86-0028
414	48242	ZA	43	86-0029	ZA	43	30CF	70	CF6-50C2	04.03.1986	25.04.1986	KC-10A/USAF	86-0029
415	48243	ZA	44	86-0030	ZA	44	30CF	71	CF6-50C2	25.03.1986	09.05.1986	KC-10A/USAF	86-0030
416	48297	FM	3	N308FE	FM	4	30F	3	CF6-50C2	16.04.1986	28.05.1986	FX	N308FE
417	48244	ZA	45	86-0031	ZA	45	30CF	72	CF6-50C2	07.05.1986	23.06.1986	KC-10A/USAF	86-0031
418	48245	ZA	46	86-0032	ZA	46	30CF	73	CF6-50C2	29.05.1986	18.07.1986	KC-10A/USAF	86-0032
419	48298	FM	4	N309FE	FM	5	30F	4	CF6-50C2	19.06.1986	31.07.1986	FX	N309FE
420	48246	ZA	47	86-0033	ZA	47	30CF	74	CF6-50C2	11.07.1986	27.08.1986	KC-10A/USAF	86-0033
421	48247	ZA	48	86-0034	ZA	48	30CF	75	CF6-50C2	01.08.1986	30.09.1986	KC-10A/USAF	86-0034
422	48299	FM	5	N310FE	FM	6	30F	5	CF6-50C2	22.08.1986	30.09.1986	FX	N310FE
423	48248	ZA	49	86-0035	ZA	49	30CF	76	CF6-50C2	15.09.1986	31.10.1986	KC-10A/USAF	86-0035
424	48249	ZA	50	86-0036	ZA	50	30CF	77	CF6-50C2	06.10.1986	30.11.1986	KC-10A/USAF	86-0036
425	48250	ZA	51	86-0037	ZA	51	30CF	78	CF6-50C2	28.10.1986	24.12.1986	KC-10A/USAF	86-0037
426	48251	ZA	52	86-0038	ZA	52	30CF	79	CF6-50C2	18.11.1986	31.01.1987	KC-10A/USAF	86-0038
427	48303	ZA	53	87-0117	ZA	53	30CF	80	CF6-50C2	05.01.1987	28.02.1987	KC-10A/USAF	87-0117
428	48304	ZA	54	87-0118	ZA	54	30CF	81	CF6-50C2	09.02.1987	17.04.1987	KC-10A/USAF	87-0118
429	48305	ZA	55	87-0119	ZA	55	30CF	82	CF6-50C2	16.03.1987	26.05.1987	KC-10A/USAF	87-0119
430	48306	ZA	56	87-0120	ZA	56	30CF	83	CF6-50C2	21.04.1987	30.06.1987	KC-10A/USAF	87-0120
431	48307	ZA	57	87-0121	ZA	57	30CF	84	CF6-50C2	27.05.1987	21.08.1987	KC-10A/USAF	87-0121
432	48308	ZA	58	87-0122	ZA	58	30CF	85	CF6-50C2	01.07.1987	17.11.1987	KC-10A/USAF	87-0122
433	48300	FM	6	N312FE	FM	7	30F	6	CF6-50C2	06.08.1987	30.09.1987	FX	N312FE
434	48267	TG	3	HS-TMA	TG	3	30	163	CF6-50C2	11.09.1987	01.12.1987	TG	HS-TMA
435	48290	TG	4	HS-TMB	TG	4	30	164	CF6-50C2	16.10.1987	22.12.1987	TG	HS-TMB
436	48315	JD	1	JA8550	JD	1	30	165	CF6-50C2	20.11.1987	30.03.1988	JD	JA8550
437	48316	JD	2	JA8551	JD	2	30	166	CF6-50C2	05.01.1988	29.07.1988	JD	JA8551
438	48319	TG	5	HS-TMC	TG	5	30	167	CF6-50C2	02.02.1988	26.05.1988	TG	HS-TMC
439	48309	ZA	59	87-0123	ZA	59	30CF	86	CF6-50C2	01.03.1988	24.08.1988	KC-10A/USAF	87-0123
440	48311	FM	7	N313FE	FM	8	3OF	7	CF6-50C2	29.03.1988	28.05.1988	FX	N313FE
441	48310	ZA	60	87-0124	ZA	60	30CF	87	CF6-50C2	25.05.1988	30.09.1988	KC-10A/USAF	87-0124
442	48312	FM	8	N314FE	FM	9	30F	8	CF6-50C2	23.06.1988	26.08.1988	FX	N314FE
443	48313	FM	9	N315FE	FM	10	30F	9	CF6-50C2	22.07.1988	29.09.1988	FX	N315FE
444	48314	FM	10	N316FE	FM	11	30F	10	CF6-50C2	19.08.1988	28.10.1988	FX	N316FE
445	48317	BG	1	S2-ACR	BG	1	30	168	CF6-50C2	19.09.1988	30.12.1988	BG	S2-ACR
446	48318	WT	3	N3042W	WT	3	30	169	CF6-50C2	17.10.1988	27.07.1989	WO	N117WA

Marienne, **DC-10-30 N82NA of National was the backdrop for a ceremony to mark the 200th DC-10 delivery, in June 1975.** McDonnell Douglas

Chapter Seven

MD-11 – The Legend Lives On

Already in 1979, production of larger models of the efficient DC-10 was under consideration at McDonnell Douglas in Long Beach. Using the same nomenclature as the DC-8 series, Douglas had three different versions under study. The DC-10 Series 61 would be a domestic-range model, while the Series 62 and 63 would have intercontinental ranges.

Both the Series 61 and Series 63 tri-jets would be 40ft (12.1m) longer than the 182ft (55.4m) length of the existing DC-10s, and the Series 62 would be 26.7ft (8.1m) longer. Maximum capacity of these new variants would be over 500 passengers, compared to the maximum of 380 for the DC-10s in service today.

Plans of the extended fuselage DC-10s called for a 5ft (1.5m) tip extension on the wings and powerplants in the 52,000 to 55,000lb (231 to 244kN) thrust range. The new DC-10s would consume less fuel and offer lower operating costs, per seat mile.

Although these planned series did not make it into production, it was a clear sign of what Douglas had in mind as a DC-10 successor. As noted in the Introduction, the DC-10 was to be the last aircraft built by McDonnell Douglas with the 'DC' prefix. In 1983, a name change, which would incorporate the company's full name, was decided upon by the Douglas management. All commercial aircraft would carry the designation MD, for McDonnell Douglas. The name was introduced on the successful Super 80 family, the Super 81 and 82 series being renamed the MD-81 and MD-82. The first aircraft to carry the new name from the start of development was the MD-83, later followed by the MD-87 and MD-88.

With DC-10 production entering the last stages, Douglas was ready to launch a new series of wide-body tri-jets. It followed that the successor to the DC-10 would receive the designation MD-11.

The official MD-11 launch date was 30th December 1986 and assembly of the first aircraft started on 9th March 1988. On 10th January 1990 MD-11 N111MD made its first flight from Long Beach and Federal Aviation Administration (FAA) certification for the type was granted on 8th November.

In the past VASP was a DC-10 operator. The Brazilian carrier presently has a fleet of nine MD-11s, PP-SOZ illustrated. McDonnell Douglas

Photographs on the opposite page:

The manufacturer used a Continental Airlines DC-10-10 N68048 to flight test the winglets for the MD-11. 'Experimental' stickers were placed beside each entry door. McDonnell Douglas

Federal Express Corporation was the launch customer of the full freight aircraft, the MD-11F – N601FE illustrated. McDonnell Douglas

Within a year of the maiden flight the first aircraft was delivered to Finnair on 7th December 1990. Not only did other airlines, such as Alitalia, KLM, Martinair and Swissair, choose the MD-11 as a replacement for their DC-10s, the MD-11 also attracted many new customers. The new tri-jet was also ordered by China Airlines, China Eastern Airlines, Delta Air Lines, EVA Airways, LTU, Saudi Arabian Airlines and VASP. Some airlines have both the DC-10 and MD-11 in their fleets, for instance Federal Express, Garuda Indonesia, Japan Air Lines, Thai Airways International and VARIG.

At the Farnborough Airshow in the UK in September 1996, Lufthansa Cargo announced an order for five MD-11Fs with an option for seven additional aircraft. Lufthansa has the largest cargo service of any passenger airline in the world. Selection of the MD-11F by Lufthansa was viewed by McDonnell Douglas officials as a major milestone due to the airline's reputation as a world leader in the air cargo business.

More than an Extended DC-10

Not merely an extended DC-10 able to carry more passengers, the MD-11 incorporates the state-of-the-art technologies of the 1990s and offers an increase in range of over 25%. Since computerised system controllers perform automated normal, abnormal and emergency checklist duties for the MD-11's major systems, the flight crew requirement was reduced from three to two persons.

The two pilot flight deck features the latest advances in electronic control technology. The Electronic Instrument System (EIS) consists of six identical colour cathode ray tube displays (CRTs) which display flight instrument and aircraft systems information. The dual Flight Management System (FMS) automates the lateral and vertical navigation to reduce pilot workload and to enhance precision control of the aircraft. To provide simple and positive aircraft control, dual Flight Control Computers (FCCs) are installed.

Using former Continental Airlines DC-10-10, N68048, extensive flight tests were conducted to test the application of the new winglets. Further aerodynamic improvements include a redesigned wing trailing edge, a smaller horizontal tail with integral fuel tanks and an extended tail cone. The aerodynamic features contribute to higher fuel efficiency, reduced drag and added range.

Again, General Electric and Pratt & Whitney are the suppliers of the engines for the MD-11, with the following being offered: the GE CF6-80C2D1F, and P&W with the PW 4460 and PW 4462. The new high thrust engines not only achieve a maximum in noise reduction but are also instrumental in securing a low fuel consumption.

A major decision was taken by McDonnell Douglas to build the fuselage sections for the MD-11 in-house. The first MD-11 fuselage built from barrels produced at the Long Beach plant was completed in July 1996. Until then the fuselage sections of the MD-11, and of course of the DC-10, had been produced by General Dynamics at their Convair Division in San Diego.

MD-11 Specification – Passenger aircraft, general

Capacity

Passengers	250 - 410	
Cargo holds (bulk)	6,850ft³	194m³
Cargo holds (containerised capacity)	5,566ft³	166ft³

Dimensions

Wingspan	169ft 5in	51.7m
Length with GE CF6-2080C2D1Fs	201ft 4in.	61.4m
Length overall P&W 4460/4462s	200ft 8in	61.2m
Height overall	57ft 8in	17.6m
Wing area (ex winglets)	3,648ft²	339m²
Winglet area (each side)	40ft²	3.7m²
Sweepback	35°	

Landing gear

Tread (main wheels)	34ft 7in	10.6m
Wheel base (fore & aft)	80ft 8in	24.6m

Engines

Three General Electric CF6-80C2D1F turbofans thrust of each engine	61,500lb	273kN
or three Pratt & Whitney PW 4460 turbofans thrust of each engine	60,000lb	266kN
or three Pratt & Whitney PW 4462 turbofans thrust of each engine	62,000lb	275kN

Weights

Max take-off	602,555lb	273.318kg
Max landing	430,000lb	195,045kg
Max zero fuel	400,000lb	181,437kg
Empty	286,965lb	130,165kg
Fuel capacity	258,721lb	117,354kg
Weight limited payload	113,035lb	51,272kg

Performance

Level flight speed	588mph	945km/h
FAA take-off field length at MTOW	10,220ft	3,115m
FAA landing field length – at Max landing weight	6,950ft	2,118m
Range (298 pax and baggage, – international reserves)	7,850 miles	12,668km

MD-11ER

Additional passenger aircraft specifications

Max take-off weight:	630,500lb	285,990kg
Auxiliary fuel tank capacity	3,060 US gallons 11,583 litres	
Range (298 pax and baggage, international reserves	8,300 miles	13,427km

---

Family Concept

Following the DC-10 concept, four different versions were offered from the very beginning. An all-passenger version, a 'combi' for mixed passenger and cargo transport, a convertible freighter and an all-freight version are available to meet customer requirements.

The flexibility of the cabin allows for many configurations. A typical three-class seating arrangement with six-abreast first class sleeperettes, seven-abreast business class and nine-abreast economy class seating can transport 298 passengers in comfort. A standard two-class arrangement accommodates 323 passengers, while up to 410 can be accommodated in an all-economy configuration.

To allow airlines to respond efficiently to changing markets, passenger cabin flexibility has been further increased with the use of tracks. These enable the quick relocation of virtually all cabin elements, like galleys, lavatories and vacuum waste system.

The combi aircraft features a large 160in x 102in (4.06m x 2.59m) cargo door in the rear port side fuselage section and can be equipped to handle four, six, eight or ten cargo pallets in combination with a one, two, or three-class passenger configuration. As an option, the combi has the capability of transporting a spare engine in the rear of the main cabin.

Below the main deck, the MD-11 provides more space for containerised or palletised revenue cargo after passenger baggage is loaded than any other airliner. Both the convertible freighter and pure freighter versions have a 140in x 102in (3.56m x 2.59m) cargo door installed in the forward port fuselage, the same door as installed on the DC-10 versions. The MD-11F has a gross payload of 202,100lb (91,760kg) and its main cabin will hold up to 15,530ft³ (440m³) of palletised cargo.

Early in 1996 McDonnell Douglas introduced the MD-11ER – Extended Range – and the first two aircraft were delivered to World Airways in March of that year. This long range version provides a maximum range of approximately 8,300 miles (13,427km) at a maximum take-off weight of 630,500lb (285,990kg). To operate the longest routes, the ER has been equipped with an auxiliary fuel tank in the forward cargo hold. The tank holds 3,060 gallons (11,583 litres) of fuel and can be easily and quickly installed or removed as required by airline operation.

A New Extender?

With the KC-10A McDonnell Douglas has provided the US Air Force with a versatile workhorse which has proven itself during worldwide missions since the first delivery in 1981. The Royal Netherlands Air Force can be considered as the 'launch customer' of the KDC-10 (see Chapter Five). Based on the DC-10-30CF, the KDC-10 conversion programme may well attract other air forces to obtain a reliable tanker/cargo aircraft.

Once more proving the versatility of its products, McDonnell Douglas followed up on the KDC-10 programme with a military version of the MD-11: the KMD-11. McDonnell Douglas is offering the same advanced tanker technology for conversion of new commercial MD-11s into tanker/cargo aircraft for future air force operations. Besides the extra range, the KMD-11 will offer an increase of 35,000lb (15,876kg) in maximum take-off weight and 8,400lb (3,810kg) in fuel load over the KC-10A.

Several hundred Boeing KC-135 Stratotankers and other specialist role versions are in service with the USAF and other air forces and it will only be a matter of time before a replacement for these ageing aircraft will be required. With no serious rival on the market, certainly not as far as performance is concerned, McDonnell Douglas again may well hold all the trumps.

KMD-11 Specification – Where differing from the MD-11

Dimensions

Cargo door	160in x 102in	4.06m x 2.59m

Weights

Max take-off	625,000lb	283,500kg
Empty*:	281,500lb	127,688kg
Max fuel load:	347,600lb	157,671kg
Max cargo load	169,800lb	77,021kg

Crew   Pilot, Co-pilot and Boom Operator/Loadmaster

* Tanker configuration with supplemental fuel tanks, centreline boom, wing pods, no cargo handling equipment

At the time of writing, 171 MD-11s have been delivered and 170 are in worldwide service with 21 operators. With the MD-11, McDonnell Douglas is offering another reliable workhorse – a proud and worthy successor to the famous DC-10!

On 31st December 1997 the MD-11 fleet in the different versions had carried 77,345,938 passengers and had flown 1,490,833,976 statute miles. A total of 3,007,278 revenue hours were completed.

Reminiscent of the DC-8 era, McDonnell Douglas intended to use the Series 61, 62 and 63 nomenclature on further DC-10 developments.

Artist's impression of a KMD-11 showing McDonnell Douglas' plans for a future tanker/cargo aircraft. Boeing maintains that there is a place for this aircraft in the new product line. Both McDonnell Douglas

Epilogue

Following the general recession and the accompanying downturn in commercial aviation in the early 1990s, airlines started facing a brighter future during 1995. With a worldwide economic growth forecast at a rate of 3.2% annually through to the year 2016, it is expected that worldwide air traffic will grow at an average annual rate of 4.9% over the coming 20 years.

To satisfy this demand the world's passenger and cargo aircraft fleet will more than double to over 23,000 jet aircraft by 2016, compared with 11,500 jet aircraft at the end of 1996. To accommodate the growth in traffic and replace capacity lost as aircraft are removed from commercial airline service, the delivery of over 16,000 new jet aircraft is required. The Boeing Company's current market outlook projects the worldwide fleet in 2016 at 23,600 jets, composed of 69.1% single-aisle, 23.5% intermediate-size and 7.4% 747 or larger-size aircraft.

In 1992, Douglas Aircraft Company unveiled their MD-12 proposal. This was the first full-length double-deck, high-capacity aircraft to be offered to the world's airlines. With a fuselage 24ft 3in (7.4m) wide and 27ft 11in (8.5m) high, it would have been the most spacious aircraft in service featuring two- and three-aisle cabin alternatives. The four-engined transport was designed for non-stop routes of up to 9,200 miles (14,805km) carrying between 499 and 579 passengers in different class configurations. Thus the aircraft would have been able to fly non-stop between the world's most distant pairs of cities, such as New York and Taipei, Los Angeles and Bangkok or Zurich and Singapore. Unfortunately the lack of equity partners terminated the project.

A further project started by McDonnell Douglas (MDC) in the early 1990s was the Blended Wing Body (BWB). The revolutionary 'flying wing' aircraft, named the BWB-1-1, powered by three 62,000lb (275kN) thrust very-high-bypass turbofans, would carry up to 800 passengers over a distance of 7,000 miles (13,000km).

Unlike a conventional cabin layout, the seating arrangement in the double deck cabins extended further spanwise than lengthwise. With a wingspan of 289ft (87.5m), 19.2% more than a conventional aircraft, the BWB would still have been able to use existing runways. MDC and NASA studies have shown that the BWB would be 27.5% more fuel-efficient than a conventional 800 passenger aircraft.

In July 1997, a 6% scale, 17ft (5.2m) wide remotely piloted BWB model was successfully flown at El Mirage Dry Lake, California. The model was designed and built by Stanford University of California. If further developed, the 'super jumbo' jet could enter airliner service by the year 2020.

On 19th October 1995 MDC launched the 100-passenger MD-95, powered by latest technology BMW Rolls-Royce BR715 engines. The new twin-jet will be rolled out in early 1998 and first deliveries will take place in 1999.

The C-17A Globemaster III is another MDC workhorse of which a total of 120 have been ordered by the US Air Force. (The C-17A shares the same flight deck configuration and shape as the DC-10.) On 2nd October 1997 the 34th aircraft was delivered to the 437th Airlift Wing and associate 315th AFRES Airlift Wing, Air Mobility Command, Charleston Air Force Base, South Carolina, who jointly operate the aircraft. C-17As are also stationed 97th Airlift Wing at Altus Air Force Base, Oklahoma.

At the Farnborough Airshow in September 1996 MDC displayed a model of the MD-17, the civil cargo version of C-17A. A production run of 30-35 of the heavy, outsized freighters is expected over the next ten years. As an alternative to the European Future Large Aircraft, the company is proposing the KC-17 tanker/cargo version of the C-17A transport. Potential customers for this derivative are Japan, Saudi Arabia, the UK, as well as other European nations.

Towards 'Day One'

When Harry C Stonecipher was elected president and chief executive officer of MDC in 1994, he proclaimed: 'If we weren't already in the commercial aircraft business, we'd get into it.'

With the battle for a 500 plus seat aircraft being fought between Airbus Industrie and Boeing, MDC concentrated on a 300-400 seat aircraft and planned to offer two versions of a new rewinged MD-11 derivative which would ultimately replace it on the production line.

The 'MD-XX Stretch' would be a 375 passenger aircraft with a 7,200nm (13,300km) range. This stretched version would be 31ft (10m) longer than the MD-11. With this aircraft MDC aimed at the 747-200 and 747-300 market. The smaller, MD-11-sized, 'MD-XX LR' (Long Range) version was intended to compete with the Airbus A340 and Boeing 777. Offering a range of over 8,500nm (15,700km), the aircraft would have a capacity of 309 passengers.

In order to be able to offer the aircraft to interested airlines and to meet the projected launch date of January 1997, a MDC board of directors approval was needed by November 1996. During the board meeting on 25th October it was decided to terminate the MD-XX programme. Contrary to his earlier statements, Stonecipher said: 'I don't see McDonnell Douglas as a major stand-alone player in commercial airliners. The investment required to make us into a full-fledged major player is probably in the order of $15 billion over the next ten years.'

If not a 'major player', would there be a co-operation, a joint venture or even a merger with another manufacturer? With Airbus pursuing the double-deck high-capacity A3XX, an airliner similar to the once planned MD-12, the European consortium has indicated that it will need significant partners for the $10 billion project.

At the time the decision to abandon MD-XX plans was announced, the Boeing Company and MDC had already been in talks about possible collaboration. On 3rd December 1996 Boeing announced that an agreement had

been reached with MDC to work together on the development of future Boeing wide-body airliner programmes. The strategic collaboration meant that several hundred MDC employees would be assisting with engineering design and analysis on the planned, meanwhile discontinued, 747-500X and -600X programmes at Everett, Washington.

The big news was yet to come. Within two weeks, Phil Condit, president and chief executive officer of Boeing, and Harry Stonecipher, president and chief executive officer of the MDC, jointly announced on 15th December that a definitive agreement had been signed for the two companies to merge into the world's largest aerospace company.

Boeing and McDonnell Douglas presented the US Federal Trade Commission with more than five million pages of documents, numerous issue papers and testimony by experts from both companies and other parties. After what is considered one of the most detailed and extensive reviews in the history of proposed mergers, the agency gave unconditional approval to the merger of the two companies on 1st July 1997.

At separate meetings in St Louis and Seattle on 25th July, MDC's and Boeing's shareholders also approved the merger. The St Louis meeting was also the last shareholder meeting for both the McDonnell Douglas Corporation and its chairman, John F McDonnell, who retired on 31st July. In his address to the shareholders and employees of the aerospace giant founded by his father in 1939, McDonnell said, 'Today fulfills the goal I set for our company when I became chairman: to become the pre-eminent aerospace company in the world. Although today is a day tinged with sadness, there is no doubt in my mind that our merger with Boeing represents the best, even the ideal, solution for our customers, team-mates and shareholders. We are surrendering our independence to be part of something greater, a new company that has the potential to become the first and only pre-eminent aerospace company in the history of aviation'.

As a part of clearance by the European Commission (EC), Boeing agreed to certain conditions to address concerns regarding the merger. This included the agreement that Boeing will maintain MDC's commercial aircraft business in a separate legal entity for ten years. Boeing also agreed not to enter into any new 'exclusive' supplier agreements with commercial aircraft purchasers until 1st August 2007, except where another aircraft manufacturer has offered such an agreement. Furthermore, Boeing agreed not to enforce the 'exclusivity' provisions in its existing agreements with American Airlines, Delta Air Lines and Continental Airlines, as described in Chapter Three. The agreements remain otherwise unaffected.

Following the final approval from the European Commission on 30th July, the merger became official on Friday, 1st August 1997. On that day the Douglas Aircraft Company was renamed the Douglas Products Division. The division reports to the Boeing Commercial Airplane Group (BCAG) and is managed as part of the new Boeing Company. Operations of the new Boeing Company began on Monday, 4th August 1997, called 'Day One'.

On 3rd November 1997, Boeing announced its product strategy decisions regarding jetliners produced by the Douglas Products Division. Whereas production of the MD-80 and MD-90 will be terminated by mid-1999, when current production commitments end, Boeing is committed to build the 50 MD-95s ordered by launch customer AirTran. On 8th January 1998, Boeing announced that the MD-95 had been renamed the Boeing 717-200. (The Series 200 designation hinting at a family of regional jets, with a smaller Series 100 to follow.) As regards the tri-jet family, Boeing will continue to offer the MD-11 in both passenger and freighter roles.

Even if the combination of the surnames of fellow Scotsmen James Smith McDonnell and Donald Wills Douglas in the future may never again adorn a new civil or military aircraft, they will not be forgotten as important aviation pioneers and manufacturers of some of the most famous and finest products in aviation history.

As a result of the cancellation of the MD-XX programme, the MD-11 will unfortunately be the last of the successful tri-jet aircraft family built by the Long Beach manufacturer, which started out with the DC-10-10 in 1971. The rigidity and reliability of the DC-10 and MD-11 however ensure that these legendary airliners will be a familiar sight at airports around the world for many years to come.

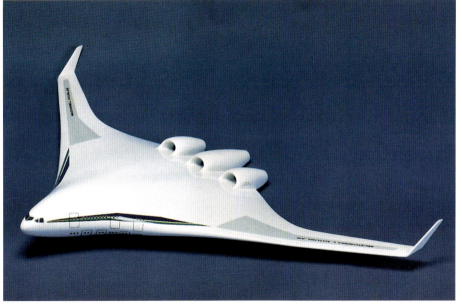

Opposite page:

The MD-XX 'Stretch' was one MDC entry for the next century. McDonnell Douglas

Photographs on this page:

Model of revolutionary Blended Wing Body shows enormous wingspan of the aircraft, the location of the entry doors for upper and lower decks and the housings of the three turbofan engines. Note resemblance of cockpit section to the DC-10 and MD-11. McDonnell Douglas

Thousands of Boeing Douglas Products Division people admired the Next Generation 737 and MD-90 side-by-side as a dramatic symbol of the Boeing / McDonnell Douglas merger in an event at the Long Beach plant on 'Day One' of the new Boeing Company, 4th August 1997. Boeing

In 1982, American author Jay Miller published his first major book, the 'AeroGraph' on the F-16. Since then there has been a steady flow of widely acclaimed books from the Aerofax line.

After many years acting as European distributors, Midland Publishing Limited have acquired the rights to the Aerofax imprint, and have commissioned many new titles for the series from a talented team of internationally known authors.

Some will continue to be produced for Midland by Jay Miller in the USA, but these are now augmented by others originated either in the UK or USA.

These softback volumes are full of authoritative text, detailed photographs, and line drawings. They also contain some colour illustrations, and cockpits, control panels and other interior detail are well illustrated in most instances.

The previous categories of AeroGraph, DataGraph, MiniGraph, and Extra are no longer applied; all new titles are simply published as 'Aerofax' books.

Some of the more recent titles are outlined alongside, whilst a listing of the others in the series that are still in print, plus details of the very latest titles to be announced, is available upon request.

Aerofax
Tupolev Tu-22 'BLINDER' and Tu-22M 'BACKFIRE'
Yefim Gordon & Vladimir Rigmant

This detailed study of Russia's two long-range supersonic nuclear-capable bomber types explodes many previously held myths and sets the record straight. It reveals how 'Blinders' were to have been used to destroy NATO's warships, plus their combat use by Libya and Iraq. Also described is the use of the 'Blinder' and the 'swing-wing' 'Backfire' in the bloody campaign in Afghanistan, plus details of cockpits, armaments, mods and test-beds, likely developments and the current force disposition. Fascinating!

Softback, 280 x 216 mm, 96 pages
c100 b/w, 54 colour photos, and line art
1 85780 065 6 **£14.95 / US $24.95**

Aerofax
F-15 EAGLE
Supreme Heavy-Weight Fighter
Dennis R Jenkins

The F-15 is regarded by many as the finest air superiority fighter to serve with 'western' air forces, from the time it first entered service in 1976. Continued improvement programs have resulted in the F-15C and 'D, and more recently the potent F-15E two-seat 'Strike Eagle' ground attack aircraft. The F-15 is still in production (under the Boeing banner), for Israel and Saudi Arabia.

Coverage includes in-depth detail on systems, engines and weapons, plus development, units and technical drwgs.

Softback, 280 x 216 mm, 112 pages
191 b/w, 50 col photos, 13 col patches
1 85780 081 8 **£14.95 / US $24.95**

Aerofax
BOEING KC-135 STRATOTANKER
Robert S Hopkins

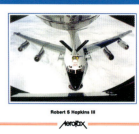

This book, written by a former USAF RC-135 crew commander, follows the development and service use of this globe-trotting aircraft and its many and varied tasks. Every variant and sub-variant is charted, the histories of each and every aircraft are to be found within; details of the hundreds of units, past and present, that have flown the Stratotanker are given. This profusely illustrated work will interest those who have flown and serviced the '-135s, as well as the historian and enthusiast community.

Softback, 280 x 216 mm, 224 pages
210 b/w and 46 colour photos
1 85780 069 9 **£24.95 / US $39.95**

MIDLAND TITLES

We hope you enjoyed this book . . .

The Aerofax and Midland Publishing titles are edited and designed by an experienced and enthusiastic trans-Atlantic team of specialists.

Although further titles are in preparation we always welcome ideas from authors or readers for books they would like to see published.

In addition, our associate company, Midland Counties Publications, offers an exceptionally wide range of aviation, spaceflight, astronomy, military, naval and transport books and videos for sale by mail-order around the world. For a copy of the appropriate catalogue, or to order further copies of this book, or any of the titles mentioned elsewhere on this page, please write, telephone, fax or e-mail to:

Midland Counties Publications
Unit 3 Maizefield,
Hinckley, Leics, LE10 1YF,
England

Tel: (+44) 01455 233 747
Fax: (+44) 01455 233 737
E-mail: midlandbooks@compuserve.com

Distribution in the USA by
Specialty Press – see page 2.

AIRLINES WORLDWIDE
Over 300 airlines described
and illustrated in colour (2nd edition)
B I Hengi

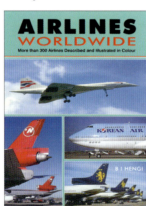

This new edition, with its superb large size full colour photographs, providing vibrant detail of airline colour schemes of the world, has been completely revised and updated to take into account the fast-changing airline business. New types have come into service, such as the Airbus 330 and Boeing 777; several famous names have quietly gone out of business, whilst there is a never-ending stream of 'start-up' operators. *Airlines Worldwide* has become a trusted reference work.

Softback, 240 x 170 mm, 320 pages
304 full colour photographs
1 85780 067 2 **£16.95 / US $29.95**

AIRLINERS WORLDWIDE
Over 120 airliners described
and illustrated in colour
Tom Singfield

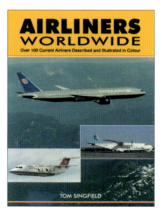

This companion volume to *Airlines Worldwide* provides large full colour illustrations of the major airliner types, ranging from the humble 15-seat feeder-liner to the mammoth Boeing 747-400. The detail given includes development, conversions and sub-series, number built and in service. There is also a listing of the airlines using each type.

The author, an English air traffic controller, has provided readers with an informative but highly readable briefing on each type of airliner.

Softback, 240 x 170 mm, 128 pages
130 full colour photographs
1 85780 056 7 **£11.95 / US $19.95**

AIRLINE TAIL COLOURS
485 colour illustrations to aid in the
quick recognition of airlines
B I Hengi

Interest in airliners, their operation and liveries has never been higher. This handy pocket-sized guide, produced in colour throughout, features a dazzling array of the colourful and artistic tail markings of 477 of the world's airlines.

Not only does it answer the needs of basic recognition, but it also provides the airline's nationality, three-letter code used for flight numbers, radio call-sign prefixes, the airline's international registration prefix, its main operating base and the aircraft types used.

Softback, 150 x 105 mm, 128 pages
485 full colour photographs
1 85780 077 X **£6.95 / US $12.95**

Index

Right: **The prototype DC-10, *Spirit of St Louis-1971* prior to its flight to the Paris Airshow, with a replica of the famous 'original' 1927 Ryan NYP *Spirit of St Louis*.** McDonnell Douglas

Overleaf: **A Condor Flug DC-10.** Photograph courtesy of Condor-Bildarchiv

General Index

In order to make this index as easy to use as possible, references to oft-quoted items such as McDonnell Douglas, Douglas Aircraft, specific DC-10 powerplants, the DC-10 itself etc have been omitted. Page numbers in this index refer *only* to narrative references.